A Western Horseman Book

PROBLEM-SOLVING

Preventing and Solving Common Horse Problems

By Marty Marten

Edited by Gary Vorhes

Illustrations by Dwayne Brech

Photographs by Sheri Gulley, Gary Vorhes, Fran Devereux Smith, and Kathy Swan

PROBLEM-SOLVING

Published by
Western Horseman Inc.

3850 North Nevada Ave.
Box 7980
Colorado Springs, CO 80933-7980

Design, Typography, and Production
Western Horseman
Colorado Springs, Colorado

Cover photograph by
Gary Vorhes

Printing
Publisher's Press
Salt Lake City, Utah

Second Printing: March 1999

ISBN 0-911647-43-0

DEDICATION

To Tom Dorrance, Ray Hunt, and Buck Brannaman,
the best horsemen and problem-solvers I know.

ACKNOWLEDGEMENTS

I have learned a great deal from my mentors,
my friends, the clinicians I have ridden with, and all the
horses and riders who have ridden in my clinics and private sessions.
Wish I could acknowledge them all, but it would take a book in itself,
and I might still inadvertently miss someone.

Among those many people who have helped and
encouraged me with my horsemanship are Margaret Stockton, Phil White,
Jim Cook, D.V.M., Mindy Bower, Larry Flemming, Mark Fitch, D.V.M., Terry
Crofoot, Bill Riggins, Joe Wolters, Bill Dorrance, Carolyn Hunt, Margaret
Dorrance, Peter Campbell, Craig Johnson, and Gary Sneed.

Special thanks to Sheri Gulley. Sheri's photos, organization,
editing, and encouragement were instrumental in making this book
possible. Thanks also to Phil White and Mindy Bower for their objective
and insightful input on the manuscript.

Thanks for providing photo locations to Lloyd and Patty Britton,
Al and Diana Green's AW Ranch, Roger and Laurie Cain's Lazy S Ranch,
Steve and Amy LeSatz's CAAR Farm, Neil and Karen Steward's ranch,
Tom and Lori Winsor's ranch, Larry Ruyball, Bob and Sindy Lindow's
ranch, Ben and Sue Weem's ranch, Twin Pines Ranch in Wyoming,
Kit Carson Riding Club, and Last Resort Equestrian Center.

Last, but not least, special thanks to Gary Vorhes,
Pat Close, Dwayne Brech, Brenda Goodwin, and the rest of the
staff at *Western Horseman* for making this book possible.

Marty Marten

MARTY MARTEN

INTRODUCTION

What this Book Is Intended To Do—What It Cannot Do

THIS BOOK includes the most common problems people consistently seem to have with their horses. Over the years, these are the most prevalent problems people have asked questions about at my clinics and individual sessions. When speaking at group and organization meetings, I often have people list their problems, and in every case, these have been at the top of their lists.

My intention is to provide you with ideas and suggestions on how to develop a plan to solve problems yourself. Read every chapter before you begin your problem-solving. Look for the common thread throughout; it will help with your understanding of your own individual situation. This common thread exists in all these approaches because they are based on the horse's instincts—how he thinks, learns, and communicates naturally. Hopefully, understanding this will help you be more creative and imaginative in solving your own problems. Even if you do not have one of these problems, understanding these principles will help **prevent** them in the future, and cross over to other problems not specifically addressed.

This book is intended to help you solve problems yourself. However, do not hesitate to seek professional help when necessary. This book is intended to augment rather than eliminate the professional trainer's role. **Accurately and realistically evaluating your situation and your horse's situation is necessary before proceeding with any problem-solving approach.**

Not every horse is suitable for everyone. The horse and rider mismatch is the most difficult problem to solve. Although the principles outlined in this book have worked countless times over the years for me, my clients, and many other people, there is no guarantee they will work for someone who is completely over-horsed. Equine activities are supposed to be fun and enjoyable, but this is difficult when the rider is constantly fearful and overwhelmed. There are times when the best solution to a problem is for this rider to find a horse more suitable to his current and potential skill level.

Dangers and Risks of a How-To Book

This book presents a philosophy and numerous suggestions, ideas, approaches, and techniques to solve various problems. However, it is extremely important to remember: **Every technique is good and every technique is bad—it's not what you do, it's how you go about it.** Even the best of techniques presented improperly or at the wrong time may not work. This is where the human's understanding is so very important—where feel, timing, and balance become obviously necessary. Avoid techniques that have a higher risk for failure, and use those with a higher potential for success.

Horses are individuals just as humans are. In the same situation, each may respond or react slightly differently. The human needs to understand the importance of adjusting to fit each horse and situation moment by moment. Work with your horse from where he is, not where you think he should be. Prepare yourself before working on problems, so you can prepare your horse. If you aren't prepared you can't expect your horse to be.

Don't just read one chapter or section of a chapter to fix your problem—it most likely won't work. Preparation is the key. As mentioned throughout, what we commonly call problems are really symptoms. Things aren't always what they seem on the surface; you may have to look deeper. This is the purpose of Chapters 1 and 2, because problem-solving starts at the foundation level. Get down to the real problem level and start there.

To remove a problem you have to replace it with a desirable behavior. Nature doesn't like a vacuum. Rather than just focus on the problem, get busy with other things, getting them better. When you come back to the problem, you may find it is smaller, because you have begun to replace it with more desirable response and respect from your horse.

The diagrams and photos in this book are a guideline to help better visualize the exercises described. However, in order to obtain the desired outcome, always be prepared to adjust to your horse's response, reaction, or resistance moment by moment as needed.

The Horse's Nature and Perspective

Horses do not want trouble—they do not deliberately try to displease us. The horse is never wrong, stubborn, bad, or obnoxious, etc. He is just doing what he thinks is right for him at the time. He may be doing this because of his instincts, or because the handler has inadvertently rewarded undesired behavior, or is miscommunicating what is wanted. The horse may be scared while we know there is nothing to fear. However, for the horse, perception is reality. We need to present ourselves to him in a manner that develops his trust and confidence in us. The horse is a prey animal and we are predators—a strange match to begin with. However,

much to the horse's credit, if we adjust our approach and don't behave like a predator, the horse—amazingly—will do almost anything for us despite his instincts.

Observe horses loose together in a pasture or corral; study their movements, patterns, and interactions among themselves. Accurately seeing and being aware of this will help you better understand how you need to present yourself to them in a way horses can best communicate with and understand you. Then try to fit yourself to the horse, so later he will fit you.

Horses, by nature, are meant to constantly roam and move around over large areas. Therefore, it is best to keep horses in as natural an environment as possible, such as a large pasture with other horses. They are happier, healthier, and have fewer problems. If this is not possible in your situation, then add even more riding with mentally challenging opportunities out in their natural environment.

The Human's Perspective

Problems are really opportunities to advance the human's knowledge and skills with horses. If you see these problems in this way, instead of as a nuisance, both you and your horse will gain more from the experience and enjoy the process. See your horse and your situation as a half-full glass of water rather than half-empty. Your horse can sense your true feelings and attitudes. He knows if you are timid or fearful of him, if you dislike or do not respect him, or if you doubt or lack confidence in him.

As Ray Hunt says: "The horse knows

when you know, and he knows when you don't know . . . he's a living, breathing, thinking, decision-making animal." See your horse for what he is—a horse. Look for the positive and build on it rather than focus on the negative. Believe in your horse—never doubt him.

If the human will make some positive changes in how he approaches, his horse will make even larger positive changes. Communicating with horses effectively will require the human to work at it. There will be periods of trial and error, success and failure, but the more you work at it, the more proficient you'll become. Develop good habits and learn to be particular about how you ride and handle the horse on the ground. Be very aware of what you are doing so your good habits become automatic and second nature. Enjoy your horse for what he is and what you can be together.

Applying These Principles

Ask, respond, release—this is as simple as it gets. There are no formulas or recipes for solving problems or any other training. However, the most basic thing a horse needs to learn is to yield to and from pressure, which is often different from what his instincts would tell him to do. This is why we need to present ourselves to the horse without bringing out his self-preservation instincts. When we are helping horses learn this, our release of pressure is the point at which they learn how to respond to our request (or stimulus).

Form a picture in your mind of what you want, then get your horse ready before you ask something of him. If you set this up correctly, you have greatly increased the odds in your favor of getting the desired response. Keep in mind that horses have an incredible ability to separate and compare different meanings within our communication, if we are consistent.

When working with their horses, people often ask what to look for, how much is enough, how much is too much, how to build from one level to the next, etc. This is learned through experience. In the process of gaining this experience, experiment with different approaches. It is also inevitable you will make mistakes, but these are really learning opportunities. Your horse won't hold these mistakes against you if you maintain a good attitude.

This book refers to using an approach-and-retreat concept—another way of saying pressure and release. It is important to develop the feel, timing, and balance of when to approach with a stimulus of some type and how much, when not to approach, when to retreat, and when not to retreat. Each chapter discusses in numerous ways the importance of why this is so fitting from the horse's point of view.

To obtain a positive response, reward the smallest change and try through release of pressure. Then move on to a higher plateau by asking for slightly more than before, releasing when you get a response. Then start again, moving on to the next plateau, elevating your expectations as your horse is able to accept more.

Learning to more accurately observe your horse and his overall body expression as you work with him will help further develop your feel, timing, and balance. Notice his eyes, ears, tail carriage, body posture, roundness, and how he places his feet. Are you getting a response or a reaction? Is it from fear and escape or confidence and respect?

In learning to respond to pressure, horses learn to yield, to give, then turn loose. They cannot do this until we help develop their trust, confidence, and respect in us. When evaluating a horse's response or resistance, try to distinguish between fear and respect. Being accurately aware of why your horse is responding or resisting will help guide you in how to proceed and what your horse needs next. This takes experience and experimenting to learn, and there is no better time to get started than now.

Firming up is okay; horses are actually happier, more content, and bond better with humans when we are consistent and clear about our boundaries, what we ask them to do, and about our follow-through. Firming up to get a response is better than constantly nagging the horse, neither getting a response nor giving a release.

When and how much to firm up is again a matter of experience and the particular situation. Each horse is different. What is firm for one wouldn't be noticed by another. When firming up, avoid getting the horse afraid or defensive. Instead, keep him in a learning frame of mind so he keeps searching for the answer.

Always give your horse the lightest communication first, then firm up as needed to get a response. Just don't wait too long or he may not make the association of you firming up with your light request. There will be times when your horse will regress or have trouble making progress. When this happens, don't get angry or try to force him to do what you want; just let him work at it until you get a slight try, then release. Never make things a contest between you and your horse. Instead, make the right thing easy and the wrong thing difficult.

If at any time you have trouble with an exercise or approach, return to something more basic you know your horse can accomplish and build on that. Rather than drill your horse at the exercises suggested, keep him fresh and attentive with frequent transitions. After he has done one exercise a few times, change to a different one. Keep things interesting, enjoyable, and rewarding for both you and your horse.

Giving Credit Where Credit Is Due

Some of the phrases and expressions used in this book have come from the people I have learned from. Those of you who have ridden with Tom Dorrance, Ray Hunt, and Buck Brannaman have heard them often. Rather than attempt to re-coin them for this book, I have chosen to include them as I use them in my clinics, which is how I have heard them said. I just don't think I can improve on them by making them sound different, as though they came from me rather than someone else. I have learned much from my mentors and their words, so instead of trying to change these phrases and expressions, I prefer to give credit to them.

—*Marty Marten*

PREFACE

THE GOOD NEWS is, you do not have to be an expert to have the ideas suggested in this book work for you. I certainly do not consider myself an expert or authority. I enjoy my horses and helping other people get more enjoyment with their horses. I particularly enjoy my horses in trail riding and working cattle ranch situations where things are interesting, challenging, and rewarding. My goal is to help people develop a willing partnership with their horses.

The bad news is, if you are like me, you will have to work at these things just as your horse at times will have to work at them. There will be periods of trial and error, good days and bad days, setbacks and successes. However, it will be a rewarding and satisfying experience, if you allow it to be. Anything worth having is worth working for. The fact that I have developed my skills to become proficient in the areas discussed in this book is evidence you can do it too!

I am very fortunate to have come in contact with others who have been more than willing to help me learn and understand more about how horses think, learn, communicate, and operate naturally. I am also fortunate to have several friends living nearby who are as good or better with horses than I and are equally willing to share their experience and help me learn more. Over the years I have learned from everyone who has ridden with me in my clinics or whom I've worked with on an individual basis. I hope I've been helpful to them too.

Certainly I don't know it all and am still learning more every day about horses and horsemanship. Writing this book has pointed out even more things I need to work on and get better at. I may never reach my goal to one day be an expert horseman; however, I am thoroughly enjoying the journey and process. I hope you do as well.

Remember, it is the little things that make the difference and mean the most. Whatever your goal, start taking action today. Don't be afraid to make mistakes; they are learning opportunities. Don't let obstacles overwhelm you or stand in your way. Instead become proactive, working on the day-to-day little things, daily chipping away at improving yourself so your horse will have an opportunity to improve. Then give yourself and your horse credit as you make those little improvements. Good luck!

—*Marty Marten*

CONTENTS

1. GROUNDWORK

It's the little things that make the difference.

Problem-Solving Starts Here

THE PURPOSE of this chapter is to establish a foundation for solving all the problems covered in this book. As you read the chapters on solving specific problems, there will be many referrals back to the groundwork. The techniques suggested in these chapters will assume the handler has read and can successfully complete the various groundwork exercises presented.

The beauty of this groundwork is its simplicity and positive results. It is useful in all aspects of training, whether working with a problem horse, starting a colt, or improving your own horsemanship. At any age or level of a horse's training, you can improve his groundwork and riding foundation.

Why Do Groundwork?

Groundwork is a confidence-builder for both the horse and the human. It is an opportunity to develop mutual trust, confidence, respect, and understanding.

The beauty of this ground-work is its simplicity and positive results.

The human can establish himself in the leadership role.

It's the little things that make the difference. Getting you and your horse handy on the halter rope makes everything easier, including catching, leading, trailering, vetting, shoeing, saddling, mounting, and all riding activities. Respect and response are as important during the day-to-day little things we do around our horses as they are in our planned training sessions.

Using this nonconfrontational approach helps establish response and control. I've found at my clinics, as people get their horses better on the halter rope, it helps every other aspect of their horsemanship. It helps them overcome many problems. In addition to a willing attitude, it develops the horse's suppleness, roundness, softness, and lightness.

On the ground, you are in a good position to watch your horse think and to learn from him. You can easily watch his feet and how he operates naturally. This groundwork will help you learn how to get and keep your horse's attention. Horses do not have a short attention span. But, to maintain their attention and earn their trust and respect, make things interesting, challenging, and rewarding for them.

Sometimes groundwork is overdone. This usually shows up in horses who have been worked in multiple circles, with few transitions. These horses have the typical glazed-over look in their eye, going through the motions physically but mentally inattentive. There is no need to drill your horse at any type of groundwork.

Use groundwork as a starting point to help the horse learn responding and yielding to and from pressure. This helps the human learn to look for the timing of the release, thereby rewarding their horse's response.

Groundwork is an excellent evaluation tool. Before starting each riding session, check to see if your horse is mentally hooked on to you. Is he responsive, supple, and attentive? A few minutes of quality groundwork can evaluate and prepare your horse. Many problems that might otherwise come up can be avoided by getting things on track with groundwork.

This groundwork will help you and your horse get handy. Everything you do will become easier and your horse more pleasurable to be around. He will be respectful of your personal space and not walk all over or push on you. You'll be

This is the rope halter I use. Notice how the knot is tied (upper right). The throatlatch should stay behind the jaw and not slip down. I tie my halter rope to the halter with a half-hitch; I do not use snaps.

This filly patiently waits for me while I get some equipment out of my trailer tack room. Groundwork will help get your horse handy, so he can help you do things.

safer. This groundwork, if done correctly, will build in a safety factor to help keep both you and your horse out of trouble. Leading him from the pasture to the saddle rack need not be a chore. This is about the horse being properly halter-broke.

When around the horse, we're always training. If a horse is not responsive, respectful, trusting, and a pleasure to be with when we're doing the little things around the barn, we're reinforcing inappropriate behavior. It will show up later on the trail, in the pasture, or the arena

11

because the horse is doing what he's learned and what he has lived. **Don't wait until you get out to the arena to think about training; it started when you went to catch your horse.**

Come back to groundwork when all else fails. When you're having trouble with your program, trying to solve a problem, or anything else, go back to these groundwork exercises to regain response, control, confidence, and respect.

As you get handy on the halter rope, this groundwork will be functional in how you handle your horse all the time. Give your groundwork a meaning and purpose. If done correctly, it will have a positive carryover into riding.

Getting Down to Your Horse's Feet

It's very important to understand the concept of getting down to your horse's feet. This means when you pick up on your halter rope or bridle reins, you should be directly connected to your horse's feet. True softness, roundness, lightness, and responsiveness should transfer directly down to his feet. Freeing up your horse's feet while doing groundwork will carry over into riding.

The objective is to get your horse willingly to yield throughout his body without any bracing. He already does these maneuvers naturally on his own out in the pasture. We're just going to ask him to willingly do them upon request. The goal is to accomplish the movements smoothly, all the way down to his feet, with no resistance. Work to get both his right and left sides equal and balanced.

If these exercises are new or seem difficult to you, first familiarize yourself and develop a better understanding of them with a tractable horse. Learn the ground-

work with the handy horse before you go to your problem horse. You'll then have a better chance to help your problem horse.

Be aware of your personal space throughout all these exercises. Right from the beginning, instill in the horse that your personal space is not to be invaded or pushed on. You determine the size of the bubble you create between you and your horse.

I use a tied rope halter such as the one made by the Double Diamond Halter Co., and a ⅝-inch halter rope 11 or 12 feet long. My rope ties directly to the halter without a snap. They are sold at many tack and saddle shops or call Double Diamond at 406-582-0706.

Moving the Hindquarters and Disengaging

Disengaging the horse's hindquarters puts him into neutral. This is like a one-rein stop, establishing control and relaxing your horse. This will help free up his feet.

Standing alongside your horse and behind his withers, first bend his head and neck toward you. See diagram GW-1. Place your hand on the halter rope 2-3 feet from where it connects to the halter. Keep a bend in your elbow, and your forearm in front of you. The bend makes it easy for him to come off the pressure by stepping his hindquarters away from the direction of the bend. Facing the rear, walk toward his hindquarters. He disengages when he steps his inside hind leg up under him and in front of his outside hind. Release when he steps his hindquarters away. Release the pressure by stopping and/or backing up, and allow him to straighten his body.

As you progress, circle your horse around several steps, bending his head and moving his hindquarters away from you. He should be moving all four feet, but reaching more with his hindquarters than the front.

Ideally, when he comes to a stop, all his joints stop at the same time, rather than bracing and pivoting on the inside front leg. Disengaging the hindquarters is still a forward movement, but the horse is not engaging. Throughout this exercise, he should remain balanced and upright. Be aware of your feel, timing, and balance throughout.

There should be slack in the halter rope while your horse is bending. If not, bump

12

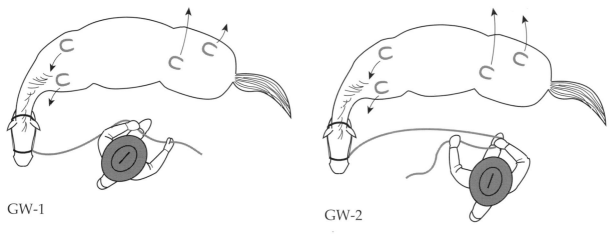

GW-1

Disengaging the hindquarters on left side with halter rope in left hand. Practice this from both sides of your horse.

GW-2

*Disengaging the hindquarters on left side with halter rope in right hand. Practice this from both sides of your horse. **Notice how the halter rope is being held by the right hand.** Generally, with all these groundwork exercises, to have more control, hold the rope so the part going back to the halter comes out the bottom of your hand.*

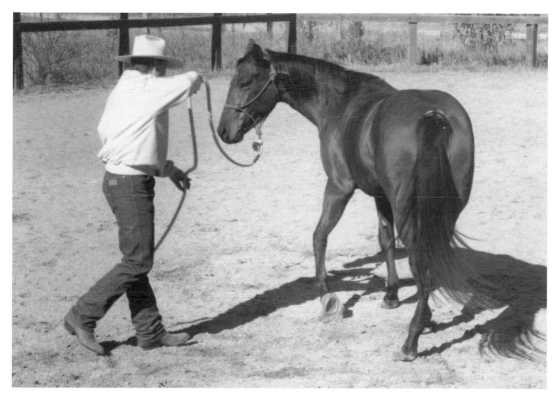

Disengaging the hind-quarters. Note my hand placement and the position of this mare's left hind leg.

his nose with a quick tug and release of the halter rope. Your horse should not be leaning or pulling against you, so make sure you're not pulling on him.

Now do this same exercise holding the halter rope in your other hand, closest to your horse's hindquarters. See diagram GW-2.

You may bend your horse's head and neck around and he might just stand there without moving his hindquarters. If so, at first, just wait, giving him time to think. Pretty soon you might need to tap him on the rump with the tail of your halter rope,

and ask him to move away from the pressure. If he's saddled, you could also bump the stirrup on his side, behind your back cinch, to help him move his feet. When your horse steps his hindquarters away from the pressure, release, then build on this.

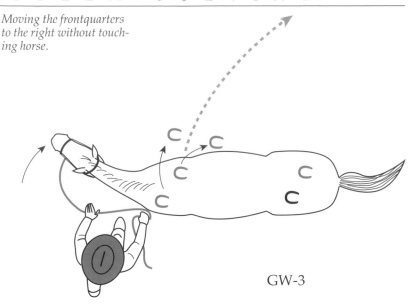

Moving the frontquarters to the right without touching horse.

GW-3

I am asking this mare to move her frontquarters to the right by placing my left hand on the halter cheekpiece and my right hand on her shoulder. The goal is to do this exercise without touching your horse, just having him move away from you as shown in diagram GW-3.

Flexing Laterally

If your horse does not bend his head to the side when you ask, you need to help him learn lateral flexion. Stand facing the same direction as your horse with your rib cage next to his rib cage, behind his withers. Put one arm and elbow over his back, holding the halter rope. Run your other hand down the halter rope a little ways, and bend your elbow. Bring your arm in, creating pressure against his outside cheek, hold and wait. When he yields to the pressure and bends his nose toward you, even if it's only an inch, release and pet him, then start again. When he flexes laterally, he should break at the poll, keeping the bridge of his nose vertical.

If your horse resists when you ask him to bend (flex) laterally, don't pull on the halter rope, just hold and wait. When he releases to your pressure, then you release. When your horse gives to you, make sure you don't pull on him. Keep building on this until he will bend his head about 90 degrees. Do this on both sides.

Your horse can learn to separate if you want him to only flex laterally or flex and move his feet. Now ask him to bend his head and move his hindquarters. The bend is now connected to his neck and feet and to his hindquarters. Although you have taught your horse to flex his neck without moving his feet, the reason to bend your horse's head and neck is to gain control and direction of his feet.

Moving the Frontquarters

Moving the frontquarters is a pivot on the hindquarters. As with all these exercises, there are a number of ways to do this.

Start by asking your horse to walk his frontquarters away. Use body language, walking to the horse with intent, so he senses he is to move away from you. See diagram GW-3. This is the way a dominant horse would ask a submissive horse to move away from a flake of hay.

If your horse has trouble moving his front feet, flex his head away, and put a slight pressure back on the halter rope. This helps him shift his weight back so moving the frontquarters is easier.

If you need to add more support, put your hand on the cheekpiece of the halter

14

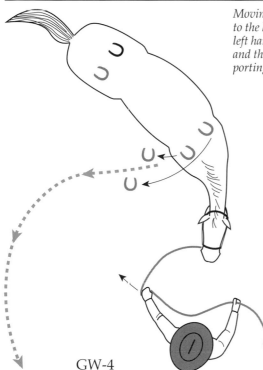

Moving the frontquarters to the horse's right. The left hand is the directing and the right is the supporting (driving) hand.

GW-4

1/ *Preparing to move frontquarters to the right. Note this mare's right front preparing to step out and back. Also note slack in halter rope in both photos.*

2/ *Her left front starts to step across in front of her right. I am walking toward her head, driving with my right hand.*

and hold the halter rope in your hand closest to his shoulder. Put a slight amount of pressure on his jaw and his shoulder, walking his frontquarters away from you. Release when he steps away.

His inside front hoof (opposite of the side you are on) should step out and back, making room for his outside foot to step over and in front as he pivots on his haunches.

If the horse backs up to evade, just go with him, maintaining the pressure. Since he's shifting weight to his haunches, he will eventually find his way off the pressure by stepping his frontquarters away; then release.

Some horses have a tendency to walk forward when you ask them to move their frontquarters. Walking forward puts more weight on the forehand, making it difficult to elevate the frontquarters. Refer to backing diagram GW-13. To inhibit forward movement, tug straight back on the halter rope, parallel to his body, shifting his weight onto his haunches. Then ask your horse to move his front end. You could also have your horse face a fence, blocking forward movement.

Eventually you will get your horse walking his frontquarters around in both directions.

*Starting position to lead horse past to the left. With slack in the halter rope, left hand is directing and right hand is supporting (driving). **Don't** pull horse forward; drive him forward with supporting (right) hand.*

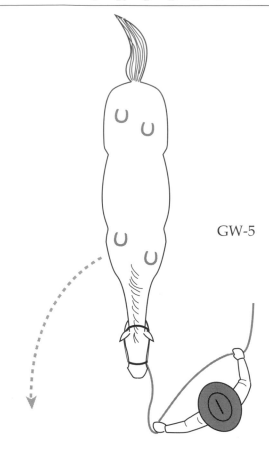

GW-5

Build to a degree of lightness and suppleness where you don't have to touch him. He'll read your body language, sense your bubble coming, and know you are asking him to move away. The horse can separate whether your body language is asking him to move or stand still.

Another way to move the frontquarters is to stand in front and to the side of your horse at a 30- to 45-degree angle (see diagram GW-4). Using your directing or leading hand pointing at a 45-degree angle off his hip, bend your horse's nose past you. This helps him rock back and get into a position to move his frontquarters, pivoting on his hindquarters.

Next move your supporting or driving hand toward his outside neck and jaw, then walk toward his neck and shoulder. As he moves his frontquarters, release and

allow him to move off and forward. You will use this in combination with the leading-past exercise.

Anytime your horse makes the slightest change, the slightest try, reward him with release, by easing off the pressure. Reinforce your release reward by reaching up and petting his neck and shoulder.

Leading Past You

Having your horse lead past you, then stopping him by disengaging his hindquarters, bringing his frontquarters across, and driving him off in the other direction includes all the essential movements and transitions. If learning how to have your horse lead past you was the only groundwork exercise you learned, assuming it was done correctly, you would be in pretty good shape.

Start by standing slightly in front and to the side of your horse, off his shoulder at about a 45-degree angle. Put your directing hand (left, in this case) about halfway down the halter rope, extending your arm out directly away from your shoulder. This gives your horse a direction and a place to go. There should be slack in the halter rope. See diagram GW-5.

If he doesn't respond to the direction and your body language, don't try to pull him past you. Instead, add support with your other hand by raising the tail of the halter rope a little higher and toward his shoulder. Always offer the lightest encouragement first. Direct (lead) first, then support (drive). Your supporting hand tells your horse to move his feet. Then when he moves away, release pressure, and let him go forward by letting the halter rope slide through your directing hand.

If he hasn't moved forward yet, you might have to flip the tail of your halter rope in the air, with an overhand rotation, toward his shoulder. If there still is no response, firm up by letting him run into the tail of the halter rope, just behind the point of his shoulder. Don't wait too long between stages, but do give him a chance to think. In elapsed time, all this should take place in just a very few seconds. How long to wait before firming up more at each stage depends on each individual horse. This is adjusting to fit the situation.

16

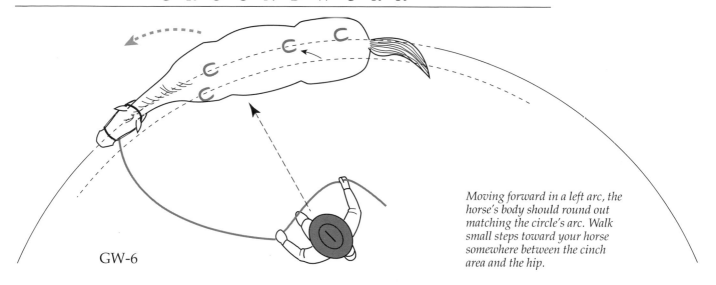

GW-6

Moving forward in a left arc, the horse's body should round out matching the circle's arc. Walk small steps toward your horse somewhere between the cinch area and the hip.

When he goes forward, he will either move out straight, respecting your space as he goes by, or he might move out and away from you. Ideally he will drift away from you as he goes forward with impulsion, reaching equally on all four quarters. When he does this, he may go out and stop, or he may just keep going in a circle. If he stops, start over until he continues the circle. If he moves his shoulder into you as he steps forward, let him run into the tail of your halter rope by swinging it as explained earlier.

Stop your horse by bending him and disengaging his hindquarters. Do this by exchanging hands on the halter rope and shortening it up, bending his head toward you, keeping your elbow bent, and walking toward his flank or tail. This creates more bend and as he begins reaching more with his hindquarters than his front, he will start to disengage. Don't hurry or try to make him stop; let him find his way to a stop while you maintain the bend. When he does, release and allow him to come to a stop with roundness, then straightening out and facing you. See diagram GW-2.

Be thinking all the time about getting him soft, light, and responsive down to his feet. The softer and lighter you start when you ask, the lighter he will be. But don't hesitate to firm up; you will need to adjust moment by moment.

When he stops, this is a good opportunity to pet him. Let him stand and relax. You'll often see a horse exhale, lower his head a little, and work his mouth. This means the horse is relaxing and understanding. Particularly when he's begin-

ning to get the idea, occasionally let him have a little "soak time" after the release. You let him relax and think about what you've been asking of him. This helps him stay in a learning frame of mind.

A mistake I often see at my clinics is that people start backing up when they ask their horse to lead past them into a circle. Doing so pulls the horse toward you, putting you in front of the drive line (at the withers). This often causes the horse to stop before you ask. This also encourages the horse to invade your space.

Usually a person doesn't realize he is backing away. The horse knows, and understands body language, and the occupation of space. If he sees the human as unsure, he may read this as submissiveness, and he may become resistant or fearful. Instead, either stand still or take small steps forward, walking toward his cinch area or rib cage. This encourages him to go forward and float out away from your bubble.

Once your horse is going forward around you, be aware of his roundness relative to the circle. The horse's body should match the arc of the circle. This is moving straight with roundness. He should reach equally on all four quarters with his inside hind reaching up under and lining up with his outside front and rear. See diagram GW-6. To have this lateral roundness, the arc of his jaw, neck, shoulder, rib cage, loin, and hip will be evenly curved, matching the circle's arc.

> You'll get to where this is smooth and fluid just like a dance.

There shouldn't be any pressure on the halter rope as he goes around. If he leans on the halter rope, or his body is not round, bump his nose. Don't pull the halter rope, which would give him something to lean or pull against. Bump the outside of his nose with a tug and release of the halter rope. Be consistent with the timing of this bump and release, and he'll carry himself with more roundness. If his rib cage drops inside the circle when you tug on his nose, you could flip the tail of your halter rope toward his rib cage to move it out. Build toward this roundness in increments.

Get this exercise good from both sides. Ask with as much lightness as possible. Fix it up and wait. As you are asking for a change, fix the situation so your horse can find what you are asking, then wait for him to make the change. However, if he doesn't look for the answer, you may need to be firm to keep him searching for the release. Adjust to fit your horse.

Now add reversing direction. Refer back to moving the frontquarters, diagram GW-4. When your horse disengages and stops after leading past you and circling, you will be standing slightly off to one side, with him facing you. Bend his nose past you with your directing hand, bring your supporting hand around to his other side and walk toward his neck and shoulder. You are looking for him to rock back over his haunches, step his inside front out and back, bringing his outside front across and over. He'll then move off away from you onto the circle. His body arc should change from one side to the other.

Do these exercises mostly at a walk. Trotting a small circle creates too much torque on horses' legs, especially younger horses. Occasionally tip your horse up into a trot, then back down into a walk, for the benefit of transitions.

You'll get to where this is smooth and fluid just like a dance. Your horse will develop more of all the characteristics mentioned and you'll be a team, a willing partnership. See diagram GW-7.

Frequent Direction Changes Keep Your Horse Interested and Attentive

Keep your horse attentive and interested by changing direction often when having him lead past you on the circle. Don't drill your horse with these exercises. If he stays round and supple you don't need to keep working him on the same circle. He'll get bored and his mind will start to drift, making groundwork unproductive.

Keep his attention and interest by varying the tasks and exercises, increasing his awareness and responsiveness toward you. Be aware of your horse's mind; if his attention wanders, give him something else to think about; change direction or change exercises. Becoming more proactive and interesting to your horse builds trust, confidence, and respect, and gets his attention riveted on you. He learns to willingly look to you for direction.

Have Him Stand Away

Anytime you and your horse are just standing, get in the habit of having him stand away from you. Let him learn to respond, respect, and be comfortable at a distance as well as right next to you. Have him stand at a specific place. If he moves, put him back. If he is standing quietly where you want, leave him alone. Don't force him to stand there; allow your horse to make a choice. Every time he moves, put him back. That way he will learn to stay where you put him.

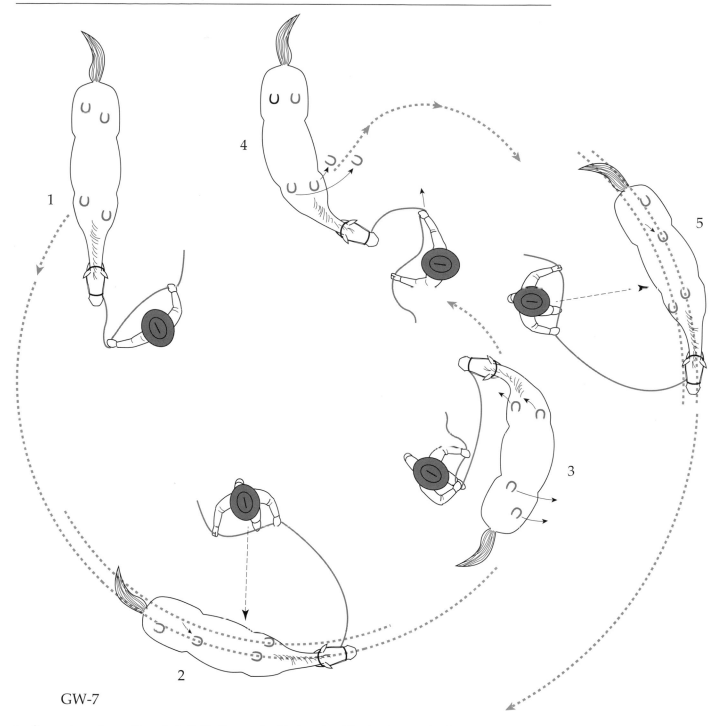

GW-7

Leading past you forward in a circle (1, 2), disengaging hindquarters (3), stopping, moving frontquarters across (4), and off the other direction (5)—putting it all together. Do this exercise making many directional changes (transitions). Keep your horse in continual motion through the direction change, except stopping only momentarily, allowing him to shift his weight from front to hindquarters before asking him to step frontquarters across. Sometimes when you ask your horse to stop, walk up and rub him before leading him past you the other direction.

1/ I am directing this filly to lead past me to my left.

2/ Still directing to left, stepping to shoulder and flipping tail of halter rope in right hand toward shoulder to ask her to move her feet forward following my directing hand.

3/ As she moves forward I step toward her rib cage.

4/ Notice slack in halter rope and roundness of her body as she moves around to my left.

5/ I have changed hands on the halter rope and now disengage the hindquarters, preparing her to stop.

6/ She has stopped and I ask her to tip her nose past me and bring her frontquarters across to my right.

7/ I use my left hand to support (drive) her frontquarters across.

8/ As she steps across, I allow the halter rope to slip through my right hand so she can move forward in a right circle.

9/ Notice she is already rounding out to her right. I am still allowing rope to slip through my right hand so she can move forward farther away from me.

Changing directions often keeps horses attentive, interested, and fresh.

Your horse can be comfortable and responsive at a distance. Get in the habit of having him stand away from you, yet remain attentive.

Halter Rope Over the Hocks to Circle

This exercise helps build more flexibility and responsiveness through the hindquarters. If presented correctly, it teaches your horse to come off his own pressure. It also helps him get comfortable with changing eyes, with you momentarily in his rear blind spot. This works best with a halter rope 11-12 feet long.

Standing on one side of your horse, take the halter rope over his ears. Hold onto the rope with one hand where his neck and shoulder meet. Holding the tail of the halter rope, slide or flip it over his hip and let it drop down to just above his hocks.

Let the rope rest above his hocks. If this troubles your horse, you could let go of the tail of the rope and still have control by bringing the rope in your hand under his neck toward you. If your horse is calm, release the rope under his neck, slowly back up at about a 45-degree angle in front of your horse. Don't pull your horse around; the objective is for him to find his way off the pressure. You're asking him to make a 360-degree turn. By backing away from his hip you can move yourself out of

1/ *Position the halter rope around the hindquarters just above the hocks. Note I still have the halter rope in my right hand.*

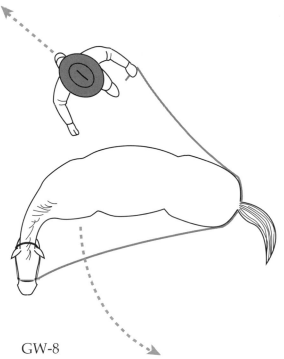

GW-8

Halter rope over hocks to circle.

the line of fire should he get bothered and kick at the halter rope. See diagram GW-8.

Don't hurry this by trying to pull your horse around. If he does not bend his neck away, you may need to help him the first time. With your hand on his jaw, bend his head away from you in the direction of the halter rope. As he bends, just take the slack he gives, and eventually he'll begin to shift his hindquarters. Keep backing, and when he completely rotates and is facing you, stop, lead him up to you, and pet him. Do this exercise from both his right and left sides.

If your horse is troubled by the rope around his hocks, get him accustomed to it by continuously flipping the tail of your halter rope back toward his hocks, letting it slide down around his feet. Do this until he accepts it from both sides.

This over-the-hocks circle is an excellent exercise, but use common sense. If presented correctly, it helps you develop your feel, timing, and balance, while helping your horse learn to yield to and from pressure. This exercise develops softness, roundness, and builds toward the one-rein stop.

2/ *I have released the halter rope from my right hand. The mare is starting to bend to her left. I am **not** pulling her, rather waiting for her to come off her own pressure.*

3/ I am backing up as she steps around, leaving slack in the halter rope.

4/ She comes around with softness, responding to the feel down the halter rope.

5/ She has made a 360-degree circle and is now facing me. I will lead her to me and rub (pet) her.

If your horse is troubled with your halter rope around his hocks, you can build a loop in your lariat, putting it over his back, letting it rest just above the hocks. Use an extra-soft nylon lariat. You can also use the tail of your halter rope instead of a lariat, or a flag (see Chapters 6 and 9) to touch him around his legs until it no longer bothers him.

Semicircle

Start with your back to a fence. With your horse in front of you, lead him past you to your right toward the next post over, probably about 8 feet away. Since he can't go in a full circle, he'll stop with his nose at the fence, roughly perpendicular or slightly facing you. Reverse your hands on the halter rope, and ask him to lead past you in a semicircle out and around you, back to the fence, on your left side. Reverse directions several times. See diagram GW-9.

Ask him to stand at each spot a few seconds to give more meaning and purpose. If he does not stay there waiting for your next direction, just keep redirecting him back to where you want him until he stands there quietly. Don't let him stop until he stops where you want. Allow him to work at it. When he does, then give him a breather.

A variation is having him stop, facing you, at any point on the semicircle. Pick a spot for him to stop, let him stand there for a moment, then send him on around. This exercise will have many applications later on.

Leading Past Between You and the Fence

Stand facing the fence, 6 to 8 feet from it, and lead your horse past you. Change hand positions on the halter rope, tip his nose back toward the fence, ask him to disengage his hindquarters and stop facing you. Then send him between you and the fence again the other direction. Rather than have him circle around, stopping him as you would on the semicircle allows for more transitions. Hold your ground, make sure your horse doesn't push you as he goes by. See diagram GW-10.

Continue changing directions and sending him the other way. As he gets good, take a step closer to the fence. Gradually work your way close enough to the fence to simulate the width of a straight-load, two-horse trailer stall. This added confinement is good trailer-loading preparation.

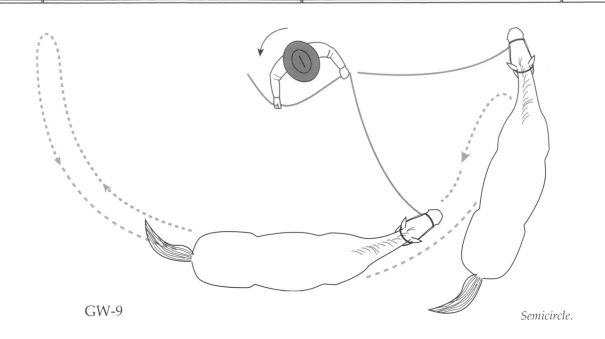

GW-9

Semicircle.

1/ *Directing with my right hand, I ask this mare to walk a semicircle to my right, getting her to move her feet forward by driving her with the tail of the halter rope in my left hand.*

2/ *Note slack in halter rope. She is leading past me to the right on the semicircle.*

3/ *I ask her to follow the arc around. I won't pull on the halter rope to stop her. The fence will stop her, I just guide her to the fence and release.*

4/ *I allow her to stand for a few seconds. I've changed the halter rope to my left hand, preparing to ask her to walk a semicircle to my left.*

5/ *She is starting to depart onto the left semicircle.*

6/ *She is completing the left semicircle. Preparing to stop, her left hind leg will step in front of her right hind, disengaging her hindquarters.*

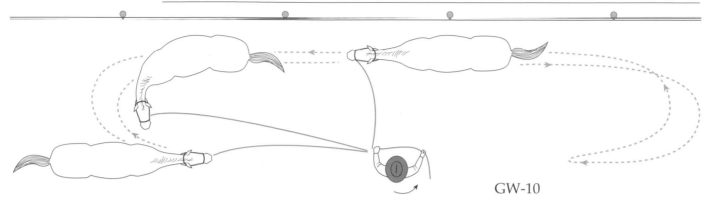

GW-10

Leading past between you and the fence.

1/ *This mare is leading past me to my right between me and the fence. Note slack in halter rope. If necessary, I'd drive her forward with the tail of my halter rope in left hand.*

2/ *I change the halter rope to my left hand to bend her to her right so she can stop.*

3/ *As she rounds out preparing to stop, she disengages her hindquarters to her left. Note her right hind is stepping in front of her left hind. If necessary, I would step to my left toward the fence to help her bend more and stop.*

4/ She is now leading past between me and the fence going to her left.

5/ Changing the halter rope to my right hand, she is already starting to round out to her left, preparing to stop facing me.

6/ Completing the stop. My right hand is already in position to ask her to lead past me to my right again. If necessary, I would drive her forward with the tail of my halter rope in my left hand.

7/ She moves forward between me and the fence. Note the tail of my halter rope is subtly communicating to move her feet. If necessary, I would firm up and flip or swing it toward her to liven her up.

Leading past through gate.

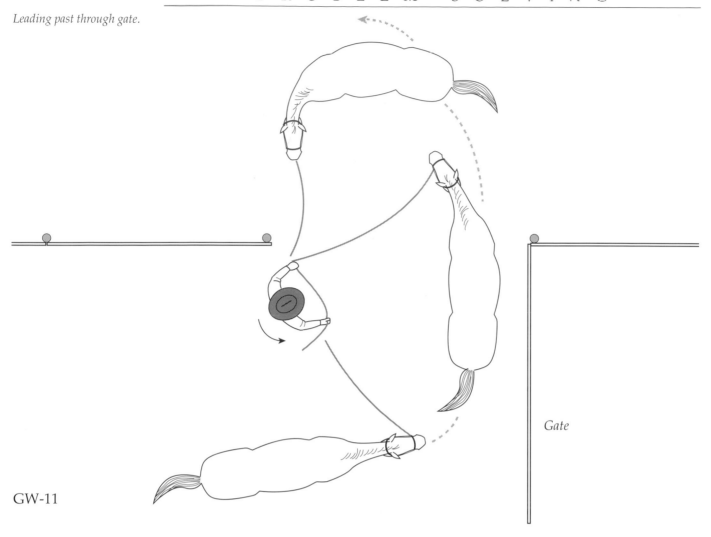

Gate

GW-11

Directing with my left hand and supporting with my right hand, I ask her to lead past me through the gate. You can also do this in or out of a stall.

Gates

Gates provide an opportunity to get your horse handier and build more roundness. Lead your horse up to a gate. Have him stop 6 to 8 feet behind you, leaving you some working room to open the gate. When the gate is open, stand on either side of the opening and lead your horse past you through the gate. See diagram GW-11. When he walks through, he'll round out his body, turn 180 degrees, and stop facing you.

Working your horse through a gate, or in and out of a stall door sets up a situation very similar to trailer-loading. All these groundwork exercises are about getting your horse halter-broke, getting his feet freed up. Most problems start because horses are not properly halter-broke.

A variation is to set up two traffic cones about 4 feet apart. Drive your horse between the two cones as if they were the

1/ *This shows my hand position to ask her to lower her head. I am **not** pushing down; I'm applying just a very slight pressure. I will release pressure immediately when she lowers her head even an inch. Note slack in halter rope; it is draped over my left arm.*

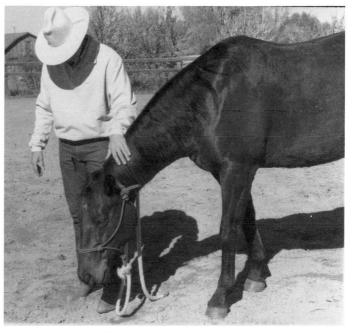

2/ *Eventually she will put her nose clear down to the ground. I don't hold her head down; my hand is lightly rubbing her neck as a reinforcement to the release reward.*

gate. Stand in various locations near the cones and drive your horse through them from wherever you are standing. Use the semicircle rather than letting your horse circle around. Lead your horse past you over a log or cavaletti on the ground, or between two barrels 4-6 feet apart.

Challenge yourself to be creative. These exercises get you and your horse handy and responsive for solving problems ahead.

Lower His Head and Flex His Jaw

Lowering your horse's head helps him relax. When horses get anxious and excited, they carry their heads higher than when they are more relaxed.

Flexing at the jaw and throatlatch area helps prepare for haltering and bridling, and relaxes and softens the horse mentally.

Place one hand behind your horse's poll, and the other on the bridge of his nose. Apply very slight downward pressure. When he gives, even the slightest amount, release and pet him, then start over. If he resists lowering his head, move his head side-to-side slightly with the hand on the bridge of his nose, while continuing the slight pressure on his neck. When he drops his head, even a little, release.

3/ *This shows my hand position to ask her to flex at the jawline to the right. Left hand is placed where the neck and jaw meet.*

The first few times your horse may only drop his head an inch. Release and take your hand away, and if his head comes up, just ask him to lower it again. Continue to do this, without forcing him to leave his head down. Eventually he'll put his nose down close to the ground.

1/ *This filly has lowered her head, making it easy to halter her.*

2/ *At a clinic, I am demonstrating lowering the head to bridle. Note I have unhooked the breast collar to make lowering her head easier. I have the tail of my mecate tied around this filly's neck with a bowline knot. Usually I would have the tail of my mecate draped over my left arm. I have my loop rein in my right hand with the headstall.*

3/ Bridling is easy when your horse helps you.

When asking him to lower his head, if he tries to back up or move away from you, go with him, allow him to drift, continuing the pressure while he's moving his feet. Keep your feet in time with your horse's feet. Maintain this position so his evasion is not rewarded. He'll begin to relax as he feels less confined or threatened. Pretty soon he'll stop. Release and start again. He'll feel more sure of things and won't need to escape. Allow him to attempt these evasions, learn they don't work for him, yet learn he doesn't need to fear what you are asking. Soon he discovers he doesn't need to protect himself. Be patient and allow your horse to make a mistake. This concept will work in many other areas. You are building trust, confidence, and respect.

Similar to lowering the head, ask your horse to laterally flex at the jawline throatlatch area. Put one hand on the bridge of his nose and your other hand at the edge of his jaw, at the throatlatch. Ask him to flex at the jawline with slight pressure at his throatlatch area with one hand, while bending his nose toward you slightly with your other hand. Flex both right and left by changing sides.

4/ I'm demonstrating how to work on a bridling or a lowering-the-head problem from a saddle horse.

Notice this when your horse is leading past you around in a circle. Some horses have their jaw pointed toward the handler. To match the circle's arc, they should be bent at the throatlatch, and their nose closer to you than their jaw. If his jaw is pushed toward you, he's defensive; it's a brace.

You'll find that a horse who is not soft and flexible through the neck and jawline in groundwork will be the same way

1/ *I ask this filly to step her hindquarters over to her left, parallel to the fence, by bumping straight up on the halter rope. As she steps over, I release.* **Timing of the release is the key**.

2/ *I rub on her to reinforce the release reward. I could now mount from the fence.*

3/ *Sitting on the fence is a good place to work on lots of things, such as swinging a rope. If you don't have a lariat, swing the tail of your halter rope. While sitting on the fence, get your horse accustomed to a slicker, flag, rope, etc.*

when you are riding. Pay attention to your horse's alignment during groundwork and while riding.

Lowering your horse's head and flexing the throatlatch will help when you're trying to halter, bridle, or saddle him. If you take care of this early on, you won't have a problem.

Sit on the Fence

Sitting on the fence, drive your horse in semicircles as described earlier. Teach your horse to lead parallel to the fence, to mount him from the fence. Often, he comes close but he won't line up perfectly, swinging his hindquarters away. Lift the halter rope straight up, bumping his nose, lightly at first, until he steps his hindquarters closer toward you and the fence. The moment he moves his hindquarters the slightest step in your direction, release, and pet him. Then start again. Soon he will hunt this spot. Your **release**, properly timed, is how he learns

where to move his feet.

While you're on the fence, be creative. Have your slicker, flag, and rope up there with you. Rub him with the slicker and rope coils, swing your rope and flag around, etc. If he gets scared and moves away, realign him and start over more slowly. If these things are too troubling to your horse, start on the ground before you get on the fence.

Leading

Once you free up your horse's feet and place them where you want them with the initial exercises, leading is not difficult. If your horse doesn't lead up well, don't pull him; you will be teaching him to drag and/or pull back. You may need to go back to the leading-past exercise to free up his feet more.

When leading, it doesn't matter

35

1/ Leading my horse forward, I ask her to stay about 6 feet behind me.

2/ When I stop, she should stop. If she didn't stop, I would back her by bumping back on the halter rope or swinging it toward her chest or legs to get her back. Eventually you could do this same exercise holding the halter rope right at the end, from 10 to 12 feet away from your horse.

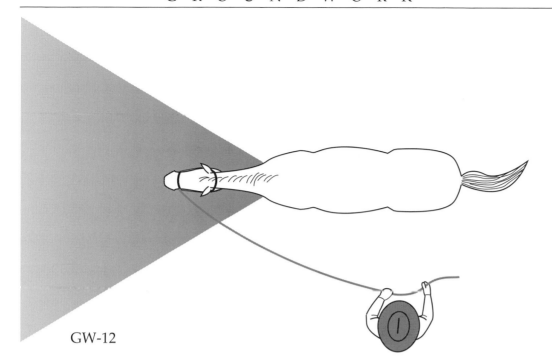

GW-12

If your horse pulls back, rears, or tries to pull away, stay out of the front triangle. Instead, get to his side, bend his head and neck around toward you, driving his hindquarters away, or drive him straight forward, or both.

whether your horse is in front, behind, on the right or left, near, or on the end of the halter rope. However, if your horse is not where you want him to be, it's the wrong place. Lead your horse from all these positions so you both get sharp and handy.

Holding or leading with your hand close to the halter is ineffective, and creates a stiff and pushy horse. Trying to control a horse by pulling or jerking downward on the halter is also ineffective, contributing to more problems.

Avoid Front Triangle

If a horse pulls back, rears, or attempts to pull away, keep yourself in a leverage position. To regain control, the best leverage position is getting off to the side and bending his head toward you so you can get him to roll his hindquarters away. Don't stay in front of your horse or hold him at the halter. See diagram GW-12.

Instead get farther out on the halter rope and get control of the horse's feet.

Start leading your horse about 6 feet behind you. If he comes closer, put him back as you continue walking forward. You do this by bumping back sideways on the halter rope or swinging the tail around toward his chest or knees to encourage him to stay back.

When you stop, your horse should stop. If he continues on, put him back by bumping the halter rope back alongside his body. This is similar to back-up exercise GW-13, except you will still be in front of your horse. This doesn't have to be harsh or abusive; just be quietly matter-of-fact and businesslike. Walk off, then stop, and walk off again. Lead from both the left and right, to achieve balance and control on either side.

Get your horse so hooked on to you mentally that he is moving and stopping in time with your body language. Whether riding down the trail, gathering cattle, or leading your horse, create an atmosphere where he is paying attention and ready to do what you ask. He is content doing his job and looking for your direction in a positive way.

Sidepassing down fence to the right. My hands are spread wide apart to drive the frontquarters and hindquarters equally.

Side-Pass Down A Fence

Start with your horse's nose at the fence. Stand off to his side, and move toward him. First move his hindquarters away from you a step, then his frontquarters away from you a step, then hind, then front, then both together.

Use the tail of your halter rope to help move him only when needed. Do this in stages until you can put it all together and he will side-pass smoothly down the fence.

Backing

Start by standing beside your horse's head. Reach under his jaw; take hold of the halter with your thumb pointing down. Your forearm will be along the side of his head. Face in the direction of his hindquarters. Apply a slight amount of backward pressure. When you feel him try to back—taking a step or just rocking his weight back—**release**.

Start again and ask for one step back. When he starts to pick up his foot, that's the time to release, not after he has backed and set a foot down. Then the release would be too late. Release when he **thinks** about backing. Time the release to his mental commitment to respond. This exercise demonstrates the importance of feel, timing, and balance of the release. The quicker the human grasps this, the quicker the horse will respond with respect and lightness.

When backing your horse, look for him to reach equally on his diagonals. Your horse backs like he trots forward—on a left and right diagonal. He should back straight. Both diagonal hoofs should leave and strike the ground simultaneously. If he doesn't reach equally, it is a sign of being stiffer on one side. He should also flex at the poll when backing.

IMPORTANT: If your horse does not back away from a light feel backward, don't add more back-up pressure. It gets his feet more stuck in the ground, and you

1/ *This is my hand placement for backing with my hand on the halter. Notice my thumb is pointed down and the bottom edge of my hand is right next to her jaw. She is stepping back, so I have released pressure even though my hand is still on the halter. If she did not back up, I would move my hand **side to side** to free up her feet, rather than push backward.*

2/ *Backing from the left. Notice where my forearm is in relation to her head. Just like when riding, I want my horse to back with a soft feel, with the nose in and down with longitudinal flexion.*

begin to lose the lightness and softness. From the horse's point of view, it becomes force. Instead, add **side-to-side motion** while maintaining a little backward pressure. This helps untrack his feet and makes it more difficult for him to resist. If you just try to push him backward, he will learn to resist you. In contrast, the side-to-side movement doesn't give him anything to lean against. When his feet come loose, release. Make sure your horse doesn't drop his shoulder into you when backing.

Incrementally build up to backing your horse several steps, releasing with each step back. It may take you awhile, depending on your own feel, timing, and balance. Do this gradually, instead of asking for several steps the first time.

Each time you start this or another exercise, ask with the lightest amount of pressure possible. Then build up to more until you get a response. Assume your horse will respond to lightness. If he doesn't, then add more side-to-side pressure until you get a response. Your goal is to have your horse back up with the slightest feel.

Once your horse is good backing straight, start backing quarter-circles. Both diagonal hoofs should leave and strike the ground simultaneously. Bend his head a little away from you after he is backing. His hindquarters will step away from the bend as he is backing. Start with a few steps and eventually he will back a quarter-circle.

3/ *Backing a quarter-circle (arc) to the right. I have the mare's head turned (flexed) slightly to the right. Note her right front is stepping out and back to the right, and her left hind is stepping out and back to the left. A right quarter-circle is backing front-quarters to the right, hindquarters to the left, reaching equally on all four quarters.*

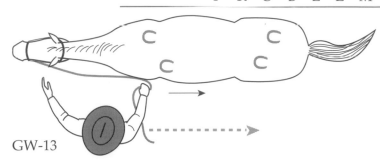

GW-13

Backing from the side.

Here's another way to back your horse. Stand facing your horse's side looking over his withers. Have the halter rope in your hand closest to his hip. See diagram GW-13. With your forearm in front of you and elbow bent, move your hand back. He should stay straight, so place your other hand by his head to block him from bending his head in your direction. Release when he steps back, then repeat. Eventually you can stand farther away from his side and he will back to your slightest feel down the halter rope.

With the correct approach, eventually your horse will back from just your body language. You can be at the end of the halter rope and back him with just the slightest movement of your hand in his direction.

Back Up and Walk the Frontquarters Away

I first learned this exercise riding in a Buck Brannaman clinic. Buck had us do this horseback; however, it is also an excellent groundwork exercise. Using a fence line, walk alongside your horse's shoulder, and lead forward with your horse next to the fence. Stop. Still facing forward, start backing him parallel to the fence by softly tugging the halter rope backward while holding it alongside, parallel to his body, with your hand next to his shoulder. After a few steps, turn into your horse, and start him backing in a quarter-circle, until he is perpendicular to the fence. Now walk toward your horse so he moves his frontquarters away from you, pivoting on his hindquarters. When he's parallel with the fence again, start walking forward. You've reversed directions, and now you're between your horse and the fence. Do this from both his right and left sides. See diagram GW-14.

Let Him Stand Tied

People who really use their horses, particularly out in the country working cattle, on trail rides, or pack trips, have many occasions to tie their horses for long periods of time. The horse needs to feel content and safe while tied.

At the beginning or the end of your daily session, get in the habit of letting your horse stand tied for a while. Use a safe tie post, tying him high with some

1/ *From the side, I am in position to ask her to back. My right elbow is bent, with my forearm in line with the halter rope. My left hand will block if she turns her head to the left. As I take the slack out of the halter rope, she will back up and I will release to reward. If she didn't back, rather than pull her back, I would firm up by bumping back on the halter rope with my right hand. Incrementally position yourself farther forward until you can back your horse from the position shown in the next photo.*

2/ *Backing with body language.*

GW-14

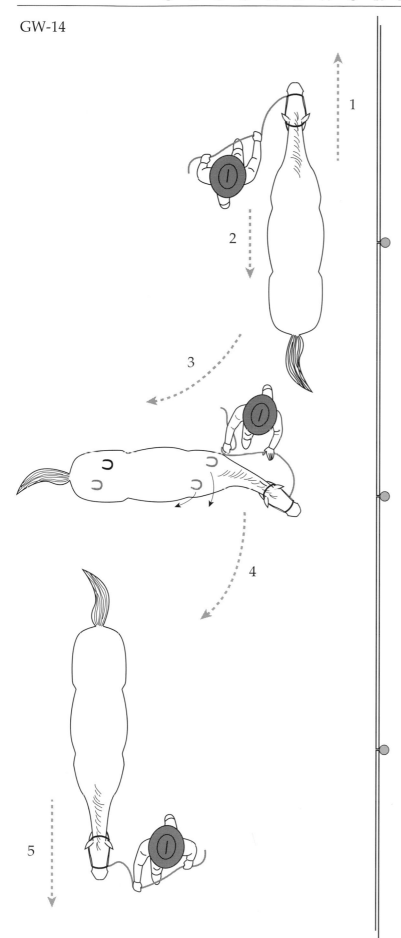

1

2

3

4

5

*Back up and walk the frontquarters away—along a fence line. 1/ Lead horse forward and stop straight. 2/ Back straight. 3/ Turn toward horse, back a right quarter-circle, stop with horse facing perpendicular to fence. 4/ Walk frontquarters quarter-turn to right. 5/ Lead horse straight forward. Do this exercise from both sides. Get familiar with this so you can **do it horseback**. This is very similar to turning with a cow.*

You'll find the handier you get with these exercises, the better your horse will be.

I am brushing her hind leg and she is helping me by standing quietly. Note halter rope draped over my arm. Through these groundwork exercises, getting horses handy on the halter rope makes everything we do easier and more pleasurable

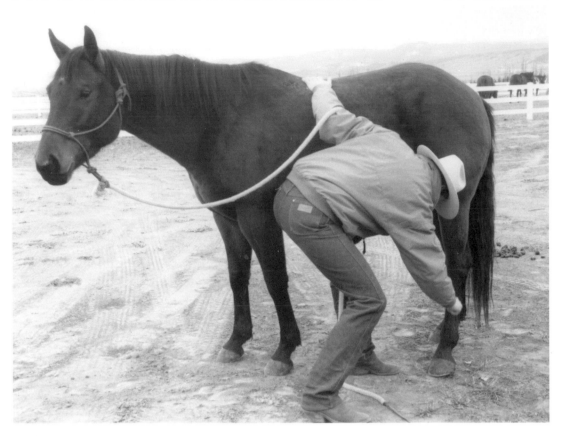

slack still in the halter rope. Tie short enough so he can't get his foot over the rope, but long enough so he can move side to side without feeling overconfined. CAUTION: This assumes your horse is already tie-broke and doesn't ever pull back. See Chapter 9, Pulls Back When Tied, for more suggestions.

If your horse is not used to being tied, or if he frets when tied, start with 10 or 15 minutes and add 5 to 10 minutes each day, until your horse can stand for several hours or all day.

Often, if a horse is impatient, he resorts to pawing or fretting. Don't untie him when he exhibits this behavior. Observe him from a distance. When he quits

pawing and is standing with a leg cocked, head lowered, and relaxed, walk up immediately and untie him. Observe him doing the right thing, untie, and put him up. It's a way of rewarding and praising him for the behavior you want.

His pawing is saying, "I want to be somewhere else." When he exhibits the behavior you're looking for, he gets to do what he wants. This may be a test of your patience as well as your horse's.

Conclusion

You'll find the handier you get with these exercises, the better your horse will be. These exercises are not complicated, and are useful for everything from halter-breaking, starting a colt and problem-solving to helping any level horse become sharper and more attentive.

People who have attended my clinics over the years have given me positive feedback about the value and functional usefulness of this groundwork. It has helped them gain confidence, understand their horses better, and get a clear picture of how their horses move and operate naturally.

The groundwork described here, if presented and practiced correctly, can serve as the foundation to solve all horse problems. Continually stretching you and your horse out of your comfort zone is imperative to advancing horsemanship and solving problems. This groundwork is a good place to start, since you can control the variables. It is also an excellent way to learn to become more **proactive; learning to be ahead of your horse mentally with direction, rather than reactive to his actions.**

Having my horses good on the halter rope is a way of life for me. I wouldn't have it any other way. Handling a horse who stays out of your space, is soft, light, responsive, attentive, and stays hooked mentally is truly a pleasure. Handling a horse who is pushy and drags on the halter rope is not much fun, and creates or perpetuates other problems.

People ask how many repetitions they should do of these exercises. The answer is to read the horse accurately and adjust to his individuality. After your horse has responded correctly a few times, then do something else. This is just a guideline; it's not etched in stone. **Don't drill** your horses at this. Instead, incorporate this into everything you do. It is more important that your horse learns to have trust, confidence, and respect for what you are asking him to do.

There are no single, quick, or magic cures for any one problem. **Your overall program and the manner in which you approach your horse will determine how things go.** Think of possibilities, get creative, and try variations of all these exercises. Have a clear picture of your goal in mind and then ask the horse to match it. Make things interesting, challenging, and rewarding for your horse.

My mentors pointed out to me early on that when trying to solve a problem, it is too easy to get overfocused on the specific problem (which is really a symptom of a deeper problem) and possibly make things worse. Rather than focus on the problem, work on something else with the horse and concentrate on getting that better. When you come back to the original problem, it may not be nearly as bad as it was.

It is never too early or too late to begin effectively communicating with your horse. Fortunately for us, even an older horse's foundation can be improved.

Getting a horse good on the halter rope is about getting him soft mentally and physically, responsive down to his feet. This is the real essence of having a halter-broke horse. What you achieve will carry over directly to your riding and solving problems, and toward a willing partnership with your horse.

2 RIDING FOUNDATION

> Give your horse a job to do.

THE EXERCISES outlined in this chapter are basic for continuing the development of a strong foundation of trust, confidence, respect, communication, response, and control—fundamental to all problem-solving. They will apply to any situation or horse, whether solving a problem, starting a colt, or any other activity. For some this information will not be new, just a review.

What we consider problems are actually symptoms. Anytime we are around our horses, we are reinforcing positive behaviors or inadvertently reinforcing unwanted behaviors. Problems often arise because the human is unaware of his role in creating or reinforcing these undesired behaviors.

When we have a problem, it is easy to become focused only on what is going wrong. However, getting away from the problem and working on other things will often help both horse and rider get more in tune with each other. Then, when you start to work on the problem again, sometimes all or a major portion of it has already been resolved.

At my horsemanship clinics, people ask me what to do when their horse exhibits a particular problem, such as won't cross water, gets chargey, balks, etc. My response is that, generally, there are some actions to take when they're in the middle of the dust storm. However, taking a developmental approach is a more permanent solution. Then when faced with the problem they're dealing with, the horse has more recent, positive experience to build on. Instead of resistance or flight, the horse learns to rely on the human for direction and self-preservation.

Get your horse prepared before you attempt to solve the problem (symptom), rather than waiting for the problem to surface and then dealing with it; be proactive instead of reactive. Having your horse good on the halter rope and hooked on mentally to you in the round corral will carry over into riding. Developing more trust, confidence, and respect when riding will carry over into problem-solving. Putting more time and effort into preparation shortens the time it takes to solve the problem.

As the rider becomes more proactive, the horse will begin to willingly wait and look for guidance, staying in a learning frame of mind. The horse learns to go with the rider's flow and the rider with the horse's flow, and they'll be right on.

Make Every Ride an Adventure

Make every ride an adventure, have fun, and stretch both you and your horse out of your comfort zones. Sometimes we think our horse is good at everything else except a specific problem. Yet, I've found this is rarely the case. Some riders think this because they stay in a familiar routine, seldom face many challenges, or don't present new challenges equal to or greater than the problem. Practice building your horse's confidence by incrementally heightening your expectations. As your horse becomes comfortable with these new situations, add another dimension. If you look for new things to experience, both you and your horse will gain new confidence.

The best way to resolve a problem, after you have established a solid groundwork and riding foundation, is to get out and ride your horse. Make every ride an adventure, finding interesting and challenging opportunities, incrementally expanding your comfort zones.

Give your horse a job to do. Allow him to build his trust and respect responding to you, as you develop your feel, timing, and balance in knowing when, where, and how much to ask to solve the problem.

Communication Suggestions

Here are some things to keep in mind when doing these riding exercises:

1/ Never get angry, frustrated, forceful, or tentative. If your horse gets troubled, resistant, or afraid, stay relaxed, positive, and confident. When things really fall apart, stay in the eye of the storm, helping your horse return to a better frame of mind. Be willing to adjust to fit the individual horse and situation.

2/ Impulsion—without it everything will be more difficult, if not impossible. Keep life in your horse's feet, and the drive coming from behind.

3/ Focus—have a plan, then pick out an object and ride toward it; look where you are riding—it will help direct your horse.

4/ Seat—subtly communicate speed, gait, direction, slow down, and stop through your seat bones. Your horse will appreciate it when you communicate with pressure the weight of a fly landing on his skin.

5/ Legs—communicating lateral movement with legs is a skill often underdeveloped.

6/ Reins—support the directing communication given through your seat and legs with the lightest pressure possible. **Avoid using the reins to stay balanced in the saddle.** Being able to ride through all your horse's gaits and back down to a halt on a very loose rein is important for developing confidence and control. Minimizing rein pressure keeps your horse's feet freed up so he stays mentally soft and light—a soft feel.

Set Things Up

With these exercises, prepare and get your horse ready before you ask him to slow down, speed up, stop, or turn. Give him a choice, but make the correct choice easy and the wrong one difficult. Offer your horse a good deal first, then firm up as needed to be effective. If he resists, you'll be in a position to make resisting difficult without forcing him to do what you want. Set it up so he sees resisting as putting pressure on himself instead of you putting pressure on him; horses understand the difference.

When you make the wrong thing difficult, don't make it unbearable, just allow him to work at it; keep him searching for the answer. When your horse yields to his own pressure, release pressure immediately. Your release, properly timed, will reward and reinforce your horse's correct choice. It's not necessary to be harsh or offensive to get a response; stay positive, smile, and relax. Don't think in terms of punishing, disciplining, or correcting. Instead, develop discipline in yourself, and redirect your horse. Be dependable in showing your horse the path of least resistance. Learn to do less to get more from your horse so pressure becomes feel.

Each horse is an individual and needs to be ridden as such. The exercises suggested will be most helpful when the rider is willing to adjust to fit the horse and each situation. Never make anything a contest with your horse; instead make both you and your horse winners.

One popular expression is there's nothing like lots of wet saddle blankets. This is true: Horses today generally do not get actively ridden enough, and this is a factor in many problems. However, **it's not what you do, it's how you go about it**. **Increase both quality and quantity in your riding.**

Get out and ride your horse, smile and enjoy yourself, it will all work out. Focus on the good and the not-so-good will just go away.

Drifting the Hindquarters

The purpose of this exercise is to develop willing control of your horse's feet with lateral bending (flexion) and disengaging his hindquarters. This builds toward the one-rein stop, but emphasizes impulsion too. It also develops suppleness and lateral roundness.

Start by riding your horse straight in a ground-covering walk, with lots of life in his feet (impulsion), all four quarters reaching equally. Start a circle, bending your horse, keeping him moving forward with the same impulsion. Gradually increase the bend 1 or 2 degrees with each step. Keep slack in the outside rein. Your circle will gradually get smaller, corkscrewing down as you bend your horse more. Winding him down gives your horse time to think and respond.

Do not lean to the inside while you are bending him. Stay balanced over your horse so he does not drop his shoulder and fall into the circle. As he bends more, you will feel his hindquarters step more to the outside, from engagement to disengagement. Immediately release the rein and let him walk off straight on a loose rein, his reward for yielding and disengaging.

You are not asking him to stop, just to disengage one step. You have gone from engagement, to disengaging one step, back to engagement. Start again, repeating this on the other side. This should be soft, smooth, and fluid like a dance.

Disengaging

Disengaging the hindquarters means your horse is stepping his inside hind leg up under himself and in front of the outside hind leg. This is similar to engaging on a circle. However, in disengagement he does not push off forward with power as in engagement. Instead you will feel his forward energy drop off and his hip drop slightly.

Disengaging is putting your horse into neutral, taking him out of gear, even if for just a moment.

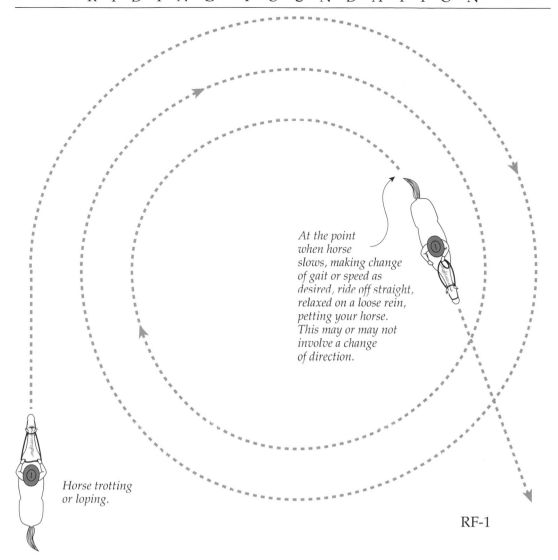

Winding down the circle to slow. Trot to a walk, lope to a trot or walk, etc. When horse changes gait or speed, ride off straight, relaxed on a loose rein.

At the point when horse slows, making change of gait or speed as desired, ride off straight, relaxed on a loose rein, petting your horse. This may or may not involve a change of direction.

Horse trotting or loping.

RF-1

Winding Down Circle to Slow

Your horse will not disengage his hindquarters during this exercise, just slow down. Vigorously trot your horse straight, then begin a large circle. Relax, slowing down your body rhythm, as you gradually make the circle smaller. As soon as your horse slows to a walk, release him out of the circle and walk off straight, relaxed. Rub him as he walks out. Alternate directions each time you start over. Diagram RF-1.

If you are riding a chargey horse and he starts speeding up to a trot or lope after you walk off on a loose rein, begin winding him down again the other direction. Repeat this until he will maintain a walk on a loose rein, waiting for your communication.

Your horse is learning to follow your body rhythm, and the smaller circle is making trotting difficult and walking easy. This exercise works really well with a high-energy horse because he does not feel too confined while learning to get in time with his rider.

Lateral flexion to the left. Note slack in rein. I'm preparing to release the rein. If your horse is not familiar with lateral flexion, he probably won't flex this much to start.

Lateral Flexion

Refer to Chapter 1 Groundwork section on bending (flexing) laterally. Ask your horse to laterally bend (flex) his head and neck while you are mounted. Remember not to try to pull your horse's head around when you take the slack out of your rein. If he does not give, hold and wait, allowing him to come off his own pressure. If your horse won't stand still while you ask him to bend (flex), you may be pulling on him or asking for too much. Ask for just a slight bend, release, and build to more

incrementally. Pretty soon he'll willingly bend (flex) his head past 90 degrees. When bending, his head should stay vertical, flexing at the poll, not laying his head parallel to the ground. When he bends (flexes) around far enough, reach down and pet his head.

As he is getting soft and light, very lightly tap him with your inside calf just before you ask him to bend. It will draw his attention that direction, and one day he will look in that direction when you lightly tap him—without you touching the rein.

One-Rein Stop

The one-rein stop is an emergency stop. When things turn to chaos and all else fails, rely on your one-rein stop. If practiced correctly, it will build trust, confidence, and respect between you and your horse.

You will ask for a complete, disengaged stop, in a slow, deliberate, smooth, and fluid movement. Trot your horse off straight, then reach down and shorten one rein, bending (flexing) your horse's head and neck around to one side. Move your inside leg back behind the cinch to help your horse step his hindquarters out away from the bend and disengage. The frontquarters should continue forward in a smaller arc, and not stop before the hindquarters do. Allow your horse to find his way to a stop; don't force him. When he comes to a complete stop, release your leg and rein, letting him stand quietly while you rub (pet) him. Be sure your horse is not pulling on the rein when you release. Practice this on both sides.

Maintain lots of slack in your outside rein throughout a one-rein stop. When you bend (flex) your horse with the inside rein, he should be soft and yielding, not pulling against you. Don't lean down or forward to shorten your bending rein. Instead, use your outside hand to pull the rein through your inside hand to shorten up.

Caution: Avoid teaching your horse to drop his inside shoulder. ***Do not lean to the inside*** as you are bending your horse,

1/ I carry a coil in my mecate. When making a one-rein stop, I lift the coil in one hand, pulling the slack through the other hand, which allows me to stay balanced instead of leaning forward to get short on the bending rein. Although I prefer to ride with a mecate, any rein setup you ride with will work equally well with these exercises.

2/ I am bending (flexing) this mare to the left. She is preparing to bring her left hind up under in front of her outside hind, and to disengage.

and don't snatch his head down and around. Keep your bending arm up and in front of you; don't let your hand drop down and behind. Keep your elbow bent. Be smooth and fluid, and stay balanced over your horse.

The one-rein stop can have a positive mental effect on your horse when he learns you can help get him out of trouble and control him without force or pain. Keep your approach positive and nurturing, not punishing. Don't overdo the one-rein stop, spend more time drifting the hindquarters. However, don't wait until you need it to practice; that's too late. Practice the one-rein stop until it becomes an automatic response, so when needed, it's there.

A variation of the one-rein stop is a simple exercise for the antsy horse who won't stand still when asked. When he moves off at a fidgety walk, put your hand down one rein with slack in the other. Bend (flex) his head and neck about 45 degrees, resting your hand on your thigh and sit quiet in the saddle. Allow him to circle until he stops, then immediately release the rein. If he fidgets and moves again, bend him the other direction, wait, then release the rein when he stops. After several repetitions, this horse will start standing quietly until the rider asks him to move.

3/ My left leg is back to ask her to disengage her hindquarters by moving them to the right. I'll remove leg pressure as she does. When she stops, I will immediately release my rein.

I recommend a plain snaffle bit (no shanks) for solving riding problems. I use an egg-butt snaffle bit. Snaffles work best for lateral bending, but work equally well for straight stops, backing up, etc. It is a good habit to often back up a step or two after you stop.

This is how I carry the tail of my mecate while riding. It runs over the horn and through my chap belt. If I came off my horse unexpectedly, it could pull through my belt without hanging up. I would remain in control of my horse by grabbing the end. When dismounting, I simply lift it off my horn, step down, then cross my loop rein over the horn. The mecate tail is then my lead rope.

Why a Plain Snaffle Bit?

Problems are best resolved riding in a plain snaffle bit (without shanks—any device with shanks is a curb bit, regardless of the mouthpiece). Use a plain snaffle for these exercises because lateral bending in a shank bit will inflict pain. It would be punishing your horse for doing the right thing. If you currently ride in a curb bit, mechanical hackamore, or a shanked snaffle, your horse will easily accept the changeover to a plain snaffle.

Snaffles work off the corners of the mouth, and control is mainly achieved through using each rein independently, not by pulling back evenly on both reins. Working through these exercises, you'll realize you have more control in a snaffle, yet still develop better communication, retaining more softness and lightness. If later you wish to go back to your curb bit, your horse will handle it better than before.

The curb bit is designed to be a signal bit for subtle communication and refinement. When a horse is ready for a curb bit, control should not be an issue. Good straight stops and advanced levels of refinement can still be achieved while your horse is in a plain snaffle.

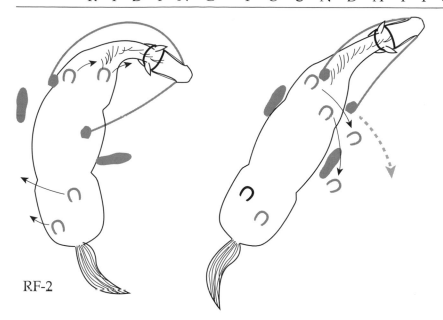

*Moving the hindquarters and frontquarters with the approximate hand and leg positions. This is like a one-rein stop, but adds moving the frontquarters. (The term **approximate** is used, as you have to read your horse and adjust to fit him moment by moment, including hand and leg positions. This also applies to the other suggested hand and leg position diagrams.)*

RF-2

Moving the Hindquarters and Frontquarters

Walk your horse forward with lots of life, then bend him to the right. When he disengages his hindquarters, just as he stops, partially release the inside rein, keeping him slightly bent. Keep his energy up. Quickly looking up and back to your right, open up with your right leg by taking it off your horse, bringing your left leg and rein against him. Slightly lean back and to the outside, your left, so he can shift his weight back to his haunches. Using mostly left leg pressure, bring his frontquarters across to the right, pivoting on his hindquarters. Release and walk him forward. See diagram RF-2.

Now bend him the opposite direction, disengaging his hindquarters to the right, and bring the frontquarters through to the left. Your feel and timing are important to get this to work fluidly and smoothly.

Observe the similarity between this and the groundwork exercises of leading your horse past you, then bending him, asking him to disengage his hindquarters, stop, then bringing the frontquarters across, and walk off the opposite direction.

As with starting colts, it may be helpful to have a friend flag your horse (see photos) to develop your feel, timing, and balance in this exercise. This exercise will have many applications later on.

Tip the Nose Toward a Fence To Slow the Feet

This is a good exercise to help your horse mentally connect a rein down to his feet. It is also excellent to help a chargey horse who won't maintain gait on a loose rein.

Walk your horse to the right in the arena, parallel to the fence. Ask him to trot forward on a loose rein. Bend (flex) his nose slightly toward the fence, maintaining forward motion, with slack in the other rein. The fence will keep your horse from turning. As he begins to slow to a walk, release the bending rein and continue walking forward on a loose rein, petting him.

Repeat this trot-to-walk both directions around the arena several times. Bending his nose into the fence makes trotting difficult and releasing makes walking easy. The timing of the release is when you feel your horse preparing to walk, not after he walks. This will help you both mentally connect your rein down to his feet.

1/ This sequence is like the one-rein stop, but adds moving the front-quarters. I am bending (flexing) this mare to the right, moving my right leg back, to step her hindquarters to the left, disengaging, and releasing leg pressure as she starts to step over behind.

2/ Note slack in outside rein. She is getting ready to stop.

3/ She has stopped, I've partially released her head as I sit back slightly. My left leg and rein are now asking her to step her front-quarters across.

4/ She is slightly flexed to the right, and stepping her right front out and back. She will then step her left front across in front of her right.

1/ Flagging a colt's hind-quarters. I am using a flag (rod with canvas tied on the end) to assist Kristi Plutt with one of her young horses in training. This helps a colt begin learning the feel of leg and rein without his rider putting pressure on him. This also gives my horse a job to do.

2/ Flagging the colt's frontquarters.

53

I have this filly's nose tipped toward the fence waiting for her to slow to a walk. I'll release immediately as she starts to walk.

Soft Feel

Ride your horse encouraging responsiveness, roundness, lightness, softness, and flexibility throughout his entire body. Soft feel is how your horse responds mentally; willingly yielding, giving, and turning loose. It begins with your horse flexing at the poll when you take the slack out of both reins, yielding to your hands through the bit. It's a mental willingness, not just physical.

Horses are naturally soft and light; they are all very sensitive. People often develop hardness in their horses through the reins. Learn to be soft, light, and sensitive for your horse. As Ray Hunt describes it: "It's a soft firmness—not a dull hardness." This begins on the halter rope, and carries over into riding.

We don't need to teach our horses to be soft, we need to teach ourselves to be soft. This is achieved by rewarding the horse for turning loose to our soft firmness, rather than pulling on or releasing to the horse's resistance, creating a dull hardness. Develop your horse's softness throughout his body down to his feet. The priority is to have your horse soft in his feet, not just soft in his face.

Flexing at the poll is one component of collection. However, collection comes from the hindquarters, from back to front, not vice versa. Moving forward with more drive from the hindquarters has been the goal, starting from the groundwork on the halter rope, carrying forward to riding.

First, ask for a soft feel while sitting balanced on your horse in a neutral position, your body language communicating to stand still. Shorten both reins, with your arms outstretched, and your hands wide apart, about the width of your horse's shoulders. Take the slack out of the reins by bringing your elbows back, with a slight pressure on the bit. Don't pull, see how little it takes. Be patient; just hold and wait. **Your hands should be short enough on the reins to stay in front of the saddle horn.** Release the moment you feel your horse give, flexing at the poll and yielding to the bit without backing up. Release by straightening your elbows, then ask again, or turn loose to put more slack in the reins.

The way you handle your reins makes the difference whether your horse feels offended and resistant or willing and open to your communication. Avoid pulling, causing overflexing past vertical, coming behind the bit. Your timing is critical. Release before his head is vertical. Your horse should flex at the poll, not just elevate his neck at the shoulder. Adjust to fit the individual horse, and have a picture in your mind of what you're looking for in your horse.

The soft feel is a way to check in mentally with your horse, keep him attentive, and in a learning frame of mind. You will use this to alert your horse to prepare for a transition, to sharpen up and get ready to do something.

When the soft feel is good at a halt, get it good at a walk. Walk out on a loose rein, pick up a soft feel for a stride, then release it. Let the horse go for a few strides on a

1/ *Asking for a soft feel or vertical flexion. Notice my elbows are bent and hands wide apart. Don't bend your wrists; keep them straight. She has flexed and I'll immediately release. If your horse is not familiar with this, he may not flex this much to start.*

2/ *Releasing rein pressure by straightening my elbows. If your horse is not familiar with the soft feel, don't wait for this much flexion before releasing. Instead reward the smallest try and build on it.*

loose rein, then ask again. Keep the life in his feet (impulsion) when you ask for the soft feel at the walk. If he slows, liven him up with your legs, keeping him moving out. Once the soft feel is good at the walk, move on to the trot. Your progression from the trot to lope may take awhile. There is no hurry; take lots of time. Initially, release to the soft feel immediately. As your horse progresses, incrementally hold the soft feel longer at each gait.

Next, carry the soft feel down to a slower gait, releasing when he makes the transition. At a walk and trot, pick up a soft feel, stop your body rhythm, and carry the soft feel down to a straight stop, then release. If at any point you lose the soft feel, just hold steady (don't pull) until you get it back, then release. To advance further, ask for the soft feel at the halt and carry it up into a walk, then release immediately. Then from walk to trot, etc.

To advance and develop more collection, add more drive with your seat and legs. It's important to remember to not attempt to collect your horse by pulling on his face. When your horse drives more from behind, he coils his loin, elevating his back and shoulders as he reaches deeper

3/ *Carrying the soft feel at a walk, driving forward with seat and legs. Build up to this in all gaits.*

with his hindquarters. When you feel him elevate his back even slightly, release, allowing him to walk off on a loose rein.

Eventually you can carry the soft feel with more collection longer before you release. However, build up very slowly, allowing your horse to learn to accept the confinement that more collection represents. Proceed gradually, and don't hesitate to adjust to your horse. Slow down or return to earlier steps if he becomes troubled at any stage.

The most basic way of thinking about training horses is that they need to learn to yield to and from pressure. The soft feel is another form of the horse yielding to and from pressure.

The soft feel is a starting point. It's a way of riding without resistance, you and your horse responding to each other with the most subtle communications. Utilize the soft feel throughout all your riding activity. It's the same type of feel you want on the halter rope—lightness and responsiveness down to your horse's feet. Lateral flexion with one rein is the same as a soft feel with two reins. It's all interrelated, part of the whole.

The ultimate goal is to ride your horse with impulsion, responsiveness, and lightness throughout his entire body. The soft feel is an important part of the mental harmony and unity horse and rider achieve in developing a willing partnership.

Communicating Through Body Rhythm

Body rhythm or body language is simply your activity level horseback. It starts with your seat and legs. Although it's so subtle it may be imperceptible to the human observer, the horse reads it loud and clear if you are consistent. At first you may need to exaggerate to communicate your body language. Riders often unwittingly follow their horse's body rhythm, encouraging the wrong thing—for example, getting in time with a jigging or chargey horse. Instead, develop a habit of

maintaining the rhythm you desire, setting it up so your horse finds your rhythm the most comfortable one to follow.

Learn to use your reins as lightly as possible in communicating with your horse. Use the reins to support your horse and as a backup to your more subtle seat and leg communication. Using your seat as your principal means of communication can be developed to a high degree of subtlety (feel). It is not very difficult or advanced, it just requires awareness and practice. Your horse is very sensitive—he can feel a fly or mosquito land on him. It is up to us to communicate with him in a way that acknowledges and respects his sensitivity.

To slow down, develop a habit of quieting your body activity, seat, and legs. To move out or speed up, get more active, subtly pushing forward with your seat bones and legs. Your horse will begin to associate your seat and leg activity with the desired response. Pretty soon, you and your horse will communicate with very little rein pressure, through feel instead of pressure.

To experiment with this, trot your horse actively on a loose rein. Continue the trot long enough to build up your horse's desire to slow down. Then change your riding rhythm from trot to walk and see if your horse will slow to a walk without need of your reins. If he slows to a walk, pet him and walk forward relaxed, then start again. If he doesn't walk, sit quietly in the saddle, then start drawing on the rein until he walks. Practice this exercise with all gaits, but start with walk-to-trot-to-walk first.

To request a trot, increase your body activity, pushing forward with your seat bones and legs. If he does not trot out quickly, follow up by bumping with your legs (not heels) and/or the tail of your mecate. Your horse will learn quickly if you are consistent with the sequence and your timing. He will associate that your seat bones pushing forward comes before your legs or mecate bump him. Rather than make him move, make it difficult for him to not move. He would prefer you not bump him, so he will move out from your seat activity. The horse needs your communication to be consistent and dependable.

Using feel, timing, and balance, someday you will sit on your horse and he will rock forward and back as you request, not moving his feet, without you touching the reins.

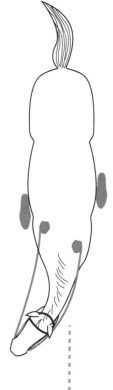

*Partial bend to slow the feet. This is similar to tipping the nose to a fence to slow, but using inside leg and outside rein pressure to keep the horse straight. Release immediately when the horse's feet start to slow down. Ride with your **hands wide apart** when more control is needed. This gelding was somewhat unsure coming through the creek between the willows and being away from his buddies.*

Partial bend to slow the feet; approximate hand and leg positions.

RF-3

Partial Bend To Slow the Feet

I use this in many, many situations where I want to communicate control to my horse, especially when circling or a one-rein stop is either unnecessary or undesirable. This exercise is helpful with a chargey, jigging, or rushing horse on a narrow road, trail, narrow water crossing, riding out in open country, and in many other situations.

Walk your horse forward with straightness, then move up to a trot. Slow your body rhythm, tip (flex) your horse's nose slightly to one side with one rein. Use your outside rein to limit the amount of bend (flex), and your legs to keep him tracking straight. Fix it up and wait for your horse to come off his own pressure. Bending makes trotting difficult, and your release makes walking easy. When your horse slows to a walk, release your reins and legs, and continue to walk forward on a loose rein, rubbing him. Alternate sides each time you ask your horse to slow his feet with this exercise. See diagram RF-3.

With a chargey or troubled horse,

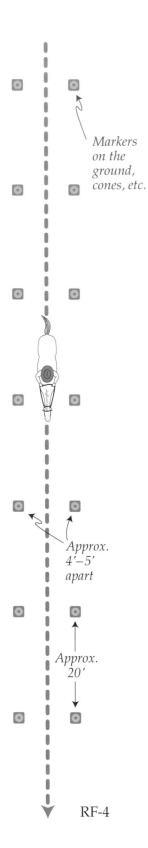

Markers on the ground, cones, etc.

Approx. 4'–5' apart

Approx. 20'

RF-4

Riding straight exercise. Markers 4-5 feet apart.

Being able to ride your horse straight is essential. Here I am loping this filly through a set of cones about 4 feet wide. Don't overlook this exercise; it isn't as easy as it may sound. First get it good at a walk and trot.

pulling back evenly on both reins without bending laterally often creates more resistance, stiffness, and a brace. When a horse keeps his skeletal and muscle structure straight, he has more power. As you bend him, his power lessens as muscles do more of the skeletal structure's job. This exercise gives you an alternative, and you are set up to bend him into a one-rein stop if everything falls apart.

Ride with **your hands wider apart** as more control is needed, about the width of your horse's shoulders. This is very important to understand.

Straightness and Riding on a Line

As you ride, be aware of your horse's straightness. What is his body alignment? Is he walking straight or wallowing around? Is there enough drive coming from behind? Can you ride him on an imaginary line? When you ride him on course, is his body aligned properly, tracking straight, round, and true?

When you ride in a circle or turn him, does his body match the arc of the circle? To maintain proper lateral roundness, he needs to reach his inside hind leg up under himself and line it up with his outside front. When he reaches up under, he should push off, driving forward, because his inside hind is his primary driving leg on the circle.

Pick out an object or point in the distance and ride toward it. Pick another object before you change directions. Experiment with picking out two distant objects, lining them up like rifle sights, and see how straight you can ride toward them. Don't ride with a narrow focus; keep your peripheral vision active, taking in all the scenery.

Your focus plays a large part in your horse developing straightness and alignment in his body as he travels forward. When he is "right on," meaning straight and mentally with you, he operates between your hands and legs where there is the least resistance. When he gets off track, your seat, leg, and rein serve as a block to direct and support him back on track. When he does, ease off again, and give him the choice and opportunity to stay on track without holding him there. Don't try pulling him back on track with your directing rein. If he drives forward off track, pushing to the outside, either bump with your outside leg, use your inside leg to move his hindquarters over so he can follow his nose back on course, or two-track him back on line.

If he loses the alignment again, then fix him and release. You may have to fix him 50 or 100 times before he'll stay on course. Stay consistent, releasing each time he is back on track, and he'll eventually choose to stay aligned. If horses are held in straightness, they never have freedom to stay straight on their own. It takes patience and persistence from the rider, but it's worth our being disciplined. The lateral response exercise will help with developing straightness.

One exercise to test you and your horse's straightness is to set out 10-12 markers about 4-5 feet wide and 20 feet apart. See diagram RF-4. Walk, trot, and lope your horse in a straight line down the middle. Don't get discouraged if your horse doesn't do it perfectly; this is a great learning opportunity. Just keep working at it, and he'll get better with practice.

As you and your horse get better at riding on an imaginary line with straightness, you will develop greater understanding, cooperation, and communication. It's up to you how well your horse learns straightness and staying on track, going where you direct him. Show your horse where the path of least resistance flows, then go with his flow.

Lateral Response

Two-tracking is a basic interim step for developing suppleness and lateral response. When starting a colt, within the first few rides, I start developing lateral response. But it's never too late to develop this, or get any age horse better at lateral movement. What I call two-tracking is similar to leg-yielding.

When two tracking, your horse is moving laterally at a 45-degree angle from the direction he is aligned. He will be looking in the opposite direction of travel. It is like combining side-passing and traveling straight forward. Good impulsion is necessary, and if it's lost, you must get it back quickly, or this isn't going to work. Generally, develop this before side-passing, because it's less confining and restricting to the horse. He can pick up the side pass quickly if he can two-track.

Working cattle requires frequent use of two-tracking. For example holding a cow out of a rodear, or driving a cow through a gate. If she wants to turn back, you have to move right or left laterally, and give ground to the cow to block her. When giving ground, keep your horse looking at the cow. This lateral movement is two-tracking.

Here are two exercises to develop and practice two-tracking. Start with the one that you think best fits you and your horse. Remember to maintain the soft feel throughout.

Ride your horse in a circle, from 25-35 feet in diameter, at an energetic walk or trot; for this example a right circle. Your horse will have a uniform bend through his body, matching the circle's arc. Start two-tracking left by applying right (inside) leg pressure behind the front cinch, asking your horse to spiral out-

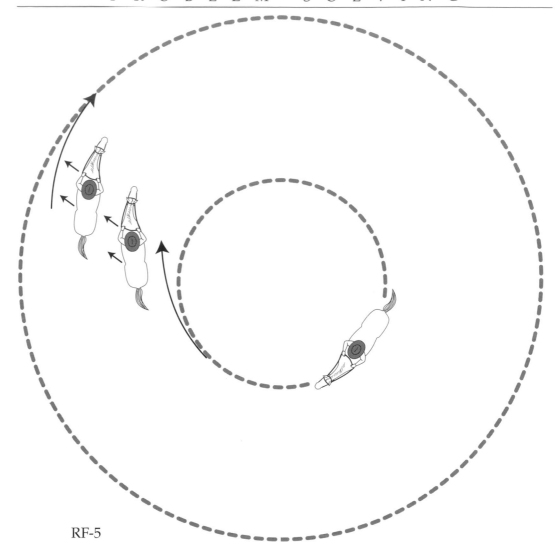

Two-tracking to the left on a circle.

RF-5

ward. Your horse's head is flexed to the right (inside) enough for you to see the corner of his right eye. Use your left (outside) rein to limit the bend and keep your horse balanced. When he two-tracks to the left a step or two, release leg pressure, continuing in the larger circle, on a looser rein, then start again.

Ride this two-tracking spiraling circle exercise both directions to keep your horse supple and balanced on both sides. Start at the walk and trot, then later at the lope on a larger circle. See diagram RF-5.

On a left two-track movement, your horse's inside hind leg (right hind), reaches up under and in front of the left hind leg, and drives forward. The right front steps in front of the left front. Everything will be just the opposite when two-tracking to the right.

Next two-track riding straight, rather than in a circle. While riding straight, start two-tracking to the right by flexing your horse slightly left, enough to see the corner of his left eye. He is flexed in the poll and jaw, with only a slight bend in his body. Avoid overflexing by using your right (outside) rein to limit the bend and to keep your horse balanced. Your left leg is back, supporting his movement to the right and forward. Sit balanced and straight. See diagrams RF-6 and RF-7.

When your horse will two-track one or

two steps to the right, release and let him walk straight a few strides on a loose rein, then ask again the same direction. Build on this by incrementally asking for multiple steps. Maintain light leg pressure to communicate continued lateral movement. Then release and walk him forward several strides on a loose rein before asking again.

Be aware of your horse's alignment; it will tell you how to position your legs and reins to help your horse stay on course. Adjust your legs forward or back to support the shoulder or hindquarters as needed. For example, if the hindquarters are lagging behind, you may need to move your driving or inside leg farther back to create more reach and drive. You may also need to hold your outside rein a little more firmly.

If your horse does not respond, ignoring or pushing against your leg, a crop or spur may help with this. Leg means using your upper leg, calf, and seat without collapsing your waist. If you use a crop or spur, here's the sequence I recommend. First ask for lateral movement with your seat and leg. If the horse doesn't respond, support your leg by quickly tapping him with the crop on the side you are applying leg pressure. With a spur, roll your toe out and your heel slowly inward, letting your horse run into the spur. When your horse moves one step laterally, immediately release your leg and crop or spur simultaneously. Start again, initially asking for just a step or two.

I can't overstress the importance of forward impulsion. If your horse bogs down, free up his feet, get him moving out forward, then ask again for lateral movement. If your horse breaks gait when you ask him with one leg to move laterally, just slow him down and start over. Pressure from one leg means to move laterally. Two legs applying equal pressure means go forward straight. Your horse can separate this if you are consistent.

Two-tracking is an excellent basic exercise for developing suppleness and lateral response to leg communication. It also helps with riding your horse straight. If he gets off course you can two-track him back on line. Use two-tracking to get your horse back on track if he drifts to the inside while loping circles.

Practice two-tracking by riding down a jeep or irrigation road, back and forth, side

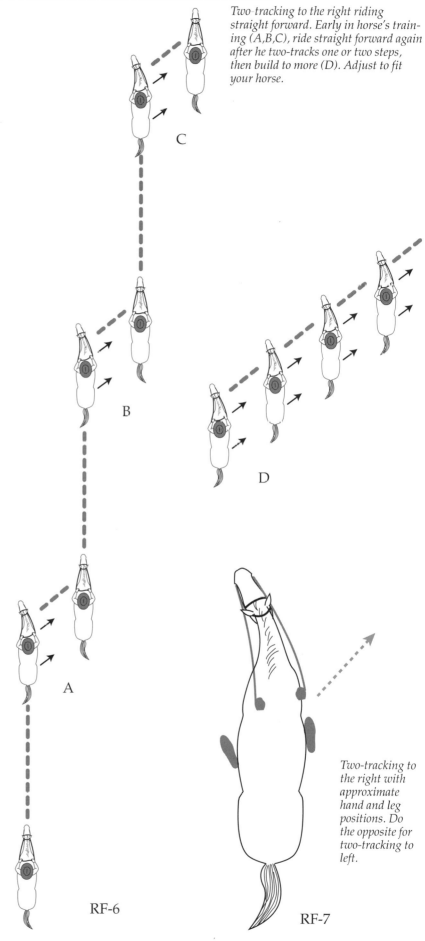

Two-tracking to the right riding straight forward. Early in horse's training (A,B,C), ride straight forward again after he two-tracks one or two steps, then build to more (D). Adjust to fit your horse.

C

B

D

A

RF-6

Two-tracking to the right with approximate hand and leg positions. Do the opposite for two-tracking to left.

RF-7

1/ Lateral response; two-tracking through markers, responding to right leg pressure to move to the left. Notice bend in horse's body in these photos.

2/ Two-track trotting to the right, laterally responding to left leg pressure.

3/ Two-tracking to the left.

4/ *Giving ground to a cow (blocking) makes use of two-tracking, here to the left.*

to side, from track to track. If you're out riding pastures or on the trail, you may need to sidestep a badger hole. Use this opportunity to two-track your horse. Ride around a tree, rock, yucca, or sagebrush, two-tracking occasionally. Ride him straight toward the obstacle, two-track past it, then ride straight again. This gives more meaning and purpose to lateral movement, as does working cattle.

Serpentine pattern.

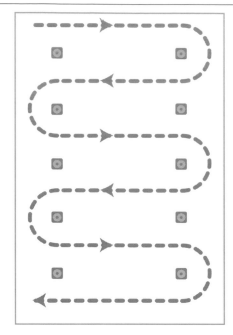

RF-8

Zigzag pattern.

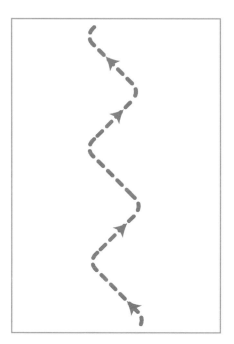

RF-9

Serpentines

This serpentine exercise is a good opportunity to see how straight you can ride your horse and how well you communicate direction. These serpentines are made up of straight lines and uniform half-circles for direction change. Do this at a walk or trot. Create a pattern using markers such as traffic cones, rocks, milk jugs, or buckets filled with water or sand. This design creates a variety of other patterns you can ride. See diagram RF-8.

A Common Mistake

Beware of overuse of the directing (leading) rein. This is by far the most common technical mistake I see people make. Don't pull your horse where you want him to go. Keep your horse's drive coming from behind—this is what turns him. Stay balanced over your horse; look where you want to go. This directs your horse and helps keep his feet freed up. If you ride one-handed (neck-reining), don't let your hand go too far past your horse's midline. Be careful that his nose doesn't tip to the opposite direction of travel. If it does, use your other hand to tip his nose into the arc with a quick, light tug (not a pull) and release of your directing rein.

Zigzag Pattern

This is an exercise you can do in the arena, out in a pasture, or open area. On as loose a rein as possible, swing or turn your horse 45 degrees and ride him straight, then swing him back and ride him straight. This forms a zigzag pattern or snake trail. See diagram RF-9. Change directions occasionally as you ride around your area. This is an excellent exercise to give your horse a job to do with lots of transitions, whether riding in an arena or out in open country. If you are riding with friends, ride opposite directions and weave in and out as you pass each other.

Backing Up—Straight and Quarter-Circles

Your horse should readily move forward with impulsion and softness before you concentrate on the back-up. Experiment with these steps to develop softness as you back your horse. Pick up a soft feel, sit down, drop your heels and wait for him to rock back, then release. Repeat, now waiting for him to take one step back. Release as his hoof leaves the ground. Repeat several times, releasing with one step. Stop and let him relax, rub him, then start again.

To develop more back-up, give a partial release by straightening your elbows with each step back. Get your release in time with your horse's feet. Don't pull your horse into a back-up, it will bog him down, getting his feet stuck. He won't back with collection or impulsion. As you progress, feel for his back to elevate as he prepares and backs up. This means he is backing more collected. Be aware of the timing of your release—when his back is elevated,

1/ *This mare is backing a quarter-circle to the right. Note how her right front is stepping out and back, as her left rear steps out and back.*

2/ *Notice the tracks in the sand as she backs an arc to the right, reaching on her diagonals.*

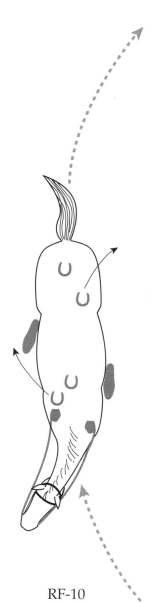

RF-10

Backing quarter-circle (arc) to the right; hand and leg positions. The horse's right front steps out and back as the left hind steps out and back. In a right quarter-circle or arc, the frontquarters move to the right as the hindquarters move to the left. The opposite for backing to the left.

Backing up a small hill or mound will help your horse get better at using his hindquarters.

Develop a fast walk in your horse—it's a great way to cover country.

66

not hollow. Getting horses good at backing helps develop good stops too.

To back an arc or quarter-circle to the right, start backing straight, then bend your horse's head to the right enough to see the corner of his right eye. Use your left rein to limit the bend. Move your right leg back and your left leg slightly forward. Backing right circles means the horse's hindquarters are reaching to the left and frontquarters to his right, reaching equally on his diagonals. When backing, he should move his feet in the same cadence he does when trotting. Left arcs or circles are the opposite.

An advanced maneuver is to walk your horse forward in a right arc, stop, then back in a right quarter-circle, without changing his body alignment, carrying a soft feel throughout. See diagram RF-10. Backing quarter-circles gets the horse up into a good position to bring the front-quarters across.

To help your horse further develop and use his hindquarters, back him up a small mound or hill. This helps him learn to reach his hindquarters deep up under himself. Start at the top, walk down a couple steps, then back up to where you started. Don't overdo this at first. Back up just a few steps until your horse builds strength for this exercise.

Develop a Faster Walk

A fast walk is a real asset for covering ground, especially on trail rides and when riding pastures. Some horses come by this naturally while others will need your help to develop a fast walk. Ride on a loose rein and encourage your horse to step out. Get your body rhythm more active and your legs in time with your horse. Look down to observe his shoulders when he walks. When the left shoulder is extended all the way forward, his right shoulder is back and his right front hoof is poised ready to leave the ground. Just as his right front starts to leave the ground, bring your right calf against him with a squeeze or light bump. Go out and inward with your leg, not forward and back. This will encourage him to extend his reach as his leg leaves the ground. Alternate both legs in this manner while pushing forward with your seat bones in time with your horse's movement.

Later, you can time your alternating leg pressure with his rear legs, but the front hoofs may be easier as a start. When your horse walks out faster, slightly ease off your leg pressure, but keep him moving. If he starts to break into a trot, lean back, quickly ask him back to a walk, and immediately start again. If he slows, lean just slightly forward, and add more drive with your seat and legs.

Having your horse walk out fast is truly an enjoyable means of travel and covering country. Your horse can learn to separate walking both fast and slow. In driving and working cattle, it will be necessary to ask your horse to slow down and walk slower at times, as cattle naturally walk slower than horses.

Covering ground at a trot is also enjoyable and a good way to cross lots of open country in a short time without overly tiring your horse. Trotting a modified zigzag pattern, weaving through the sagebrush can be fun and offer interesting transitions for your horse. Intermittent loping provides a good change too. However, generally, loping is more tiring for the horse than trotting when covering miles of open country.

Get Out on the Trail— Get Your Horse on Cattle

The best place to practice these exercises is out on the trail or in the pasture. Start in an arena if you have one, but get outside as soon as possible. Both you and your horse will enjoy it more. Be creative and make every ride an adventure. When out on a trail, where possible, get off the trail and give your horse various jobs to do so he doesn't get hooked on the trail. Keep him mentally hooked to you.

Also, getting your horse on cattle will give him a real job, a meaning and purpose to his training. At my cow-working and working ranch clinics, both people and horses seem to make great improvements and advances in their horsemanship. Perhaps it's because both horse and rider enjoy the opportunity to be out in open country with animals and other like-minded people.

Heading up the creek—the best place to practice these exercises is out on the trail or in the pasture.

Getting your horse on cattle will give him a real job to do.

Weaning calves at the Lazy S Ranch near Gardner, Colorado.

Cattle work builds confidence in you and in your horse.

Sorting pairs in Wyoming.

Have Your Horse Wait for Your Direction

Anytime your horse gets ahead of you by making a transition on his own, discipline yourself to return to the original speed, direction, or gait. I often see this when a rider allows his horse to walk off or go from a walk to a trot before asked to. Even if you intended to walk forward, stop your horse, let him stand on a loose rein a second or two, then ask him to walk forward. The same applies if you are already walking out and your horse starts to trot or lope without you asking. Slow him back down to a walk. If trotting seems like a good idea, while he is walking forward on a loose rein, ask him to trot. Your horse will learn he gets what he wants when he waits for your direction. Disci-

pline yourself and redirect your horse; you will build willing cooperation and communication.

Another approach is to put a high-energy horse to work doing very active exercises with transitions. But get him busier than he wanted to be. Make something productive and positive out of your horse's desire to move his feet. Soon your idea will be your horse's idea, and he will wait for your direction.

A related problem occurs on the trail when riding across ditches or narrow arroyos. Often, as the horse goes down he builds up speed, then rushes up the other side. To head this off, stop before moving downward. Then as you proceed, if your horse is preparing to rush, stop at the bottom and turn him parallel to the banks. Have your horse wait for you to ask him to turn and walk up and out. This will also give you a chance to get yourself in the best saddle position to make it easy for your horse to walk up the ditch bank.

Ride Your Horse Up and Down Steep Hills

To help your horse develop and use his hindquarters more, ride him up and down steep hills. To prepare your horse before starting up or down a steep hill, ask him to stop first, then proceed under control. Have him on course, walking slowly, straight, and aligned, not allowing him to get hollow or chargey. Keep his life and drive (impulsion) coming from behind.

Learn to stay in the proper riding position to help him move efficiently. Stay vertical and plumb. While headed downhill, one test of your control is to stop your horse and stand for a moment. If you need to stop for a longer period, turn your horse perpendicular to the fall line. When going uphill, use your horse's mane to balance yourself rather than the reins or saddle horn. Riding your horse in the hills helps him develop collection.

Lots of Transitions and More Exercises

Lots of transitions are essential to developing willingness and control between horse and rider. Do all these exercises with a soft feel. Take every opportunity to make numerous transitions of speed, gait, and direction. Just as in groundwork, the tran-

1/ Going down into a steep arroyo. Note hands wide apart for more control and to support the horse.

2/ Have your horse wait for your direction. If your horse gets in a hurry going down a bank, stop him at the bottom, parallel to the ditch. Rub him while he waits for you.

1/ *Get up off the cantle going up a steep hill, and hold on to the mane for balance instead of the reins. Riding up and down steep hills helps horses use their hindquarters.*

2/ *Staying balanced going downhill. Stay vertical like a pine tree on a hillside.*

sitions are important to accomplish before you attempt to solve a problem. Here are more exercise suggestions. See diagram patterns RF-11. I cannot take credit for coming up with all of these exercises. Most I've learned from my mentors.

• Trot 10 strides, walk 5. Get him ready to walk before the 10th stride. Be aware on which stride he makes the transition. Be particular without being critical.

• Change directions while you maintain the 10-5 combination.

• Walk 10 strides forward, stop your horse, then back up 5 steps (back up just 1 or 2 steps at first if your horse is really green). Step the hindquarters a quarter-turn to your left and walk the frontquarters across a quarter-turn to your right, walk or trot forward and stop again. Repeat in the opposite direction; hindquarters a quarter right, frontquarters a quarter left.

• Trot forward, swing a half-circle using your seat and legs as a guide, changing directions. Just before you make the turn, look up and back over your shoulder in the direction you want to turn, pick out an object, and ride to it. Maintain the drive (impulsion) through the turn.

• Trot forward, swing a full circle, continuing on the same direction. Use your focus as above, to help keep your horse on course.

• Trot an "S" turn. Swing wide, not short, to make the two equal half-circles.

• Ride patterns after a fresh snowfall or in a sandy area after a rain shower. You can see how straight, round, and accurately you can direct your horse.

• Count cadence while you ride. Start at a walk. Just as your horse's left front leaves the ground call out "left." Alternate to all four feet, one at a time. The hind feet may be more difficult. If you have trouble, have a friend ride behind you and call out each time a hind foot leaves the ground. You can concentrate on the feel of this until you have it. Knowing where your horse's feet are is very important in all horsemanship maneuvers.

• Back your horse and step one front foot to the side, asking as it is ready to leave the ground. Walk your horse forward, stop, back up, and ask him to move the other front foot to the side.

• Standing still, ask him to step one front foot to the side and walk forward.

• Move the hindquarters one or two steps to the side while standing on a loose rein. If he moves forward when you put your leg on him, pick up the reins with a soft feel, stop, back up, release, and start over.

• Standing still, ask him to step his hindquarters over one step and push off forward with his inside hind leg and walk forward.

• Refer back to the groundwork exercise GW-14. Walk your horse forward with the fence to your right. Stop him, back up straight, then start backing a quarter-circle to the right. When perpendicular to the fence, stop, walk the frontquarters a quarter-turn to your right without moving the hindquarters. Walk your horse forward parallel to the fence.

• Walk your horse in about a 10-foot circle, with lots of life in his feet. As you feel him start reaching in with his inside front, pick up a soft feel, still keeping him slightly bent to the inside. Stopping the hindquarters, lay your supporting rein against his neck, moving his frontquarters across with your outside seat and leg. When he steps across one or more steps, release and walk forward on a loose rein. Slowly, incrementally build up to more steps before you release and walk forward. Be sure your horse is moving freely when you release.

• Find a large pasture or long, wide trail with good footing where you can lope your horse relatively straight for a long distance. Lope your horse off on the left lead for 100-150 feet, then back to a trot for just a few strides. Then lope off on a right lead for 100-150 feet, then back to a trot for a few strides. Repeat this sequence for a long distance. This is helpful in reinforcing consistency and timing of leads. This is also an excellent exercise for a chargy horse.

These are just a few suggestions. Be creative and come up with your own combinations of transitions. Think down to your horse's feet. Think about his body alignment. As Ray Hunt says, "You are arranging the life in his body, through his mind, down his legs to his feet."

RF-11

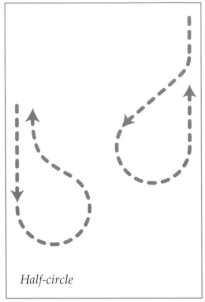

Half-circle

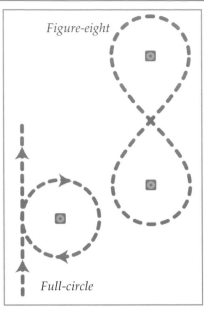

Figure-eight

Full-circle

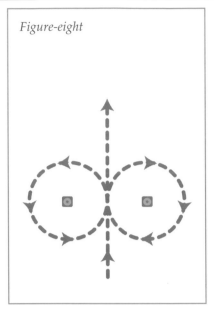

Figure-eight

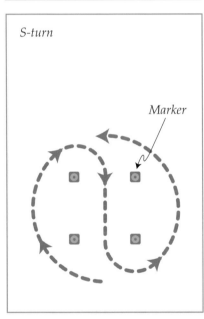

S-turn

Marker

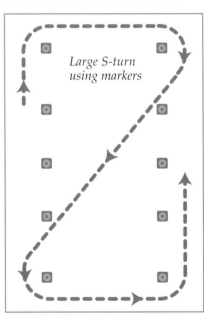

Large S-turn using markers

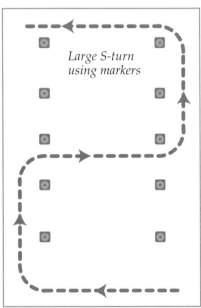

Large S-turn using markers

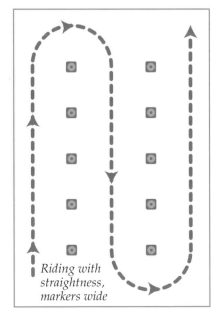

Riding with straightness, markers wide

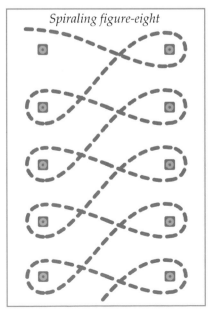

Spiraling figure-eight

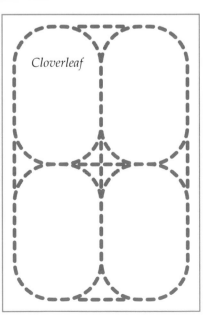

Cloverleaf

1/ *Practice these exercises riding around obstacles. This gives your horse a job to do, making a ride interesting, challenging, and rewarding. Practice your awareness of knowing where your horse is going to place his feet, but let him do his job.*

2/ *Riding through and around obstacles.*

1/ These six tires are cut in half to avoid getting a horse's hoof hung up. Start out by riding your horse perpendicularly over the tires. Continue crisscrossing the tires, incrementally changing the angle each time until you can cross them in a straight line.

2/ She is placing her feet inside or on top of each tire as we go down the line. If this troubles your horse, you could start with just one or two tires.

When riding these various exercises, think of them as giving your horse a job to do. As mentioned previously, think how you can ride these exercises in a pasture and out on the trail as well as in an arena. Practice them while riding around trees, rocks, yucca, sagebrush, oak brush, up and down ditches, in and out of arroyos and other obstacles. You and your horse will really start to get in harmony with each other.

Obstacles

Become creative at home—make your own obstacles:

Tires—cut in half like a donut

Teeter-totter—three 2 by 12s 16 feet long

Back through an "L"—start at the finish line

Tarp—attached to a frame, the tarp won't wad up around your horse's legs

Poles on the ground

Three large parallel poles, narrow and wide

Barrels placed close together.

76

1/ Like the tires, ride across the teeter-totter perpendicularly before riding over it in line. Here the teeter board is flat on the ground. This will make it easier for your horse at first. Teeter-totters are a good foundation for creeks, bridges, etc.

2/ Stopped on the downhill side.

Conclusion

There are many variations to the basic exercises outlined in this chapter. These are just a few of many you can use to get you and your horse handier. Building a better foundation with your horse before you head out to solve a particular problem is working on solving the problem. By reviewing or becoming skillful at these basic exercises, you might also head off another problem from developing later on.

Have a plan solidly in mind, but be willing to adjust to fit your individual horse. Give your horse a job to do (one of these exercises) and let him work at it while developing response with respect, without fear. This helps you both be successful in whatever problem or difficult situations you later encounter.

Look for the common thread throughout this book. Remember, it's the day-to-day little things that make the big difference. These exercises are designed to help the rider become more aware of what he or she is doing to obtain a positive or negative response, and for the horse to understand his responsibility to wait for the rider's direction. This means the rider has to be mentally ahead of the horse; to be proactive instead of reactive. The more proactive the rider, the safer and more enjoyable this horse experience becomes. The

3/ *Balanced on the teeter-totter. You can also rock your horse forward and back, touching each end down. Try this without moving his feet.*

4/ *Approaching the teeter-totter from the elevated side, asking her to push the board down, then cross.*

78

rider is the leader, but horses are never our slaves.

While you're working on these exercises, solving a problem, or involved in any other activity, don't forget to enjoy yourself and make every ride an adventure. Have a good time and make things interesting and rewarding for your horse. Always see you and your horse's glass of water as half-full, not half-empty. He will respond to your optimistic, positive outlook. The horse becomes more content knowing his security and comfort comes from the rider. When your horse knows he can trust, respect, and depend on you, you have a willing partnership.

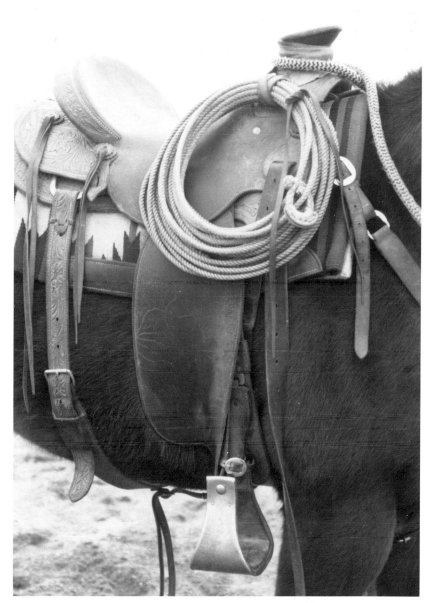

Buckaroo twist: The stirrup leather was turned by the saddlemaker to create a twist so stirrups always stay in place. Note: 1) latigo on off side (in addition to near side), making adjustments easier, latigo keeper right front string, 2) cinch keeper at middle string right side, 3) loop rein crossed around horn while dismounted, leather wrap on horn. This is a Chas Weldon saddle on a Wade tree.

Watering up at a windmill tank during a good day trail riding. Enjoy yourself and see problems as opportunities.

Give your horse a job to do. Brownie is helping open this tough Wyoming gate. Even if you don't rope, you can teach your horse to do this. (See Spooking chapter.)

Make every ride an adventure, have a good time making things interesting. Your horse will respond to your optimistic, positive outlook.

*Checking cattle at the
Lazy S Ranch, Gardner,
Colorado.*

*When your horse knows
he can trust, respect, and
depend on you, you will
have a willing partnership.*

3 TRAILER LOADING

It's not what you do, but how you go about it.

NO OTHER PROBLEM universally causes people more stress and anxiety than the anticipation of trailer loading a reluctant horse. No other horse activity causes human tempers to flare so quickly. It is equally frightening and difficult for the horse. The approach described in this chapter is the method I have used with hundreds of horses over the years. It has been successful every time on every horse I have worked with.

It's not what you do, but how you go about it. Even the best techniques may fail unless you present yourself appropriately to your horse. The key to your success is not only learning and understand-ing these concepts and techniques, but more importantly, developing your feel, timing, and balance. Develop your ability to observe and read your horse, remain patient and calm, yet be proactive. Be willing to adjust to fit the individual horse you are working with and your progress moment by moment.

Although this is a problem-solving book, the approach outlined in this chapter applies equally to the horse who has never been near a trailer and to the horse who has had a bad experience that caused the loading problem. Look for the common thread.

Goals of Horse and Human

Goal for the horse: Learn to load consistently without resistance, trauma, fear, or stress. Be mentally and physically relaxed and comfortable in the trailer. Stand quietly while the handler slowly closes the door. Haul quietly, comfortably, and relaxed, and unload calmly at the destination. Then, willingly reload to go home.

Goal for the human: Learn to consistently load your horse by yourself, without force or bribery, using only a simple halter and halter rope. Learn how to line up your horse straight so he will load himself.

There are many similarities between solving trailer-loading problems and solving all other horse problems. Developing your trailer-loading skills will accelerate your understanding of equine behavior and communication in virtually all other aspects of horsemanship.

Trailer-loading resistance can cause great stress for both human and horse.

82

The Horse's Perspective— Why Horses Don't Want To Load

Self-preservation is very strong in the horse. Your horse is not trying to displease you when he won't load. Entering a small enclosure such as a trailer goes against his instincts. Horses are naturally claustrophobic animals who perceive anything that represents restriction and confinement as threatening to their safety. Their only real defenses are escape and flight. A green or problem horse may think that once he goes into the trailer, he will never get out. We obviously know we are headed somewhere and will promptly unload upon arrival. However, the horse doesn't know what the human knows! When forced into a trailer and shut in, his fear and flight can cause panic and injury.

Fortunately, horses can overcome their natural flight tendencies. However, we must approach them in a manner to help them learn and understand that they will be safe and comfortable doing what we ask. Riding in a trailer is something we ask our horse to do without us—he is pretty much on his own and he needs to feel secure. The trailer is not a safe place for the horse unless he perceives it as safe. Your horse's perception is what's most important.

Most trailer-loading problems are a combination of the horse's fear and resistance. Resistance is reinforced when the human is unsuccessful getting the horse into the trailer. The horse will build on being rewarded for not loading. If the human lacks confidence, the horse knows it. Humans may anticipate problems and have failure expectations. The horse reads this and responds accordingly. If the human attempts to force the horse to load, it validates and escalates his fear and resistance level. If the handler lacked patience, got angry or frustrated during a previous loading session, the horse may justifiably be reluctant to load the next time.

Your horse's overall trailering experience can be broken down into three distinct parts—loading, hauling, and unloading. If any of these is an unpleasant experience for your horse, problems eventually surface, usually during the loading phase.

Horses remember bad experiences, and will remember a traumatic or unpleasant trailer ride. How you drive is critical to the horse's perception of the trailer. Poor driving, poor trailer design, and the horse not being prepared mentally to accept trailer confinement can cause more problems. Unloading can be a problem if the loading and/or hauling was a bad experience, or the horse was not properly prepared to unload. Human error during unloading also causes problems.

The major reason horses do not consistently load is human error. This chapter outlines the concepts and skills needed to help your horse feel safe and comfortable while calmly loading, hauling, and unloading.

Evaluate Yourself and Your Horse

Before starting this project, do a thorough evaluation of yourself and your horse. Starting with your horse, ask yourself what the real problem is. Is your horse green, never before having been in a trailer, or is his problem due to a bad loading, hauling, or unloading experience?

Balance fear and respect. Is your horse afraid of the trailer, or does he not respect your direction to load? Often it is a combination of both.

Is your horse very active, willingly moving his feet, although not into the trailer? You may feel out of control at times with this type horse, yet this type is typically easier to load. Conversely, is he naturally lethargic, with little impulsion? The answers to these questions will help you know what groundwork areas to emphasize. If your horse is dangerous to you and/or himself, and after all the groundwork exercises you still feel unsafe, you may want to consult a competent professional.

Horses willingly load when they have developed trust of the trailer and respect for the human.

Trailers with a dark interior are less inviting for the horse.

This leads to evaluating yourself. Don't be discouraged if some of this is new to you. There is no better way to learn feel, timing, and balance than by working with your horse on a real project. Understanding how horses think, learn, and communicate is critical for your success.

Throughout this project remain patient, yet proactive. Most unsuccessful trailer loadings result from the two extremes: people getting impatient, angry, and forceful; or people too inactive or passive, not able to ask their horses for more response.

Time constraints often cause failed expectations. Be willing to devote ample time to this project at each session. Depending on your own skills and your horse, it may take only one session to make tremendous progress. Regardless, even after your horse is loading, plan for several ongoing developmental sessions, allowing time for setbacks, which always occur in all phases of training. Allow as much time as you can possibly budget. Start early and devote all day, in case your horse regresses or some steps take you longer than others.

Familiarize yourself with the groundwork so you can consistently make the right thing easy and the wrong thing difficult without creating fear or resistance in your horse. When the horse is struggling and resisting the most, keep him working at struggling against himself rather than against you.

If you are unfamiliar with these concepts and techniques, you may want to practice first with a horse who is not a problem until you get more comfortable. Also, have a friend who has read this information observe you and give you feedback on your feel, timing, and balance. Stay calm and relaxed. The horse will reflect the human's relaxed, calm, and easygoing attitude. The moment we get a little uptight, our anxiety starts to show in what we are doing. Impatience and frustration are detected by the horse and he will perceive loading as less desirable. Staying patient and positive through the peaks and valleys of the learning curve will help you maintain perspective.

Before You Take Your Horse to the Trailer

The groundwork exercises in Chapter 1 serve as your foundation for solving trailer-loading problems. Trailer loading is an advanced form of groundwork. To be successful, develop your skills at directing and supporting your horse to lead past you, back up, move his frontquarters and hindquarters. This groundwork helps you and your horse develop mutual trust, confidence, understanding, and respect.

After you get started, if you are having trouble, you may need to take your horse away from the trailer for more groundwork. You may need to turn up the volume in terms of more quality and intensity. Pursue more difficult tasks that stretch you and your horse out of your comfort zones.

The Setup

This discussion refers to using a two-horse, straight-load trailer. The only equipment is a halter and halter rope—no pulleys, butt ropes, or food as enticement. I use a Double Diamond rope halter with a ⅝-inch halter rope 12 feet long, tied together with a half-hitch; no snaps.

These techniques and principles directly cross over to loading horses in a slant-load or stock-type trailer.

Asking the horse to move to my right with a directing (leading-right hand) and supporting (driving-left hand) motion.

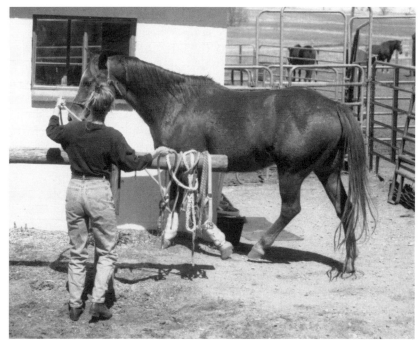

Do some quality groundwork prior to trailer-loading training—get creative as Julie Quinlan has here to simulate a trailer by leading her gelding between the building and the tie rail.

85

I recommend you have all the doors closed in your trailer with the exception of the back door. Keep the escape or feed manger doors closed. These openings may assist you in getting the horse to load because he sees a way out. However, if he goes into the trailer thinking there is an exit at the front, you are fooling your horse. He may get confused when he loads and finds there really isn't a forward exit. I have heard many stories where horses loaded, panicked, then went through the escape door, requiring a call to the vet, a welder, or both. By the time the horse heals, a severe loading problem has developed.

If your trailer is dark inside, it might be helpful to paint the inside white so it looks less confining and more inviting. A trailer with a light-colored interior is cooler and feels more open and comfortable.

The description to follow is not a recipe or a mechanical method. Moment by moment, the human needs to adjust to fit the individual horse and situation. Sometimes you need to go slower than described or move along quicker. You may need to really firm up with your horse while other times you'll need to ease off.

When I use the word "ask," it means using directing (leading) and supporting (driving) motions with your body language and halter rope. Remember the importance of the timing of your release. Recognize fear and resistance, and adjust to fit. The key is accurately reading your horse, observing what he's thinking, learning, and communicating back to you.

There are three priorities to always keep in mind while you are working through this process.

• First, your horse should maintain his impulsion forward.

• Second, he should not invade your personal space.

• Third, he should never pull back on the halter rope.

As long as you can maintain these priorities, continue to proceed with loading your horse. If you cannot, you may need to work on these basic groundwork problems away from the trailer.

Now Just Do It

At this point I will outline an approach-and-retreat strategy, teaching your horse to load and unload in increments, assuming you won't encounter major problems. Following this, I will discuss additional problems you may need to address.

It's time to take your horse to the trailer and put into action all of the preparation you have done on the halter rope, intended to help free up your horse's feet. Lead your horse to the trailer, leaving the door closed. Take up a position on the left side of the trailer, where the trailer door hinges. Direct your horse in a semicircle to your right, letting the side of the trailer stop him. Let him stand there for a few seconds. Reverse your hands on the halter rope, lead him past you in a left arc directly up to the trailer door. See diagram TL-1.

Do this several times until your horse gets familiar with moving around the trailer and develops more acceptance. You could also ask your horse to lead past you in semi-circles on the other side of the trailer.

Perhaps leading your horse to a trailer may be more than he can handle. If you are having trouble just leading your horse to the trailer, find a place where he can accept getting closer, stop, and lead him away from the trailer. Sometimes you will find a horse, particularly one with a bad experience, is very ticklish about even

Semicircle at trailer with door closed, see GW-9. Lead your horse past you to the right, to the side of the trailer. Then lead him past you to the left up to the closed trailer door. Let him stand there a short while before reversing the semi-circle, then repeat again. Do not circle the horse around you, between you and trailer.

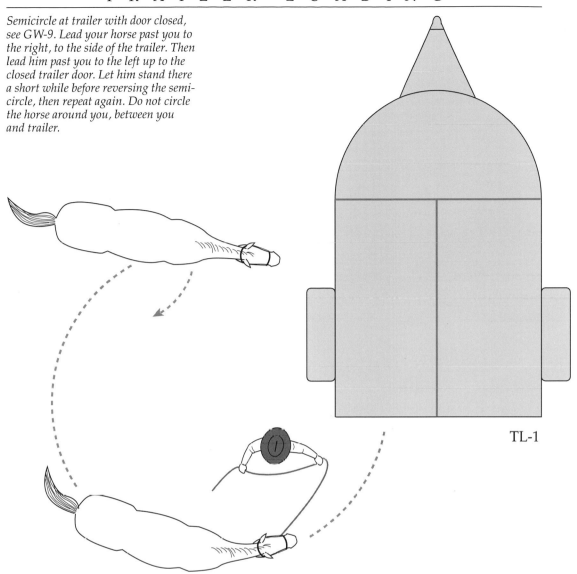

TL-1

approaching the trailer. Keep stretching his comfort zone, but go slowly enough that he stays in a learning frame of mind. Lead the horse away from a trailer, keeping him actively following your direction.

For the next exercise, refer to diagram TL-2. Step back 6 to 8 feet from the trailer, have your horse lead past you to the right and left between you and the back of the trailer. You might find some horses speed up, are reluctant to move, or even try to push you out of their way. If you are not

having trouble in these areas, it is an indication you have your horse fairly good on the halter rope.

Incrementally narrow the gap between you and the trailer to a distance the width of the trailer door. Get your horse so good at this that he's willing to move without hesitation or fear. This is a good indicator that you are ready to open the trailer door.

1/ *Groundwork at trailer prior to opening door—semicircle to left of trailer. Note: I am changing hands on the halter rope. My left hand will now become my directing hand.*

Lead past between you and rear of trailer, see GW-10.

TL-2

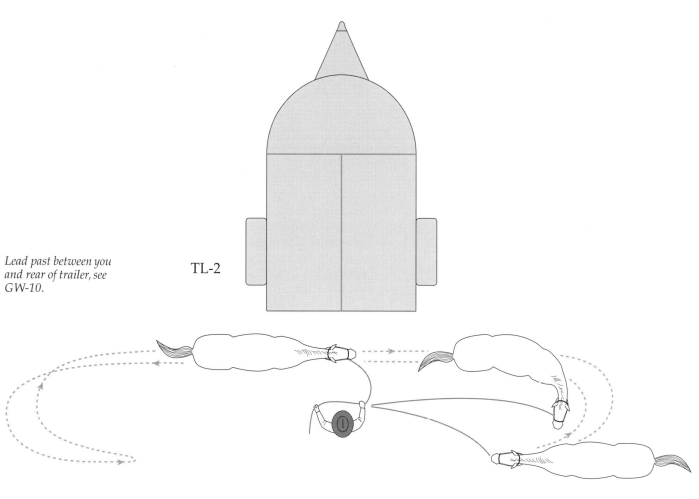

2/ This mare is coming around with impulsion.

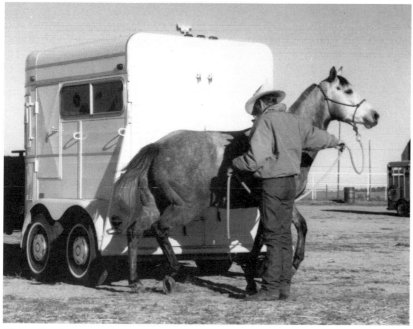

3/ Leading horse past between me and trailer. Note there is no pressure on her from my supporting hand (left) as she is moving forward.

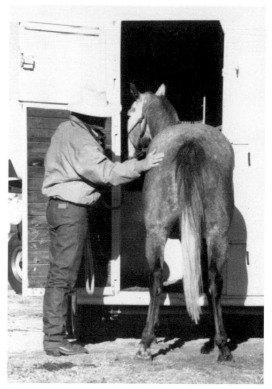

With door now open (left side), I've asked her to stick her nose inside. I'm reaching up to pet her for reassurance, then I'll lead her away while she is still interested in trailer.

1/ *The following four diagrams—TL-3, 4, 5, 6— show four ways to lead a horse away from the trailer to keep him active. Here, TL-3 shows how to lead up to, away, and back to trailer in semicircle with door open. Also refer to diagrams TL-1 and GW-9.*

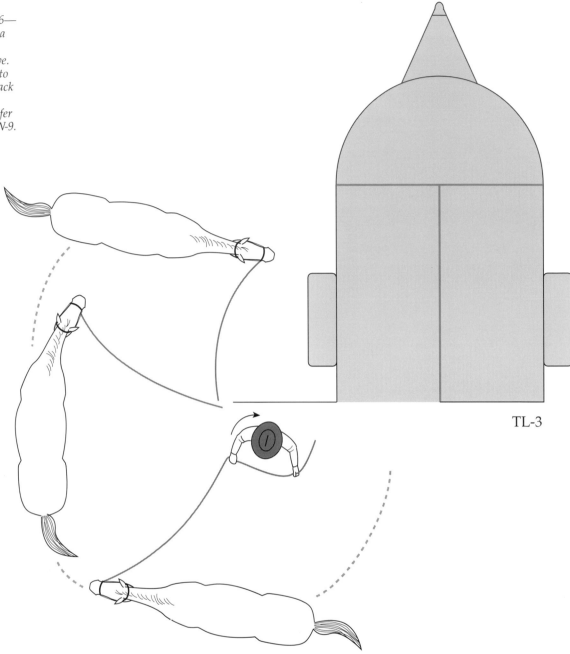

TL-3

Asking Him To Load

Open the left door and stand with your back to the door. See diagram TL-3. Maintain this position, asking your horse to do all the maneuvering around you. Stay in this position unless you need to go with your horse if he pulls away. To begin the loading, lead your horse past you to your left. Then, once he loads on the left side, the halter rope will be on the left side of the stall. This helps keep an anxious horse from trying to turn around toward the divider in a straight-load trailer.

Bring your horse up to the opening and let him stick his nose in the trailer. See if he will get curious and investigate. While he still has a curious expression in his body language, lead him away from the trailer. Leading him away while he is still interested in the trailer will take the pressure off and give him a chance to relax (this is approach-and-retreat). You don't have to go very far away from the trailer for this to be effective. Then reapproach and start again, this time asking him to stick his head a little bit farther into the trailer.

Continue building on his curiosity and furthering his level of acceptance at the trailer. Take him away several times before asking him to step into the trailer.

To lead your horse away from the trailer, refer to diagrams TL-3, 4, 5, and 6. There is nothing unique about these suggestions other than that they build on your ability to stay proactive and direct your horse. If you lead him away from the trailer in an active way, he will stay more mentally aware of your direction. These suggestions help develop your handiness, making you both sharper.

Next, lead him to the trailer and ask him to put a foot inside. If he does, just let him stand there and pet him for reassurance. Don't force him to stay. Let him relax and see that his attempts to try will be rewarded.

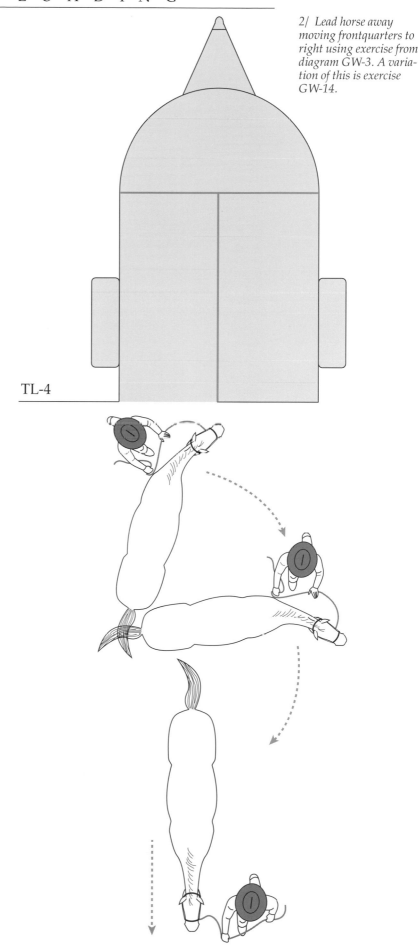

2/ *Lead horse away moving frontquarters to right using exercise from diagram GW-3. A variation of this is exercise GW-14.*

TL-4

TL-5

Pressure and Punishment

When leading your horse to the trailer and asking him to load, don't continue to pressure him with the tail of your halter rope while he is moving. If you do, in effect you are punishing him for going to the trailer. If he stops, then use the tail of your halter rope to encourage him to go forward again.

Before he moves back on his own, ask him to step back and immediately direct him to your right, in a semicircle to the left side of the trailer. Then reverse, directing him in an arc to your left, asking him to prepare to load. This time you are asking him to be bolder, to step right up and put one foot in the trailer. He might even be ready to step in with both front feet. But I wouldn't allow him to step more than two feet into the trailer at this time. He might be too willing to go forward, load all the way, get scared, panic, and then loose trust in you and the trailer situation.

Ask him to step a foot in the trailer again, immediately back him away, or let him stand there a few seconds, petting him. Again, lead him away from the trailer, using one of the examples.

Bring him back to the trailer, with the goal of loading two feet. You have to adjust to fit the horse. Some horses immediately put two feet in and others are going to take a little while longer. Adjust to fit and make sure you are staying in balance with yourself and the horse in terms of not asking too much nor asking too little. Stay proactive, keeping your horse in a learning frame of mind so he is wanting to try.

Again ask for two feet in the trailer, and let him stand there a little longer. Back him out only a step or two, then direct him right back into the trailer again.

If your horse puts both feet in the trailer with a calm expression, let him stand there for a few seconds. Then reach up with your right hand and pet him on the shoulder, neck, rib cage, and down the hip.

3/ *After the horse loads and unloads willingly, you can use a rope over the hocks to unload, see GW-8. Alternate leading away from trailer on horse's right or left side after horse is facing opposite direction of trailer using GW-4 exercise. This illustration corresponds to the photos on pages 108-109.*

If it took some encouragement on your part with the tail of the halter rope, reaching out like this might cause him to back right out. You don't want him to think every time your right hand comes his direction it means he is going to feel pressure to go forward. Therefore, if you consistently pet him with your right hand when he stops part way in, he will learn to separate that from your request to move forward and he will relax.

Pet him, then back him out. Ideally, you should back him out before he decides to. If he does back out on his own, and his fear level is not elevated, ask him to reload to the place where he was before, no farther. You are trying to build levels of acceptance.

When you lead your horse away from the trailer, it is not necessary to stay away for long. Keep in mind this approach-and-retreat strategy. Each time you take your horse back to the trailer, ask him to load a little bit farther. If the last time he had both front feet in the trailer and you were able to pet him, next time ask him to go a step or two farther into the trailer. It may seem you are going slow, not making progress as quickly as you could; however, your horse is learning incrementally, one step at a time.

Now you are ready to ask him to go farther into the trailer and/or stay there longer.

Semicircle to left, livening her up with my driving hand (right) to help her prepare to load farther into the trailer.

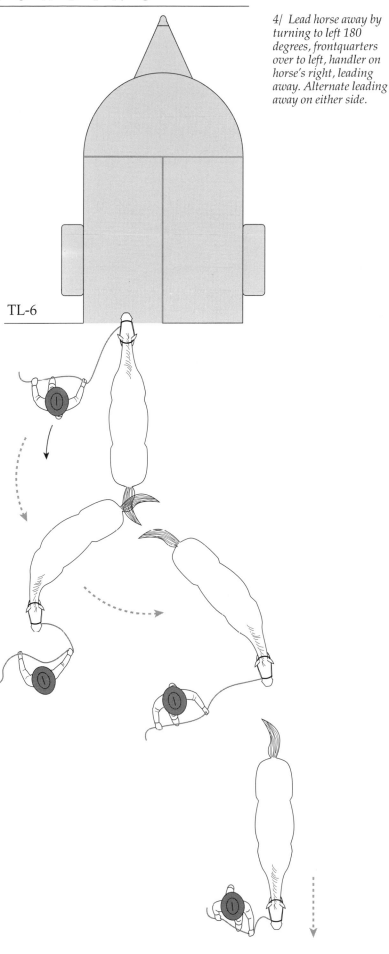

4/ Lead horse away by turning to left 180 degrees, frontquarters over to left, handler on horse's right, leading away. Alternate leading away on either side.

TL-6

1/ Starting on the left of trailer in a semicircle around to trailer door. I now ask her to step one foot into trailer.

2/ She hesitates, so I ask her to move forward with my directing hand (left) and firm up with a light flip of the tail of my halter rope in supporting hand (right).

3/ I release pressure immediately once she moves forward. She is stepping her right front foot into the trailer with impulsion. I let her stand a moment, then asked her to step out.

If, at this point, he backs out on his own and is not panicky, then ask him again to load. Use your judgment and read your horse's expression of fear, resistance, or acceptance.

What if it is fear? You might let him stand there and relax or get him to move his feet by doing a semicircle to your right, then immediately go back into the trailer again.

As your horse is able to progress farther and farther, he needs to pick up a hind foot and step it into the trailer. To accomplish this, you may need to get more impulsion, the life in the feet, farther back from the trailer. Don't let the life in his feet die as he approaches the trailer. However, don't ask him to race around at a trot, rather ask him to walk forward with life—impulsion.

If he stops suddenly before loading a hind foot, you might have to tap him on the rump with the tail of your halter rope. Start with a slight tap and build to more. This may cause him to back out of the trailer rather than go forward. If it does, do a semicircle to the right and then direct him back into the trailer again. Often, if the horse has developed a level of acceptance and is ready to do more, his impulsion will carry him forward and he

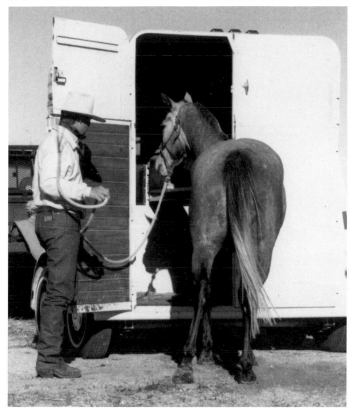

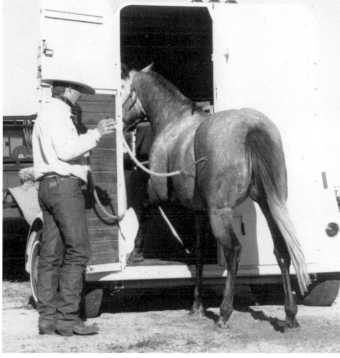

2/ She has her left front in the trailer, and I am asking her to step her right front in also. I will release by stopping the pressure from my supporting hand (right) when her right front starts to move forward.

1/ When she willingly steps in with one foot, I ask her to load two feet into trailer. I do very little directing with my left hand—the trailer helps keep her straight and she knows where she is headed. She is beginning to hesitate so I encourage her forward with a flip of my halter rope. She has lots of slack in the halter rope to go forward.

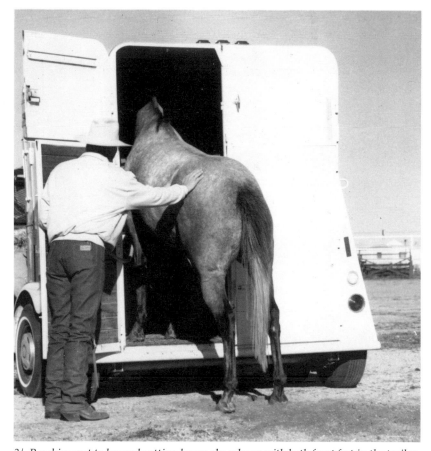

3/ Reaching out to her and petting her as she relaxes with both front feet in the trailer.

will place one hind foot in the trailer. More often than not, the horse will get right in with all four feet when this point is reached.

When the horse loads all the way, immediately ask him to unload. Up to this point you have been loading the horse incrementally through several stages, a step or two farther each time. You have also taught your horse to unload at the same time you have taught him to load. Immediately asking him to back out is important to your horse learning to load and accept being in a confined, restricted space. Once he is fully loaded, ask him to unload before he freezes up, gets scared and wonders how to get out.

Ask him to unload by first lightly tugging backwards on his tail, then use the halter rope to support or reinforce. He will learn your tug on his tail is his signal to back out. His tail is a halter rope that will always be attached to him. If your horse has a high degree of trust in you, lifting his tail to ask him to step out sometimes will help him calmly understand that the ground will be there to meet him. Let him

95

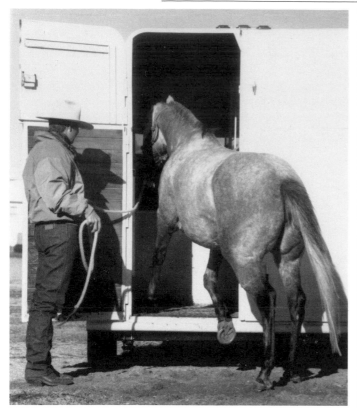

1/ Asking her to load farther in trailer.

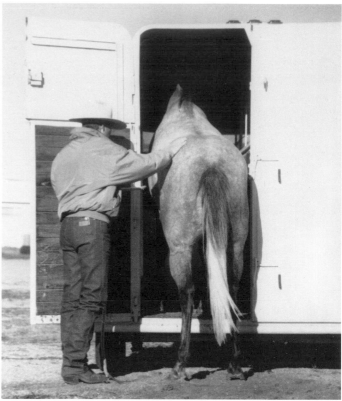

2/ I ask her to stop before she puts her hind feet into the trailer, and I pet her.

3/ With a slight tug on the halter rope, I ask her to step out. This mare is learning to unload while learning to load.

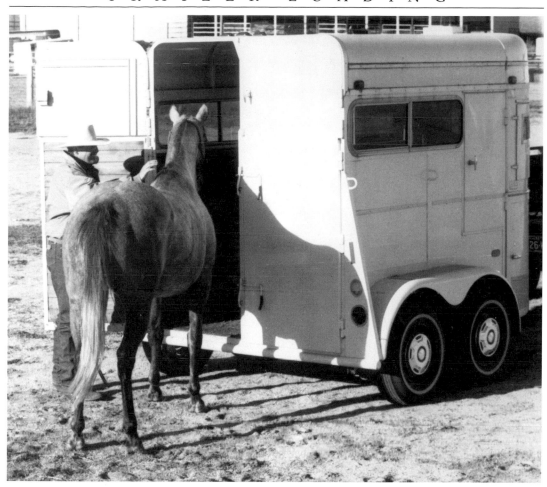

4/ *After backing her out, I keep her standing there for a while to relax.*

stand just outside with his head still in the trailer, and rub him. Let him relax and think, then walk him away.

At this point let him soak a little longer away from the trailer. If your horse's expression tells you he is relaxed and accepting, load him three or four more times, then you could quit for the day.

You know you have made a lot of progress when your horse can stand in the trailer with all four feet, cock a hind leg, and relax. You can reach up and pet him. He is in no hurry to back out of the trailer; he will wait for you to ask him to back out. He moves in and out of the trailer in total comfort, with his feet moving as freely as they move on the ground.

Soon, your horse needs to become more comfortable and able to stay longer and longer in the trailer before unloading. He should wait for you to ask him to unload, rather than come out on his own. Each time he loads, increase the time he stays in the trailer before you ask him to come out. Increasing the time incrementally reinforces your horse's awareness that he will have the opportunity to unload from the trailer.

5/ *Having led her away from the trailer, this is a good opportunity to give her a break, some soak time, and rubbing.*

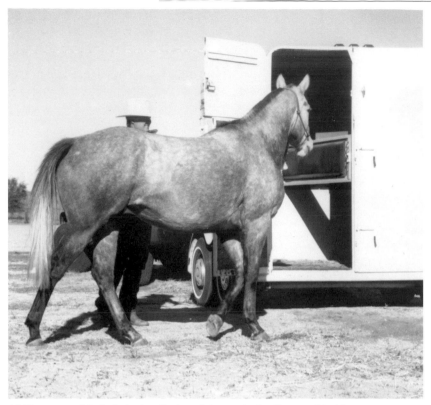

1/ From a semicircle, bringing the impulsion up for loading one hind leg.

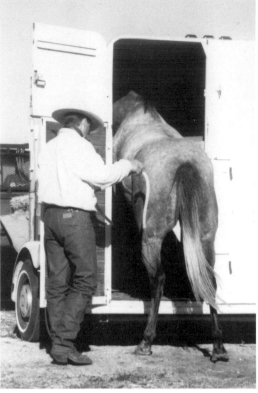

2/ Using very slight encouragement with the tail of my halter rope, I ask her to step her right hind into the trailer.

3/ I immediately released pressure as she stepped one hind leg in. From this point, I backed her out.

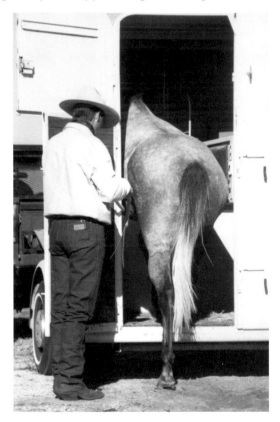

Using food as a reward rather than an enticement to get into the trailer can be a positive finish to the session. Before you load your horse for the last time, put a small amount of grain in the manger. When you load him, there will be an additional reward for him, making his experience even better. Let him eat a few bites, but back him out of the trailer before he has finished. After you put your horse up, remove the remaining grain so no food is there when you load him next time. You want the horse to anticipate there are good, safe, comfortable things around the trailer, including feed. But until your horse loads consistently for you without hesitation, don't offer feed during a loading session.

Loading a Foal or Yearling

When I am loading a foal or a yearling, I often get into the trailer with him right from the start. At that age, it can be more difficult for a young horse to learn to lead past you and be driven forward. I get up into the trailer first, preferably a stock- or full-rear door-type, then use a tug-and-release on the halter rope to get the horse to

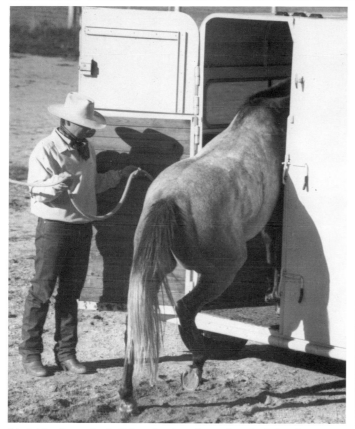

1/ Asking her to load all four feet into the trailer. She is lined up straight and headed in.

2/ I let the halter rope slide through my left hand as she goes forward.

3/ Still standing off to the side, I briefly reach up to pet her to reinforce her release reward and help her feel more secure.

4/ Standing off to the side, I immediately ask her to unload with a light tug on her tail. If she didn't respond to this, I would add a tug on the halter rope in my left hand.

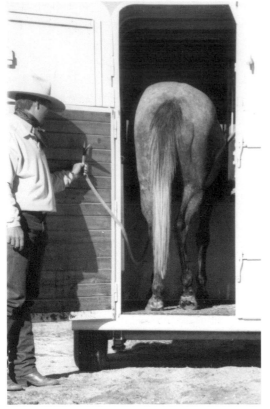

Allowing her to stay longer in trailer. Repeat loading and unloading several times, asking the horse to stay longer each time. You know you have made a lot of progress when your horse can stand in the trailer with all four feet, cock a hind leg, and relax.

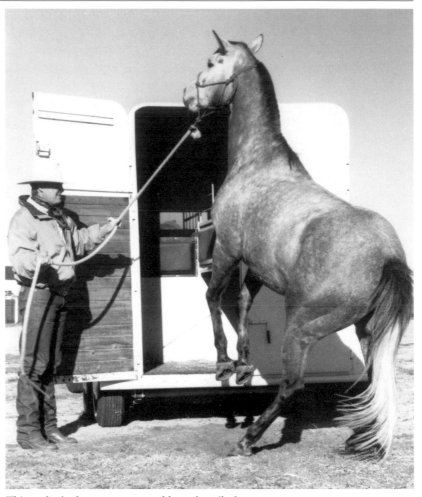

Things don't always go as smoothly as described.

come forward. This assumes you have your foal, weanling, or yearling properly halter-broke before beginning this.

My tugs are always at a 45-degree angle and not straight ahead. If you pull straight ahead, he is more apt to pull back, something you never want to encourage. When you tug at a 45-degree angle to a horse's left, you are asking him to move his left front foot forward. Then when you tug to the right, you want to move his right front foot. Release when he steps a foot forward.

Getting into the trailer often works better with a foal. You could also load the mare into the trailer first; however, I personally prefer to have the foal begin learning to follow the human's direction at an early age. Do what fits you and your situation best.

Solving Major Resistances and Problems

Teaching your horse to load and unload doesn't always go as smoothly as described to this point. Now I will discuss some problems that may arise, making your situation less than perfect. Read the entire chapter before you go to the trailer and try to implement the techniques I have described. You need to know how to handle these circumstances that might prevent you and your horse from having a successful loading experience. These problems are really symptoms, although we always refer to symptoms as problems. I will direct you more toward fixing the problem than just fixing the symptom.

As you proceed, concentrate on getting better at reading your horse. His expression and body language tell you when he is prepared to do more. If he is not ready for more, then don't press on too quickly. However, if you can see he is ready, then take advantage of this window of opportunity.

The window of opportunity is the time when the horse is in a learning frame of mind and ready to expand his comfort zone. He is ready to expand his trust, confidence, respect, and understanding of you and the job at hand. If you miss the window of opportunity by waiting too long, he will get bored or impatient and this may bring out reluctance. If the window of opportunity concept is new to you, don't get discouraged. It may be hard to see at first, but start looking for it and build your awareness.

- - - - - - - - - - - - - - - - - - - -

Offer a Good Deal

I mention tapping the horse with the tail of the halter rope for forward movement. Make sure before you make contact with the horse that you have lifted your hand and or halter rope up and given your horse some warning or some prior consideration that you are asking him to move his feet. Move your hand up and down, flipping the tail of your halter rope through the air a little before you make contact. Your horse learns you always offer him a good deal first before you firm up. But don't wait too long to make contact if he does not respond. Feel, timing, and balance are very important here. When your horse makes a change, reach out and rub him to reinforce the reward of the release. Give him the opportunity to learn, separate, and compare these different types of body languages you are offering him.

Swings Hindquarters to the Right

A horse cannot enter the trailer unless he is straight. Always encourage straightness in the horse. He has to be lined up and thinking straight ahead to get into the trailer. Often the horse will come up to the trailer straight, but at the last minute lose this straightness by swinging his hindquarters over to his right. This puts him perpendicular to the opening where you want him to load.

One solution is to direct him away from the trailer to your right in a semicircle. You wouldn't necessarily have to go all the way over to the trailer's left side; you can just swing him out a little way, change hands on the halter rope, and direct him back towards the trailer door. This will often work, but you may have to repeat it several times before the horse remains lined up straight. Also, make sure you are not standing too close to the opening, blocking your horse from going forward, discouraging straightness.

Another method I prefer seems to work a little quicker. I will continue directing him into the trailer with my left hand on the halter rope. With my right hand, I swing the tail of the halter rope toward his left shoulder. See TL-7. This may seem inconsistent, but it works really slick.

Keep bumping, tapping, or spanking him just behind the point of the shoulder until he moves his feet. He really can't move any farther to his right because the trailer is blocking him. Your left hand on the halter rope should discourage him from backing up, and encourage him to come forward. Tapping him on his shoulder tells him to move his feet. You are

Timing of the release is the key. If the horse swings hindquarters to right, a common evasion, direct with left hand and support (drive) with a tap or bump on the left shoulder. Immediately release when the horse moves left even one step, then build on this until he stays lined up.

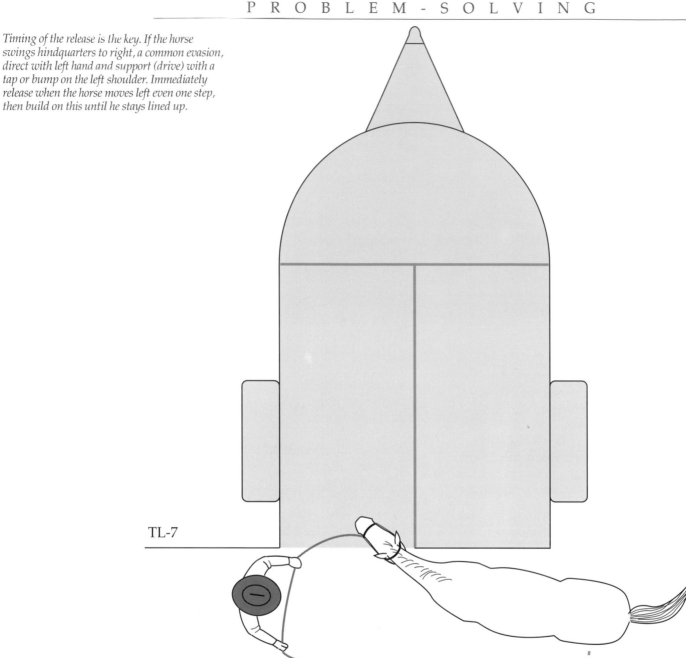

TL-7

directing him and telling him where to go when he moves. When he moves his feet a step or even a half-step to his left, immediately release the pressure on his shoulder from your supporting hand (tapping).

The key is the timing of your release. Let him stand there for a few seconds to realize what took place, then start again. He'll continue moving his hindquarters over to the left because you release pressure as he moves left. He will learn how to line himself up and stay lined up because every time he swings his hip over to the right, you make it uncomfortable. Once he has the idea, he will stay lined up. This is very similar to having your horse move his hindquarters over to pick you up off the fence, as described in Chapter 1.

If he swings his hindquarter too far to the left, tap on his left shoulder, rib cage, or hip until he lines up.

Line Your Horse Up So He Will Load Himself

Keep in mind the importance of your horse's roundness and straightness. Even when a horse's body is rounded, as in an arc, it should still be straight. That is, his body is perfectly aligned in the arc. He needs to be lined up to go in the trailer.

When leading your horse to the trailer, he should be moving with his body properly aligned and pointed towards the opening. For example, if you are standing on the left side by the trailer opening and moving him in a semicircle to your left, when he comes around, his body should be arced in the shape of the circle—with his head pointed toward the trailer.

If he is not straight, round, and moving smoothly, he will lose his impulsion and stop before loading. Avoid getting in your horse's way, such as standing in the doorway and causing him to veer off. Don't try pulling him forward with your directing (leading) hand. Instead, get active driving him forward with your supporting hand. His body should just flow into the trailer. Always be aware of your horse's straightness and roundness.

The Active Horse

You may have an active horse who needs very little encouragement to move his feet. This type horse is not only active physically but also mentally. It is very important to keep his energy and attention directed. He may move his feet quite a bit on his own without you asking, but he won't go into the trailer. However, the active horse can be relatively easy to load. You just need to stay in the eye of the storm (activity), stay correctly positioned, allow him to move his feet, but keep directing him. **Don't let him rest or stop moving his feet anywhere but at the trailer**.

When he starts moving his feet away

1/ She is swinging her hindquarters to the right, not lining up straight, and I tap her on her left shoulder with my halter rope.

2/ Timing of the release is the key to making this work. Release pressure once the horse steps over to the left.

Don't let your horse escape between you and the trailer, particularly to the left side. When a horse tries this, step quickly to your left to block his escape. If he does get by, immediately change his direction back to your right, then start him forward again.

from the trailer door, direct him in lots of transitions, keeping him working against himself. Redirect his focus, even if it is away from the trailer, so no matter where he goes, he is following your direction. As long as you keep directing all his life and energy, pretty quickly you will find this horse will load into the trailer. If he is paying attention to something to his right, then direct him to his left and vice versa. When his attention finally settles on you, and he takes the life in his feet toward the trailer, release pressure.

Don't let active horses discourage you. They are lots of fun to work with and fairly easy to load into the trailer. You will find them very interesting and they offer lots of learning opportunities.

The Sluggish Horse

The opposite is the lethargic horse. When you lead him up to the trailer, his feet just get stuck in the ground and he won't go forward. I do *not* recommend whacking on his butt endlessly and trying to get him to go forward when he is stuck, standing still. But you might want to tap him a few times on his rib cage, shoulder, or hip, to ask him to go forward. However, should he not respond, don't continue to bump him. You have to realize that what you are trying to do is **move his feet**.

If he won't move his feet forward into the trailer, get him to move them in a different direction. Direct him in a semicircle around the trailer—the exercise described earlier. As you turn him back to his left in a semicircle, ask him to really liven up and move his feet. Get his impulsion at this point to carry forward into the trailer, rather than having him lifelessly walk up then stop. Be sure your position is correct and you are not standing in his way. It may take several times to do this, but eventually the horse will liven up and start to put more effort into stepping into the trailer.

1/ This mare is very active with lots of impulsion. I just direct her energy so she will get lined up to load.

2/ This maneuver is also effective with a sluggish horse or one whose hind feet get stuck without loading.

If you find, after attempting this maneuver several times, you are still unsuccessful at getting the horse to have more life in his feet, you might want to take him away from the trailer for more active groundwork exercises to build the life in his feet—his impulsion.

3/ At this point, I have already changed hands on the halter rope, making my left hand my directing hand. With a sluggish horse, I will really liven him up from here on forward by driving with my supporting hand (right).

4/ Keep the increased energy moving forward into the trailer. Don't let it die at the trailer door. If it does, start the semicircle over (or any other exercise) to bring up the life in the horse's feet.

Hind Feet Stuck—
Keep Them Livened Up

You will find some horses load fairly readily with their front feet but won't step in with their hind feet. After you have asked such a horse to move his hind feet forward several times and he has not responded, don't just continue to smack him with the tail of your halter rope, encouraging dullness, as just described. If you just keep nagging him, he may learn to shut down, ignore you, the pain and discomfort, and still not load his hind feet into the trailer, plus he will have a negative association with the trailer.

Instead, back him out of the trailer and get him actively moving his feet somewhere else. Direct him in semicircles or any groundwork exercises fitting for your situation. However, I wouldn't recommend circling or longeing him between you and the trailer. Get his feet moving, keep him following your direction, asking for lots of transitions. Teach your horse to move his feet where you direct him, even if for now it is not into the trailer. Liven him up away from the trailer, then let him rest at the trailer. When you are successful getting him to move his feet to a particular spot, soon he'll move his feet into the trailer.

Leading Away From
the Trailer

Refer to diagrams TL-3,4,5 and 6 illustrating different ways to lead your horse away from the trailer. They will help you avoid routines. Each time you take him away from the trailer, experiment using one of these methods. This will help keep your horse's impulsion while he makes numerous transitions. It keeps his attention on you because he won't know what to expect next. This is another way of implementing your groundwork into the trailer-loading process. It keeps you and your horse sharp, while making you both handier on the halter rope.

Two of these examples will help to get your horse more comfortable and relaxed through changing eyes. One is when you back your horse out and then direct him to his left, circle him in a small "S" pattern, where you end up on his right and lead him away from the trailer.

The other is when you put the halter rope around his hocks, back him out, and swing him over to his left, with you on his right.

Rushes Out

You may have a horse who will readily load, but the instant he does, will charge or rush out. He will follow your direction to load but cannot stay in the trailer. He is telling you he is not yet comfortable with the idea. This may be the result of confinement fear, and you may need to proceed with caution. Don't force this on him; just let your horse work at it while you quietly continue to direct and support.

To get this horse to unload calmly and slowly, review the original loading section and proceed through those steps. By loading and unloading one foot at a time, he learns to be more accepting of being in the trailer, and therefore unload more thoughtfully.

Don't try to force him to stay in the trailer. Instead, the moment he steps out of the trailer, calmly ask him to go back in. You may even have to make being out of the trailer a little uncomfortable to give him a better comparison. Let him understand that when you ask him to load, the trailer is a very comfortable place.

When you ask your horse to unload, that should be very comfortable too. Anyplace you direct him, your horse should perceive as a comfortable place. When he goes into the trailer again, give him the opportunity to stay there. If you can catch him staying in the trailer for a second or two, be proactive and back him out before he decides to rush out on his own. It will be interesting to watch his body language expression while he's thinking about what is taking place. You can see the horse starting to change, starting to think the trailer is not nearly as bad as he thought it was earlier.

107

1/ *Unload and lead away from trailer by halter rope over hocks. Standing off to the side, ask her to back out by lightly drawing on the halter rope.*

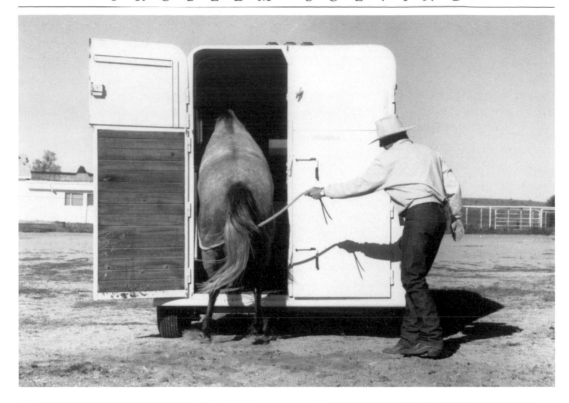

2/ *I'm not pulling her out. Rather, I'm giving her the opportunity to yield to the halter rope pressure and unload. Her hind-quarters are already starting to position to bend around to her left.*

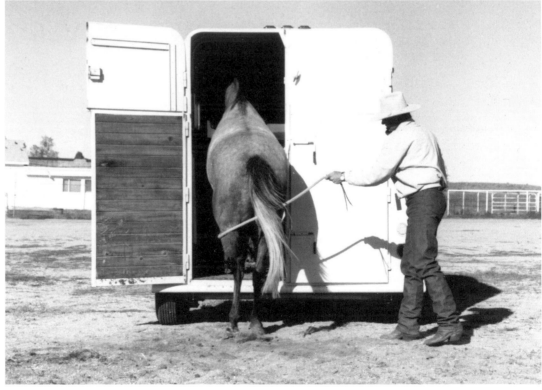

You may have to reload him many times before he will even stay there a few seconds on his own. If that is what it takes, don't hesitate to do it, but stay calm, quiet, and relaxed so your horse learns to get more confident and trusting of you. If he needs to come out of the trailer, he has a reason; he feels very uncomfortable, afraid, or both. If you try to make him stay, you are going to lose trust and confidence instead of gaining it. Don't try to overcome this too quickly, but keep him working at it. If you remain patient yet persistent, he will learn to stay in the trailer quicker than you thought.

3/ Outside the trailer, she is bending around, yielding to the halter rope.

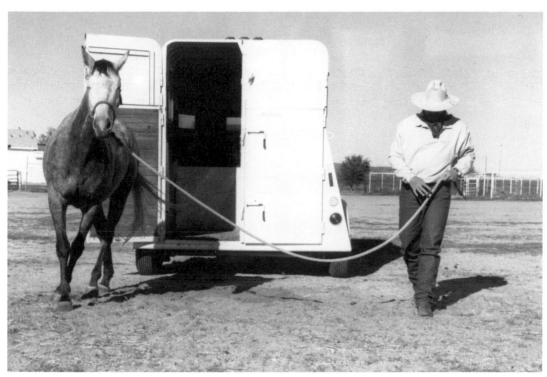

4/ We start to walk off together with slack in the halter rope, and she is tuning into me. You can now lead away from either side. See diagram TL-5

Rushes Into the Trailer

Another situation, probably less apt to happen, is when the horse rushes into the trailer. Even if the horse rushes into the trailer and comes out slowly, don't be fooled. The horse who rushes is actually escaping into the trailer. In other words, he is using his flight to get into the trailer. This is not a safe situation. I want my horse to think his way into the trailer with all four feet. I want every step he takes to be a thoughtful step, not a panic or an escape step. The horse who tries to rush into the trailer needs to learn to slow down.

Bad things eventually can happen if you let him rush in. He may panic because he doesn't know how to get out. A horse may flip over backwards or go down in the trailer. He could start scrambling, or he might jump up into the manger. If you slow your horse's feet down, in the long run, trailering will be a more positive experience for you and your horse.

If a horse is rearing, go down the side, bend the horse toward you to disengage the hindquarters, then drive the horse forward.

I am preparing to get down her right side. If a horse is evading by backing up, get down the side, and drive him forward.

As you ask him to load, be prepared to stop him with only his front feet in the trailer. Back him out a step or two and ask again. Follow the procedure described for the horse's first trailer-loading lessons. Just be sure you stop this horse from going in farther than you ask him to. In the process, he might experience a regression and for a short time, he will not load as easily as when he rushed in. However, don't be discouraged. You'll find it will be much safer for the horse to learn to think his way into the trailer step by step and follow your direction.

A horse who charges into or rushes out of the trailer has scared feet. I want him to have brave feet. I want his feet to be thoughtful and brave, and go into the trailer with a lot of confidence and trust gained from the human.

Rearing Up

Another example of resistance and fear that may arise when you are asking the horse to load is rearing up. The rearing horse is generally exhibiting both fear and a lack of respect for the human's direction. You may need to solve this away from the trailer with more groundwork. Do some exercises that stretch his comfort zone and get his feet freed up, moving forward. As with all of these, rearing up is a **symptom** of a problem. The horse needs to learn to move his feet forward instead of up when his self-preservation is threatened.

CAUTION: When the horse does rear up, don't try to pull down on his head! This may cause him to go up higher and/or flip over backwards. When the horse rears up, he could pull you backwards or come down on top of you. Don't stay lined up with him; move off to his side at the tail of your halter rope. See diagram GW-12. Be mentally ahead of him; when he starts to go up, draw his head around and move his hindquarters over. This makes it more difficult for him to rear up. The horse learning to make the choice to go forward when troubled is the solution. **He will become less troubled when he knows that if he moves his feet forward he will be okay.** This is his self-preservation.

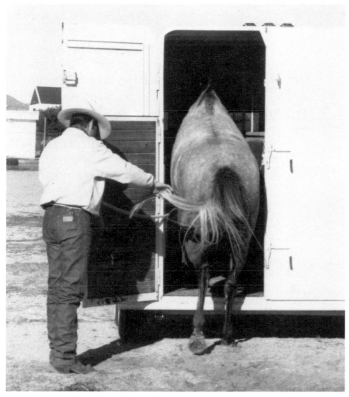

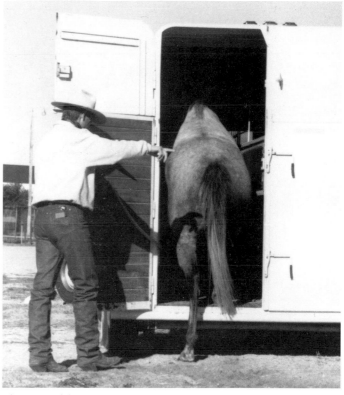

1/ Freeing up her feet. After she loads all the way into the trailer I ask her to step just her hindquarters out, then stop.

2/ Now I ask her to step in again. Note only my hand is necessary to drive her forward.

Backing Up

A similar situation is the horse who backs up instead of going forward when directed to the trailer. You need to encourage his feet to come forward, but don't pull on him. Continue directing with one hand, get active with the tail of your halter rope in your supporting (driving) hand, and go back with him. Stay off to his side driving toward the point of his shoulder, rib cage, or hip until he moves forward.

Don't stay in front of him where you would be driving him back at the same time he is backing up. Don't pull on him or hold him. You are just not strong enough to do that, and it will teach him to pull back. By pulling back, he is providing himself with a release. Your position is very important; stay to his side, always asking him to move forward.

Use all the groundwork exercises to free up the pull-back horse's feet. Be ready; when he does finally move forward, release pressure, rewarding him for his correct choice. Your horse may try to move to his left between you and the trailer. If you are close to the trailer, you don't want him to build on the idea that he can escape

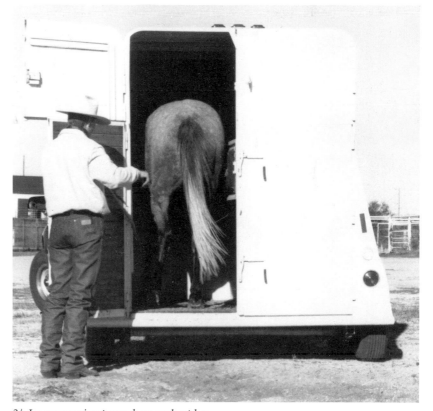

3/ I am preparing to reach up and pet her.

111

by moving between you and the trailer to your left. To prevent this, quickly move forward to your left to block his escape. If he does go by you to the left, **rather than allow a complete circle, immediately change his direction back to your right;** then start him forward again. Maintaining your correct position allows you the leverage to help your horse prepare to load and makes escape difficult.

Once your horse is dependably and predictably loading, you are both ready to move on.

Free Up His Feet Once He Is Loaded

Once in the trailer, he needs to feel that his compartment is big enough for him to move his feet forward, backward, right, and left, even though he is confined to a very small space. Keep his feet freed up when he is in the trailer. This is more critical for a straight-load, but applies to any trailer.

Start by backing only the horse's hindquarters out. Ask him to reload. You may find this difficult initially, and it might take several repetitions. Be patient but alert. Try to stay mentally ahead of him; if he comes too far out, be quick to ask him to move forward into the trailer, then start again. As you get further along, get more particular about where he puts his feet.

Next, ask him to take one step back, and then ask him to go forward without unloading. Ask him to move backward and forward as many steps as possible without stepping out of the trailer.

Eventually, as he becomes more responsive to the feel of your direction down to his feet, it will become like a teeter-totter. You'll know you have him on the teeter when he prepares to back up, you then ask him to go forward or stay, and he immediately responds to what you ask. If your horse is comfortable in the trailer and waiting for your direction, you will find he is on his way to becoming a very good loader, hauler, and unloader.

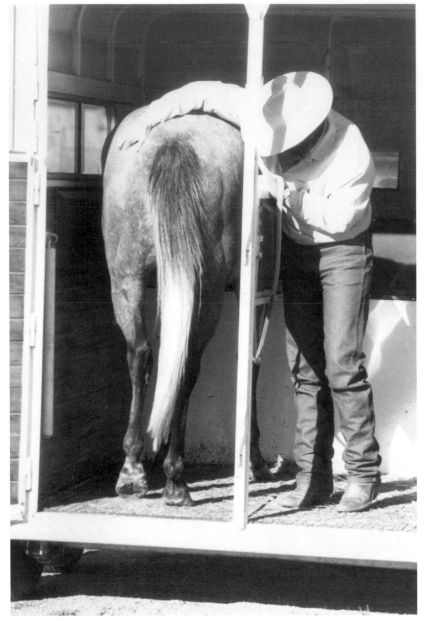

1/ *To free up the feet and mind even more, I have a horse step the hindquarters and frontquarters over laterally without unloading.* **Note: Horse is not tied in***. Her left hind is stepping over to the right. This really helps the horse feel more comfortable in a confined space. This is especially important in a straight-ahead-hauling trailer.*

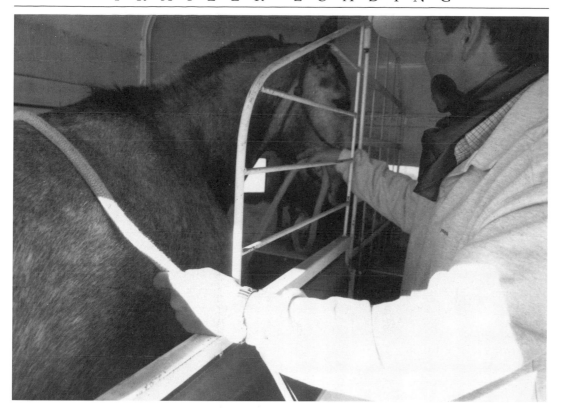

2/ *I put the tail of the halter rope around her neck and shoulder like a breast collar, and I'm asking her to move her frontquarters to her right.*

Load Yourself Into The Trailer

Your horse is now feeling more comfortable and secure in the trailer. He is standing with a back leg cocked and moving when directed. You have both made great progress.

This would be a good time for you to get into the trailer to help him free up his feet even more. Stand in the other stall and ask him to step his hindquarters and frontquarters to his right and left. Alternately, put the tail of the halter rope or your arm around his neck and his hip to ask for a side step toward you. With a light push of your hand, ask him to step his frontquarters and hindquarters left. (Note: Both rear trailer doors are open.)

Move him around in the trailer stall, even though it is a very small compartment, forward and backward, right and left. These small movements will free up the horse mentally. You are less apt to have your horse get fearful once you close the door and the trailer starts moving. Confinement fear can cause a horse to be very nervous and anxious when he doesn't

know how to move his feet. This can bring out the flight instinct, causing scrambling, jumping into the manger, flipping over backward, or other undesirable circumstances. Spending this time helps keep your horse in a more willing, accepting, positive, learning frame of mind.

When To Close the Trailer Door

If your horse accepts the previous procedures, you are probably ready to close the door. Close the door, and then, if it frightens him, open it before the horse attempts to come out. If he does attempt to come out or is panicky, you may need to do more to free up his feet.

If he backs his butt up against the door, but he is not panicky, lightly tap his butt. When he moves forward and will stand relaxed for a second, open the door and ask him out; then start again.

When your horse is standing relaxed in

Line your horse up straight so he will load himself. Once a horse is loading easily, I begin stepping back to see just how little it takes for him to load up. If you tried this and your horse ducked to the left between you and trailer, start over closer to the trailer.

the trailer, ask him to back up against the door with a light tug on the halter rope. You want him to feel the door is there, but step forward off the pressure on his own. If he continues to lean against the door, lightly tap him on the butt to move him forward. When he is standing forward, open the door and ask him to unload, then start again. Do this several times.

You are allowing the horse to learn when the door is open and when it is closed. Like teaching the horse to unload while you are teaching him to load, you are teaching him that when the door closes, it is not forever. He learns the door will open again, and he will be able to unload.

Although this may sound like a small thing, just keep in mind the horse doesn't know what the human knows. We don't ever want the horse to think that once the door swings shut, he can never get out again.

The Butt Chain

Get your horse accustomed to you closing the door before you hook the butt chain or butt bar. I've found there is usually less risk of panic and injury. The horse might panic when he sees the opening and tries to back up, unaware the butt chain is blocking his path. Many horses get reactionary when they feel the chain pressure on their hindquarters. To stay safe and minimize risk, prepare away from the trailer to get him ready for the butt chain.

The groundwork exercises earlier in the book have helped prepare your horse for this. In particular, the rope-around-the-hock exercise. You have also used this during the loading training as a method to back him out and lead him away from the trailer. When he is soft and responsive to this, the butt chain may not be a big deal for your horse.

Another exercise is to form a loop around his butt with your lariat coils or the tail of your halter rope. Tug on the loop to offer him a chance to come forward off the pressure. If he panics and

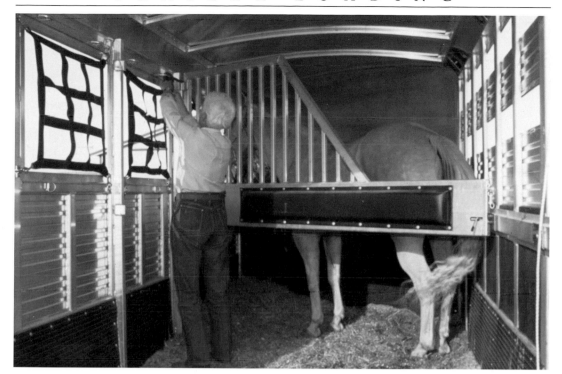

Tying horse in a slant-load with dividers. Note bars on upper divider instead of solid material make a trailer seem more open and inviting for the horse. The webbing behind drop-down windows increases air circulation, but discourages claustrophobic horses from attempting to escape. Webbing or screens also prevents horses from hanging their heads outside, which is dangerous.

kicks up, you'll be glad you didn't load him and connect the butt chain yet. You might have had a wreck. Continue to tug and release on the butt loop with each step forward. If he readily moves forward without panic, he is probably ready for the butt chain.

Load your horse, close the door, then secure the butt chain. Back him with a light tug on the halter rope into the butt chain. He should then step forward. Drop the butt chain, open the door, and back your horse out. Reload him, repeating the process several times. After he steps forward and relaxes, open the door and back him against the butt chain. Why? Some horses will try to back out if the door is open, even if the butt chain is fastened. We want a horse to move forward, off the butt chain, whenever we ask him to. For him to learn, we ask him to back up, then move forward—with the door open.

If you are unsure of yourself here, make a temporary butt chain with a rope. Tie off one end and take dallies around the center upright on the other end. If he does panic, you can let your dallies slide a little. If it turns into a major wreck, you can always let go or cut the rope. Many trailer butt chains or bars are difficult to release when the horse is braced against them. You could attach a quick-release snap on one end of your butt chain. This is just an extra precaution if there is any question in your mind about whether your horse is ready.

If the trailer door is too tall for you to reach over, find a bucket or a something else to stand on.

If your horse will back into the butt chain and step forward off the pressure, disconnect it and back him out. Repeat this several times, asking your horse to stay longer each time. Soon you can load him, connect the butt chain, close the door, and he'll be totally comfortable. Unload him, cool him out mentally and physically by walking around before putting him up. You are ready for the next step—hauling your horse.

. . . .

How To End a Session on a Good Note

After working with a horse fairly intensely, stay with him. Spend some time without asking him to do anything. Let him soak up all he has learned while you quietly groom and rub him. Really let him relax and reinforce that you are a good partner. Wait until all the sweat dries before putting the horse up. We usually think of this as a physical cool-out; however, the mental cool-out is even more beneficial. This is a positive way of sealing in the learning experience. You could also saddle up and go for a pleasant, quiet, relaxing trail ride. Make it easy for his last thoughts to be positive and relaxed. Keep this in mind with any of the problem-solving discussed in this book. It's a good way to finish a session.

To Tie or Not To Tie

For hauling, I prefer to tie my horse in the trailer, but have done it both ways. Tie his head long enough that he can look to his side approximately 90 degrees. If he were to get his head turned 180 degrees and get hung up, he could panic. Or, he might think he could turn around and go out the way he came in. Any of these could cause negative results.

Caution: In a two-horse trailer, before you tie a horse up front, make sure you have the door closed behind. Even with a horse who ties well, if the door is still open and he decides to back out and panics, it could turn into a major wreck. Be sure you have your sequence down—load him, close the door, hook the butt chain, then tie him the proper length.

Likewise, at your destination your first step is to untie him. Even if you use a trailer tie, I suggest leaving the halter rope on the horse. When a trailer tie with a safety snap is used, hook the tail of the halter rope near the rear door or lay it over the horse's back so it's handy for unloading. Make sure your ties are made with a quick release. When backing the horse out, after untying him up front, the tail of the halter rope is right there handy. You could also tie the horse up front with your halter rope. Trailer designs vary greatly, so adjust to fit your situation.

Caution: Do not tie the horse too short. This can add to his feeling of being trapped and cause him to panic. He should have enough slack that if he backs up, he feels the butt chain before the slack is out of the tie rope.

When you are going to haul somewhere, hook up your rig and trailer first, before you load your horse. This applies to practice loading too.

Prepare To Load, Haul, and Unload

Now you are ready to take your horse for a trip. At this point, he is loading willingly, standing quietly in the trailer while you slowly close the door, hook the butt chain, and tie his head up front. If he is not pawing, not troubled, and is relaxed, you are ready to go on a trip. For this first trip, you might just haul him around your pasture or around the block. After you make a circle or two, unload and reload him.

If your horse was relaxed with the first trip, then haul him two or three more times around. Unload and reload him each time. Your next step is to take a trip around the neighborhood and come back to your place, unload and reload him. Even if that was your last haul, reload him a couple of times before you put him up. Start lengthening the trip based on what the horse can handle.

I recommend at this point you haul him by himself, rather than with another horse. The buddy horse may help him relax, but someday you may need to haul him alone. Take the time necessary initially to let him learn to be confident and secure by himself. However, adjust to your individual horse and situation.

When you stop to unload on these practice trips, if your horse is pawing in the trailer or acting anxious, don't unload him at that moment. Wait until he stops pawing and relaxes, then unload. If he is pawing and fretting when you unload, you have rewarded his behavior and he might develop this habit. Catch him doing the right thing—relaxing and waiting—then reward him by unloading. Stay calm and relaxed yourself; your horse will take confidence from you.

The next step in this sequence is to haul him somewhere, unload and reload, then haul him back home. Unless you are sure of yourself, I recommend you haul to a place you are familiar with. If the horse has a major regression, have safe options in case he will not reload. If you have followed the outlined procedures up to now, this probably will not happen.

When You Haul Your Horse

Until you develop unquestioning confidence in your horse reloading, I recommend that after you unload at your destination, reload him three or four times in a row. This way, if you do have a problem, you have taken care of it at the beginning of the day. You may miss your trail ride, but at least you have time left over to get your horse in the trailer. I've been called out several times by people who have gone out on trail rides and when ready to return home, couldn't get their horse in the trailer. By the time they got in touch with me and I got out there, it was after dark. Had they reloaded their horse, it would have reassured the horse and reinforced the loading routine before they headed up the trail.

Slant-Load and Stock Trailers

Horses haul more comfortably in slant-load and stock trailers in which they can ride at an angle. Therefore, they load more willingly. If you have a slant-load or stock trailer, once your horse drives into the trailer consistently, you can lead him into the trailer from then on.

With a slant-load, you can use the divider to get him to step his hindquarters over to the right and line up in the proper position. Don't **push** him over with the divider; use it to **ask** him to step over to his right. He should be standing in the correct position before you lock the divider. If your horse feels a little claustrophobic, instead of locking the divider in place, open it to take the pressure off. Use the approach-and-retreat strategy with the divider to ask your horse to accept more confinement. Take this slow and break it down into steps to make it easy for your individual horse to accept.

When tying a horse in a slant-load with dividers, thread the tail of the halter rope through the tie ring, take it over the top of his divider, and tie off. This makes it really convenient when you go in to unload. Before you ever open his divider, you can untie him. This might prevent a wreck if he tries to bolt backward while still tied. You can prevent this situation from ever occurring.

Trailer Design

• Horses travel more comfortably and balanced in a slant-load or stock trailer than a straight-load trailer. See TL-8.

• **Dividers should not go all the way to the floor.** Not being able to spread their feet causes horses more claustrophobia and is one of the major reasons for scrambling, jumping in the manger, flipping over backwards, etc.

• If, after thoroughly working through all the procedures outlined earlier, your horse still exhibits severe problems such as scrambling, one solution might be to haul only in slant- or stock-type trailers, or to remove the divider.

• If you haul only one horse in your two-horse straight-load trailer, unhook the divider in back and swing it over to the right to make a one-horse, slant-load trailer. See TL-9.

• If you have a four-horse trailer with a divider in front that makes horses face straight ahead, either pull the divider out or swing it off to the side, making it a slant-load. See TL-10.

• If you have a stock trailer, either turn

*A two-horse, slant-hauling trailer.
Horses travel more balanced and
relaxed in a slant than a straight-ahead.*

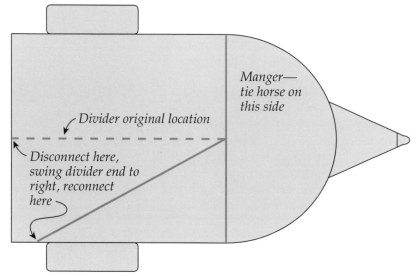

Single door,
full-width

Tack area

TL-8

*A two-horse straight con-
verted to one-horse slant.*

Manger—
tie horse on
this side

Divider original location

Disconnect here,
swing divider end to
right, reconnect
here

TL-9

your horses loose or tie them on a slant. To
prevent fighting, you can alternate tying
them head to tail, on left and right sides.

• If you have a slant-load, when you tie
your horse in, thread the halter rope
through his tie ring and tie off to a ring in
the next stall back. For added safety untie
your horse before you open his divider.

• Experiment with taking the first
divider (or all dividers) out of your slant-
load trailer and tie to the left side. If you
want to leave the last divider in, you can
swing it closed after tying the horses in.
See TL-11.

• Ramps vs. step-up: Horses can learn
to load in either; however, generally they
load and unload better with step-up trailers. Ramps can be inconvenient for humans
and some get very slippery for horses.

• On bumper-pull or gooseneck stock
or slant-load trailers, a full-width door in
back works best, with no rear tack compartment. Having to walk through a
narrow back door and passageway can
trigger claustrophobia.

• Bars instead of solid material on the
upper part of dividers give a more open
feeling to your horse. He feels less claustrophobic, less restricted and confined.

• Light-color trailer interiors are cooler
and appear less confining than dark colors.

• If your trailer has drop-down side
windows, do not leave them open while
the trailer is in motion unless web window
covers are installed.

• When hauling in a strange trailer,
load and unload your horse two or three
times before leaving.

• The cost of a safe, well-designed
trailer is money well-spent on your horse.

Driving Tips

• To warn your horses of an upcoming
stop or slow-down, lightly tap the brake
once before braking. This also serves as a
warning for traffic behind you.

• When turning, do not accelerate until
your trailer is lined up straight behind
your truck.

• When cornering, the horse on the
outside of a straight-load trailer gets

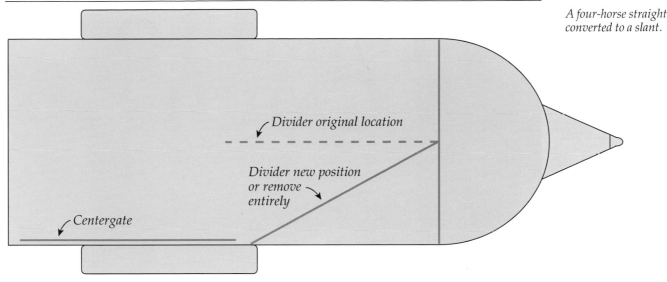

A four-horse straight converted to a slant.

Divider original location

Divider new position or remove entirely

Centergate

TL-10

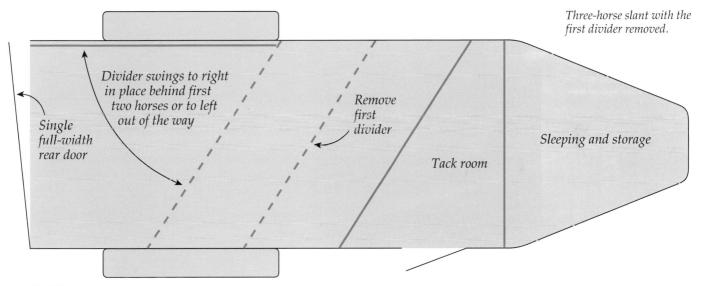

Three-horse slant with the first divider removed.

Divider swings to right in place behind first two horses or to left out of the way

Single full-width rear door

Remove first divider

Tack room

Sleeping and storage

TL-11

thrown off balance more than the horse on the inside of a turn.

• If you haul your horses in a straight-load trailer, drive slower than you think you need to. Keep your cornering speeds even slower, due to the poor balance straight-load trailers provide horses.

Conclusion: It's Mostly Feel, Timing, and Balance

The concepts and procedures outlined in this chapter are intended to give you a better understanding of your horse and how to develop his trust, confidence, respect, and acceptance in various aspects of trailer training. This is not intended to be a formula or mechanical recipe, just an outline. As I mentioned at the start, your success will depend on your ability to adjust to fit your horse and the situation. As you develop your feel for the horse, this becomes easier and more rewarding. You may find other people ask you to help them with their horses too.

As you develop your feel, you will be amazed how important it is and how much it means to the horse. Have fun and enjoy your discovery of it. Best of luck!

4

HARD TO CATCH

Learn How To Approach

LEARNING AND understanding how to approach a horse is more important than teaching a horse to be caught. Rather than thinking about catching your horse, think about getting him ready to be caught. The hard-to-catch horse will welcome our approach, or even approach us, when being with a human becomes a good place, and he associates us with safety, comfort, and leadership.

There are some common mistakes to avoid. Avoid making him feel captured or relying on using food as a bribe. Never leave a halter on a horse turned loose in a pasture or corral. People often think it is easier to catch a haltered horse, but turning a haltered horse loose invites injury.

Another example: If you have several horses in your corral and you go to retrieve the easy-to-catch bay mare, observe how your hard-to-catch sorrel gelding is reacting. If you ignore or miss observing him walk away from you or "hiding out" when he sees you coming to catch another horse, he is rewarded for his avoidance behavior. However, if you walk over and rub him before you leave the corral, it will help next time you want to catch him. This may seem like a small thing, but it's a big thing to your horse.

Starting in a round corral can make solving a catching problem easier. Your success will be determined by developing your feel, timing, and balance, not by the technique or equipment used. Understanding how to make the right thing easy, and the wrong thing difficult helps teach your horse to be consistently easy to catch. This skill is not difficult to learn or develop, but requires awareness of one's actions.

Round corral training goes beyond just solving a catching problem; it will expand your abilities in every other area of horsemanship, including riding. You and your horse will be able to operate with more lightness, softness, and responsiveness.

Working effectively with horses at liberty sharpens your awareness of the horse's subtle changes of expression before or as they occur. It is important to recognize when the horse is approachable and when he is thinking he needs to leave. By accurately reading the horse and adjusting the approach, the human will avoid mistakes that make horses difficult to catch. When the human makes small positive changes, the horse makes large positive changes.

Working in the Round Corral

This round corral discussion is not intended to be an exhaustive study; rather it is a condensed version to suggest some ideas to help with your hard-to-catch horse. Do the groundwork on the halter rope in Chapter 1 before starting in the round corral.

You do not need to buy or build a round corral. It is more important to learn the concepts, because you can apply them in any safe corral or pasture where you keep your horse, or in any situation with a loose horse. You can secure panels in the corners of a square corral to make it rounder. The

1/ Horses can be easy to catch in a corral or pasture.

2/ Easy-to-catch horses are also easy to halter.

guidelines suggested here are not a mechanical recipe. Every situation will be slightly different. Stay flexible in your approach. There are many variations of techniques to work effectively with a horse in a small area such as a round corral. Different horses provide opportunities to learn to adjust to their individuality. Do not worry about making mistakes. Mistakes are learning opportunities.

A round corral is an effective tool because it provides the human an advantageous position at the center of the horse's activity. This allows you more control of your horse's motion and direction. Horses can hide out in a larger area, but this is not as easy in a smaller corral. A round corral, about 50 feet in diameter, is large enough so your horse does not feel trapped and has a place to move his feet. Overconfinement does not build trust, but creates insecurity. This brings out the horse's self-preservation instincts, which can override his thinking about finding release, safety, and comfort in responding to the human.

The round corral is not for running your horse around until he is tired or exhausted. The objective is to reinforce a learning frame of mind, keeping your horse attentive and responsive to your body language, to get him "hooked on." This means he is not afraid. Instead, he is respectful and trusting, and wants to be with you. Mentally, he's connected to you, looking to you for answers.

This is the essence of catching your

"Hooked on" coming off round corral fence toward me.

horse and developing willing cooperation. The horse's self-preservation instincts cause him to stay attentive and aware of his environment. It is the human's responsibility to keep things interesting and rewarding for the horse.

Getting Started

Remove the halter, turn your horse loose in the round corral, and ask him to move off. Send him off with a directing and supporting motion similar to the leading-past groundwork exercise. He should leave with a good expression. It's important to be able to drive your horse away as well as to get him to come back to you.

While your horse is moving along the fence, observe his expression, observe the whole horse. What is his body language telling you? Is his tail kinked or relaxed? Is he laterally round? The curvature of his body—his jaw, neck, shoulder, rib cage, loin, and hip—should be evenly curved, matching the arc of the corral.

If his jaw or rib cage is pushed out toward you, this indicates defensiveness, a brace; he's not relaxed and comfortable. Stay aware of your horse's alignment.

Watch his eyes and ears. Are they attentive? Does he have an ear pricked toward you? Is he afraid, looking for escape, or is he looking for a place to hook on to you for safety and comfort? Does he resist moving out or does he become flighty with very little pressure? These are just a few things to be aware of.

When you ask your horse to move off, you do so through pressure. Whenever you apply pressure, regardless of which horse, first apply the slightest amount possible, then increase as necessary to get a response.

With a horse who is flighty and afraid, the slightest pressure may be enough to get more response than you really want. Sometimes a person's mere presence is more pressure than some horses can stand. Give a scared, flighty horse plenty of room to think about things, so he doesn't get more scared—trust him. Pressure is a relative thing. What's pressure for one horse might not even be noticed by another. What is enough pressure to get one horse to move might make another jump out of the round corral, buck you off, or pull away from you on the halter rope. Always start with the least and build up to more. You'll have a better chance of keeping your horse light, soft, responsive, and

The advantage of a round corral is being at the center of the horse's activity.

unafraid. The objective is to operate with your horse through feel.

Block and Draw

To gain control of your horse and get him hooked on, experiment with a block-and-draw technique. As he moves around you to the right of the corral, you can block his forward motion by moving from the center back and to your right. If you move in his direction at a sharp angle, he will probably turn into the fence to change direction. By not moving at him too sharply, he will turn toward you to change direction.

As he turns in, back away to draw him toward you. He may stop and face you or walk up to you. If he moves off the other direction rather than stop, just quietly encourage him forward and start again. Your movements should be as subtle as your horse's. Feel, timing, and balance are important. Give your horse a chance to work at it and figure this out. This will have good long-term benefits.

With him moving to the left, step back and to your left to block. As he slows and

Having removed halter, I am sending this filly off with a directing and supporting motion similar to the groundwork exercise.

123

Block and draw to left.

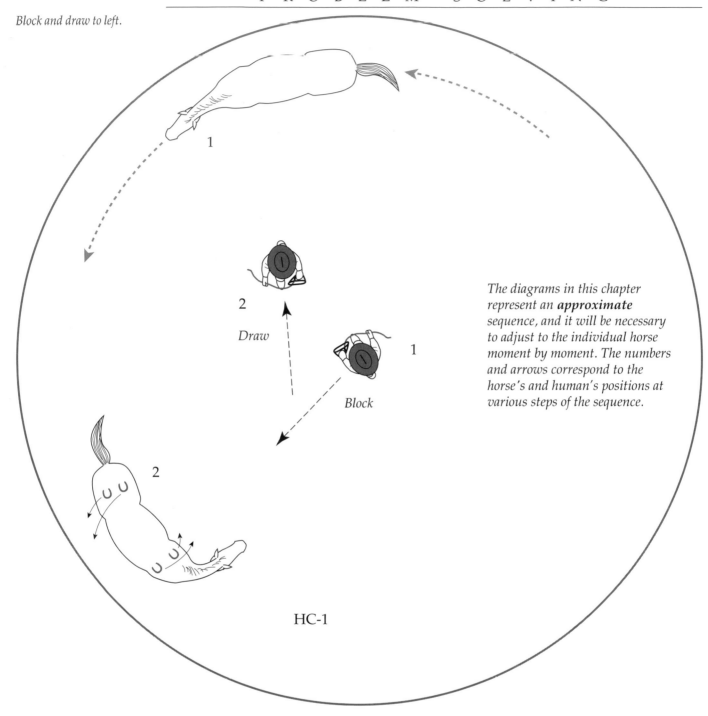

The diagrams in this chapter represent an **approximate** sequence, and it will be necessary to adjust to the individual horse moment by moment. The numbers and arrows correspond to the horse's and human's positions at various steps of the sequence.

Draw

Block

HC-1

1—In this block-and-draw exercise, the horse is moving to the left. Step back and to your left to block him.

2—As he slows and looks toward you, draw him by stepping back and to your right.

looks toward you, draw him by stepping back and to your right. This will give him the opportunity to turn in off the fence to you. Block and draw is a form of pressure and release, or approach and retreat. When working with these exercises, observe your horse's expression. Rather than look him straight in the eyes, keep your focus soft to prevent him from interpreting your actions as threatening. See diagram HC-1.

Drawing your horse releases your pressure on him and encourages him to hook on to you. Your horse will begin to associate you with his safety and comfort. You can build on this to help him become easier to catch in the future.

Sometimes a release of pressure is backing up, or stepping to your right or left away from the horse. It could be just relaxing your body posture. Maybe just relaxing your shoulders or leaning back would be enough to have the horse feel the release. You just have to experiment with this.

When you don't get the response you want, ask yourself, "How should I adjust? What can I do to communicate the response I want?"

Observe how your horse comes off the fence. Ideally he should have a soft expression and round body, rather than coming out sharp, braced, and stiff like a board. When your horse comes off the fence to face you and stops, if he's approachable, walk up and rub him. Approach at a slight angle, rather than straight toward his head, into his blind spot. If he is a little nervous, but allows your approach, it may be best to first make contact on his shoulder or neck. Each horse can be different about how he prefers to be approached and touched.

If you observe and read your horse, he will tell you how to position yourself so he can relax and stay with you. If your approach disturbs him, he may move and head out. If so, it's okay; just start over. Drive him a circle or two, and then draw him again, adjusting to make it easier for him to stay. These are great learning opportunities for you both.

After your horse is hooked on, you should be able to move him off and he should leave with a good expression. Drive him around the corral either direction, then hook him on again. However, avoid numerous continuous circles because horses can mentally check out or get lost in self-preservation. Occasionally make some transitions of direction and speed—walk to trot, lope, and back down to walk.

Initially, with a more fearful horse who doesn't know how to hook on, let him stop and turn into you whenever he wants. Later in the process, after he is readily hooking on, let him stop only when you ask. Some horses will be reluctant to go or stop when you ask them to move off, not wanting to work. Beware that your horse does not take over.

Remember, this is not a recipe or mechanical approach. This description is just to get you started thinking how to position yourself to get the desired response. There are subtleties and nuances with each individual horse. Keep adjusting to fit each situation moment by moment as your horse changes and you develop your feel, timing, and balance.

The Chargey Horse

A chargey horse will usually maintain his own forward movement in the round corral without you driving him. To help him hook on, stand in one place and toss the halter at him each time he passes the same spot on the circle. Hold onto the tail

Start Slowly

Caution: Use good judgment with a flighty and chargey horse to avoid injury or making your problem worse. If the horse is fearful, this procedure may be too much for him with an inexperienced handler. Be extremely cautious and accurately read the horse. Adjust to fit the horse moment by moment.

1/ Block and draw. I am stepping to my right to slightly block this filly's forward motion. Note her hindquarters are preparing to slow down and her right ear is indicating her attention is in my direction.

2/ Notice her right ear and her whole body expression. I am stepping back to my left to draw her in to her right toward me.

3/ She has come off the fence and her body expression indicates she is hooking on to me. I stand waiting for her. My posture is neutral.

4/ I approach in a manner that encourages her to stay and wait for me. I am preparing to make contact and pet her.

1/ Another block-and-draw sequence with a different mare. Here I am blocking to my left. Notice my mare, Dee Lena's expression indicating that she is responding to me.

2/ I have backed up a step, creating a draw. Notice she is coming off the fence with a good expression, soft and round.

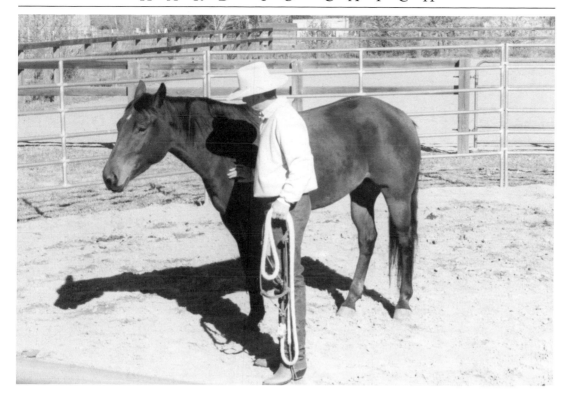

of the rope when you toss the halter. It does not have to hit him to be effective— I prefer that it does not. After a few times, he will anticipate getting into trouble (having the halter tossed at him) as he approaches that spot.

He may try to reverse directions to avoid the spot. Block this, sending him on in the same direction as before—he made the wrong choice. Next time he approaches, he may prepare to slow down or stop and face you. If you see him prepare, back up to draw him. If he doesn't stop, just send him off and around again the same direction. If he does stop and face you, the correct choice, back away, rewarding him with release and rest. Approach him, rub him and let him relax, then send him off the opposite direction and see if you can draw him off the fence to you, or repeat as above.

Another approach for a chargey horse who isn't ready to hook on yet is to repeatedly change directions or turn him on the fence several times, until he begins to prepare to stop and look at you. Use about a quarter of the corral for these turns. With this procedure, I usually turn the chargey

horse into the fence instead of the center.

These repeated changes of direction are more work, making the wrong thing difficult. Pretty quick he will be looking for a change and will be preparing to look in your direction. Don't miss observing this or you could put a great deal of stress on your horse without results. When you see him prepare, back up, drawing him toward you. He will appreciate an opportunity to be with you and rest. Be very careful with this approach. If you put too much pressure on your horse he could attempt to jump out of the corral or otherwise hurt himself. This takes feel, timing, and balance to work out. See diagram HC-2.

Blocking chargey horse using a portion of the corral.

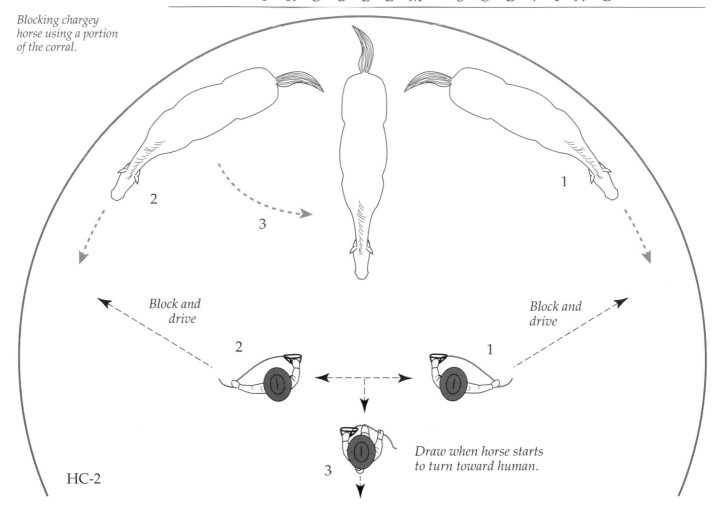

Block and drive

Block and drive

2

1

Draw when horse starts to turn toward human.

3

HC-2

Moving the Hindquarters

If your horse is moving around the corral to the right, draw him toward you. See diagram HC-3. Allow him to stop and face you. You should be in his right eye. Keep him focusing on you. Walk a semicircle toward his right hindquarters while holding his visual attention on you. You may have to do something like shake your halter rope or lightly slap your thigh to refocus his attention on you. The pressure this creates should encourage him to yield his hindquarters over to his left, away from you.

When he does, release by stopping and/or backing up. Then approach and rub him. Now move your horse off to the

left. He should leave with a good expression. Block and draw him to you. Then move his hindquarters from his left side to the right. Moving his hindquarters in this manner is a big part of being hooked on. This exercise is the same as in the ground-work chapter, but without a halter rope.

If at any time during this exercise he leaves instead of yielding his hindquarters, just quietly send him on and start again.

This maneuver requires subtle and accurate body language communication between horse and human. When you can accomplish this, you are making great progress with your horse mentally as well as making him easier to be caught. There are numerous variations on this exercise.

Next, move his frontquarters in a similar manner as in the groundwork exercise. See diagram HC-4.

With a chargey horse, to help him hook on, toss the halter toward him each time he passes the same spot.

"S" Turn and Changing Eyes

Once you can consistently draw your horse and move his hindquarters and frontquarters, you can ask him to maneuver in an "S" turn. You will find this more challenging, but well worth your effort. You will be asking your horse to change eyes when he makes the turn. See diagram HC-5.

Moving your horse along the fence to the right, walk toward his right hip, at a 30- to 45-degree angle. There are many similarities between working a horse in a round corral and moving cattle. You are asking him to round out to his right, walking toward the center. As he starts to round out, turn and go in his direction, still in his right eye.

Just before he crosses the center, step out toward his right eye, blocking, and driving him off to his left. This will get him to come out on his left eye along the fence, moving to the left of the corral, completing the "S" turn. Draw him, and have him hook on, and come out to you on his left side. Approach and pet him, letting him feel safe and comfortable standing with you.

Completing this maneuver requires your horse to change eyes. When you leave his right eye and before he picks you up in his left eye, he loses you in his rear blind spot. Being able to have him consistently change eyes without your startling

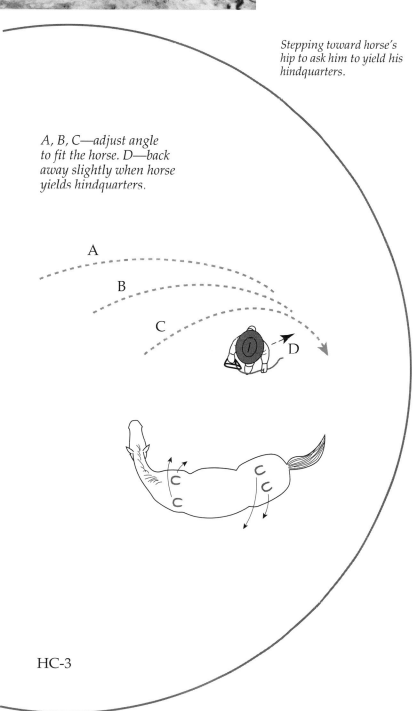

Stepping toward horse's hip to ask him to yield his hindquarters.

A, B, C—adjust angle to fit the horse. D—back away slightly when horse yields hindquarters.

A

B

C

D

HC-3

131

1/ Yielding the hindquarters while still hooked on to me. I am walking toward her hindquarters while maintaining her attention on me. She can sense my body language is not communicating for her to leave, but to stay and step over behind.

2/ She is starting to step her hindquarters over to her left. I will release pressure by stepping away just slightly.

3/ I have approached her and am petting her on the neck and shoulder.

1/ Another example of yielding the hindquarters. This is similar to the exercise in Chapter 1.

2/ She has disengaged her hindquarters and I am easing the pressure. Note how her head and neck are still bent toward me.

To get this horse's atten-tion back, I lift the halter up and down.

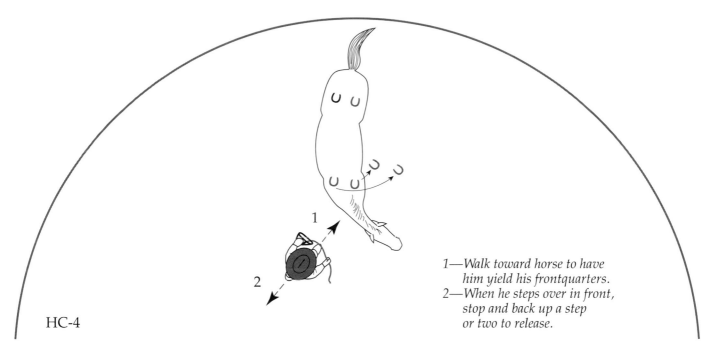

HC-4

1—Walk toward horse to have
   him yield his frontquarters.
2—When he steps over in front,
   stop and back up a step
   or two to release.

Yielding frontquarters away.

or scaring him, while controlling his movements in the round corral, will build his trust, confidence, and respect for you.

As Ray Hunt says, you are "arranging the life in the horse's body through his mind, down his legs, to his feet."

Your position, feel, timing, and balance are critical to accomplish this maneuver. It will develop your ability to drive your horse while he remains hooked on. This is important for future catching. Stay patient and work at it; it may take some trial and error to achieve this, but will be rewarding to accomplish. At my cow working clinics, I often have a horse and rider practice this same "S" turn, changing-eyes exercise with a cow in the round corral, and then out in a pasture.

1/ *Moving the frontquarters, similar to the Chapter 1 groundwork exercise. Note this filly's right front is stepping out and back.*

2/ *She is stepping her left front across in front of her right.*

You can do a similar changing-eyes exercise from behind your horse. Standing at your horse's right hindquarters with your arm over his hip, change sides to his left, moving behind his rump. Notice when you are on the right, his head is tipped slightly to his right. When you cross over behind him, he should tip his head to the other side picking you up in his left eye. He should remain calm, not concerned with your position.

Some horses are comfortable with the human in one eye, but not the other. This is going to carry over into the other things you do, particularly when you're riding. Get both sides balanced to avoid future problems. Do these changing-eyes exercises several times, starting from both sides, until it gets good. This will have a positive effect on your horse.

1/ "S" turn. This mare is moving to the right of the round corral. I am stepping toward her blind spot. My pressure is toward her right hip as though I was going to walk behind her to the other side. I am in her right eye.

2/ She has come off the fence and I am now driving her forward across the center of the round corral, still in her right eye.

3/ She has crossed the center, and my right hand is pushing on her right eye for her to change directions to her left.

4/ *She starts to move to her left as I continue to push on her right eye.*

5/ *She is making the turn to her left against the fence. At this moment, I am in her blind spot. When she turns she will pick me up in her left eye.*

6/ *She has completed the "S" turn and is moving along the round corral fence. I am in her left eye and am moving forward to block.*

7/ *I have backed up to draw her off the fence, hooking her on to me.*

"S" turn changing eyes.

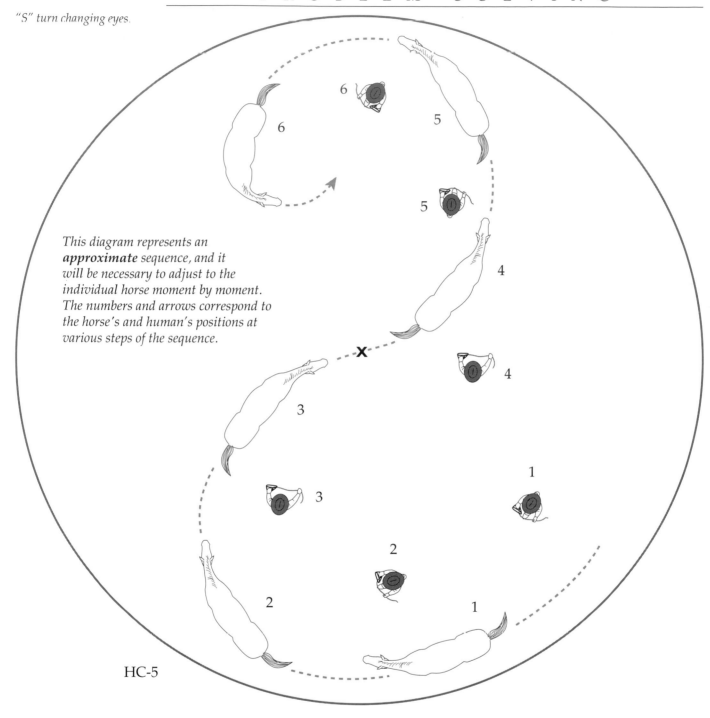

This diagram represents an
approximate sequence, and it
will be necessary to adjust to the
individual horse moment by moment.
The numbers and arrows correspond to
the horse's and human's positions at
various steps of the sequence.

HC-5

1—Here's how to accomplish the "S" turn in which the horse changes eyes.
As your horse moves along fence to the right, walk toward his right hip at a
30- to 45-degree angle.

2—As he rounds out to his right, turn and go in his direction, still in his right eye.

3—Just before he crosses the center, step out toward his right eye, blocking him
and driving him off to his left.

4—This will cause him to ease off to his left.

5—As he moves along the fence, you will now be in his left eye, and the "S" turn
is completed.

6—Draw him toward you to have him hook on. Then approach and pet him.

Catching in a Larger Arena

When you and your horse have accomplished these exercises and he is solidly hooked on to you, and you can easily catch him in the round corral anytime you wish, you are ready to move to a larger corral. If possible, practice catching in an arena or larger corral, rather than jumping to a large pasture. Work your way up in size with what you have available. You could trailer your horse to other arenas for practice too. If at any time he reverts back to being hard to catch, go back to a smaller corral and work your way up again. Even if catching is going well, reinforcing earlier training sessions in a smaller corral is beneficial.

When you practice catching your horse in a larger area, always carry your halter out in the open. Don't be sneaky with the halter or your approach. However, don't approach your horse aggressively, straight on like a predator. Let him rest and relax when he allows you to approach and stand next to him.

Have Your Horse Catch You

Teaching your horse to catch you can be fun as well as a positive learning experience. Ask your most patient friends to help you. Turn your horse loose in a large corral or arena. Have your friends each carry a halter rope, although you will be the only one catching your horse. The objective is for your friends to drive your horse to you as you slowly back away.

As long as your horse is walking on course toward you, your friends do not put pressure on him. When your horse stops or gets off track, their job is to swing their halter ropes to drive him toward you again. When he moves in your direction, they release their driving pressure, and you slowly back away from your horse. Make sure you always back up slower than your horse advances toward you. You are drawing him like you did in the round corral. This will give him a chance to hook on and catch you.

1/ *Changing eyes while standing at the hindquarters in this filly's blind spot. I lean just slightly to her right and she flexes her head and neck to see me in her right eye. Note I am touching her hip so she is aware of my presence.*

2/ *Shifting to lean over to her left, she flexes to pick me up in her left eye. My hand stays on her hip.*

1/ Changing eyes with a cow in a round corral. I am riding toward this heifer's right hip and she has come off the fence. I am in her right eye.

2/ Still in her right eye, I am preparing to position to change sides and eyes.

3/ We have changed sides and we are now in her left eye.

Horses move like flowing water, in the path of least resistance. Backing away creates a draw on your horse; he senses an opening. He'll be easier to catch if you're backing away than if you're moving in his direction. Your friends putting pressure toward him when he's off course and releasing pressure when he's on shows him the path of least resistance. When your horse's body language tells you he is looking you up, stop backing away and let him walk up to you.

Don't try to capture him once he is near you; just pet him. Let him stand there with you relaxed and comfortable before haltering him. You could quit now or turn him loose again and see if you can catch him by yourself. If so, quit for the day. If not, have your friends help you again.

The goal is for your horse to perceive you as the most comfortable place in the corral. For this to work, your friends will need to be very attentive to your horse, knowing when and how to drive him to you and when to release pressure. Your friends will enjoy this as much as you.

Walking Him Down

If you keep your horse in a large pasture and you do not have access to a catch pen (see sidebar) or other alternative, you may have to rely on walking him down to help with your catching problem. This method is the most difficult, and may require considerable time and patience. Plan ahead to devote the entire day if necessary. Start early and pack a lunch. This way you are not under the pressure of time constraints.

Head out to the pasture with your halter rope and walk toward your horse in a somewhat zigzag pattern, rather than straight at him. Maintain a very passive, casual body language, as though you have no intention of catching him. If there are other horses, you can walk up and pet them as you go by. Keep your focus on your horse, but also be alert enough to be safe among the loose horses.

Using a Pen

If you keep your horse in a large pasture, it may work out well for you to set up a catch pen. You can teach your horses to come into the catch pen for a bite of grain. The catch pen is a means to an end. This is not a bribe, it just provides a smaller area to work on catching. Do this often rather than just when you want to catch your horse for work. Work on all the fundamentals described in this chapter. Your goal is to not need the catch pen.

When your horse sees you, if he starts moving away, keep walking toward him in a blocking direction. When he stops, you stop and/or take a step backward. At this point you will have to read his body language to know if it is appropriate to walk toward him or wait before you approach him. When his body language is right, approach him a step or two. If he stays, stop and back up a step. Repeat this until he lets you walk up and pet him.

If he moves, continue walking toward him, following him wherever he goes. Don't chase or be sneaky, just keep moving in his direction. Depending on the horse and the pasture, you can also begin to direct him by switching sides, blocking right or left by walking parallel to him. You will be changing eyes similar to the "S" turn.

Keep this up. Stay patient and don't doubt yourself or your horse; it will work out. It just may take longer than you wish. When your horse lets you walk up and pet him, don't immediately

1/ Have your horse catch you. There are three of us driving this young filly to Amy LeSatz. The filly is off track looking my direction (out of photo) and I am putting pressure toward her to look back to Amy. Amy will stand still until the filly walks toward her.

2/ She is on track and Amy is slowly backing up to draw the filly to her. The rest of us are neutral as long as she is on track.

try to halter or capture him. This will ruin your efforts even if you get him caught. Instead, be slow and casual about haltering him. If you brought a small amount of grain with you, give it to him only after you have him haltered.

An excellent way to develop an easy-to-catch horse is to frequently walk out to his corral or pasture and catch him. Rub him, then remove your halter and walk away. Catching need not always mean being led away from herdmates and put to work.

3/ Amy is stopping, letting her filly walk up to her.

4/ This filly has discovered Amy is the most comfortable spot in the arena. Not in a hurry to catch her, Amy is quietly petting her.

Leading and Gates

Leading a horse from corral or pasture, especially out the gate, where there are loose horses can sometimes be a problem. When leading your horse, if the loose horses are getting too close, turn and face them with your horse behind you. The safest place to be is between your horse and the loose horses; this gives you more control. Use the tail of your halter rope to drive them off, and/or kick some dirt their way or even toss a small rock (avoiding their heads). Don't attempt to lead your

1/ *Haltering an easy-to-catch horse in a pasture. Note my right arm over her neck and right index finger and thumb asking her to tip her nose to me. Her head is lowered, making haltering easy. If I put my right arm under her neck to halter her, it would encourage her to elevate her head and neck, making it more difficult to halter or bridle her.*

2/ *All horses have the potential to be easy to catch even in a pasture. Learning and understanding how to approach a horse is more important than teaching a horse to be caught.*

horse through a gate with loose horses hanging around you. Drive them off, wait until they are standing away and won't rush or otherwise interfere with your horse going through the gate. If you drive them off and they come back, just drive them off again. They will eventually stay away and will respect you more next time. See diagram GW-11 for suggestions on leading through gates, as the human's position makes it easier to prevent another horse from escaping. By keeping loose horses from bothering your horse, he'll respect and trust you more, and understand when caught he is safe with you.

Turning Him Loose

Rather than thinking that they are turned loose when the halter comes off, I want my horses to understand that turned loose is when I walk away from them. They are then free to go wherever they want. Therefore, after removing the halter, I keep my right arm over the neck and stand with the horse for a while, then walk away. I never want a horse to pull or walk away from me while taking off the halter. Turning your horse loose with quality will have a positive effect, carrying over to catching next time. It's the little things that make the difference.

Conclusion

Good, sound catching principles remain the same regardless of your situation, size of corral, or pasture. Learning how to catch your horse in the round corral will greatly improve all aspects of your horsemanship. Start with the groundwork, then the round corral, before you move on to larger areas. Each step will help you develop more understanding of how your horse thinks, learns, and communicates. He gets easier to catch as you improve your awareness of position and approach and your ability to read your horse.

Again, make being caught easy for your horse, and make not being caught difficult. When you make the wrong thing difficult, it shouldn't be so unbearable for your horse he cannot think and make choices. Stay this side of trouble and keep your horse from feeling that he needs to use his self-preservation flight instincts to defend himself. Keep him in a learning frame of mind.

Look for the common thread throughout all the problem-solving suggestions discussed in this chapter and throughout this book. Then get creative and imaginative so you can adjust your solution for catching to fit you, your horse, and the facilities you have available. Good luck!

5 BARN-SOUR HORSES

As your horse becomes more sure of you, this problem will solve itself.

IF YOUR HORSE has barn-sour problems, don't be alarmed. Generally these are relatively easy to resolve. Keep in mind that this is really a symptom rather than a problem. The horse is a herd animal with a strong sense of self-preservation. He associates safety and comfort with the barn, where he has shelter, food, water, rest, and his herdmates. He may also have a predictable routine that he likes. Often it's the patterns and routines we set up that create these problems.

The origins of the barn-sour problem are often numerous. Usually they result from insufficient trust, confidence, and respect between horse and rider. The horse doesn't feel secure and confident enough to be away from home or his buddies. It's the rider's responsibility to provide the leadership the horse needs to feel safe and comfortable, and willingly go wherever he is ridden. Fidgety or chargey horses and horses who jig on the trail also fall into this category.

Riding back to the barn on a loose rein. If you have barn-sour problems, they are relatively easy to fix.

146

It is important to be able to ride your horse straight, wherever you direct him. At the barn before heading out on the trail, make use of obstacles and lots of transitions.

When I refer to barn-sour, "barn" means anyplace your horse does not want to leave, or rushes to go back to, except other horses, which will be discussed in the herd-bound chapter. Your barn could be where you board your horse, your property, your trailer, or wherever. When implementing these suggestions, adjust to fit your situation, your horse, the individual circumstances, your property, and how the trails lead from the barn.

Barn-sour problems are usually easier to solve than herd-bound problems. However, there is a common thread in the concepts and techniques appropriate for both problems. If you have a herd-bound problem, first read and practice the suggestions in this chapter. These principles can also be easily applied to many other situations.

Much like trailer loading and herd-bound, barn-sour problems seem to bring out the worst in the human. The concepts and procedures suggested in this chapter, as well as the other chapters, offer suggestions on how to do less to get more. The concepts should also provide more insight into and appreciation for the horse's natural self-preservation instincts.

These ideas are not a recipe. These solutions and techniques will develop the rider's confident leadership skills. They will help the human read the horse and be proactive in directing him. These concepts

Before you head out on the trail, you need to be able to ride through all gaits on a loose rein.

Too many
horses are
not ridden
on a daily or
regular basis.

are also intended to help develop the rider's feel, timing, and balance while developing the horse's trust, confidence, and respect for the rider's guidance.

I will suggest ways to set up situations where you control the variables. This provides a greater opportunity for the rider to remain calm, which allows the horse to stay in a learning frame of mind, looking to you for direction. When your horse is resistant, you can set it up so he is working against himself rather than against you. With a patient attitude and planning, overcoming this problem can be very enjoyable and rewarding. It will also advance all other aspects of your horsemanship, and develop a stronger bond between you and your horse.

Typical Symptoms

Generally, the barn-sour horse may exhibit one or a combination of the following symptoms.

You try to ride away from the barn, your immediate area, or trailer, and he doesn't want to go. If he does leave the barn, he's tugging on you all the way out wanting to return. He is nervous, anxious, it's difficult to maintain his attention, and he won't relax until you return.

It is very unsettling if, on reaching the destination and turning for home, your horse jigs, prances, and/or wants to race back to the barn. The more you hold him back, the more likely he starts tossing his head, jigging, rearing, or bucking. I've seen horses side-passing all the way back to the barn because the riders were over-confining them with the reins. Not being able to control your horse's speed or gait can set up a very unsafe situation.

Why Do Horses Become Barn-Sour?

Take an overview of your routines, which may be creating or reinforcing your barn-sour problem. Even if you don't have a barn-sour horse, the star pattern idea and other suggestions to follow could be implemented as preventive maintenance.

Too many horses are not ridden on a daily or regular basis. They may get saddled up only once or twice a week and taken away from the barn to work. Why would they want to leave, particularly if they don't have confidence in a rider who sporadically interrupts their barn routine?

Humans often unconsciously establish patterns when returning to the barn from riding. The horse knows as soon as he gets home, he gets unsaddled, turned out or put in his corral or stall, which is followed by feed, water, and relaxation. He's also back with his herdmates.

By setting these patterns, we make the barn comfortable and being with the rider, away from the barn, less comfortable by comparison.

The goal is to make both places comfortable. The rider should represent his horse's comfort zone, with stimulating mental and physical challenges along the way. Become something for your horse to look forward to. As your horse becomes more sure of you, this problem will solve itself.

Getting Prepared: Saddle Up and Get Started

As with all problems, my first recommendation is to develop more communication and understanding between you and your horse through a solid foundation of groundwork and riding. (See Chapters 1 and 2.) While still at the barn, you need to be able to ride your horse straight on an imaginary line, directing and guiding him wherever you want to go. If this isn't sharp, it's too early to head out on the trail.

Evaluate yourself and your horse. Some techniques recommended may not be fitting for the timid rider, especially with a fractious horse. The most difficult problem to solve is the horse and rider mismatch. If you feel this applies to you, approach this with caution. If at any point you feel you are over your head, consult a competent professional.

Here is a good preliminary test for working on any riding problem. Before you head out on the trail, see if you can ride your horse in an enclosed arena or round corral through all gaits, then back to a halt with a very loose rein, or better yet without your hands on the reins.

If your horse receives a rich, high-energy grain and alfalfa ration and is not ridden enough to work it off, this may be contributing to the problem. Stalled-up, hyper horses can get very excitable and chargey when ridden. This horse may be happier if he gets a cutback on his rich feed and has more frequent, interesting, and challenging riding.

Star Pattern

Riding a star pattern will serve as a general concept for preventing and solving barn-sour problems. It is a great place to start. It helps break the unconscious, unproductive routines we create. The horse won't know when he returns to the barn whether he's going to be put up or if you will just keep riding. Rather than ride out a long distance from the barn, then struggle with your horse all the way back, make multiple short trips. With the star

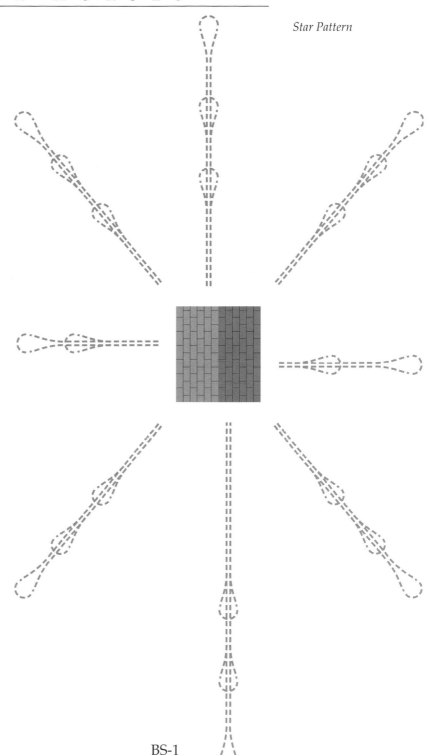

Star Pattern

BS-1

149

Using the star pattern, pick a point and head out away from the barn.

pattern, you conceivably could take a 5-mile trail ride without getting more than a quarter-mile from the barn.

The term star pattern is used just to create a visual image. It is an approach-and-retreat strategy that fits well with the horse's instincts. See diagram BS-1. The barn is in the center and the star points are the trails leading away. "Trail" means a road, pasture, lane, direction, or actual trail where you can ride your horse. As you progress, your goal is to incrementally increase the distance out on each trail point. Use your imagination and be creative.

Pick a trail and ride your horse away from the barn. Don't go too far, maybe just 50-100 yards depending on your horse. Before he gets upset, turn and ride back to the barn. When you get there, don't stop; turn and choose another point to ride to. Ride out approximately the same distance as before, turn around and head back to the barn. Determine how far out to go based on your experience and ability to read your horse. Continue repeating this until you have ridden out and back in all directions. Your horse should leave and return relaxed before you increase the distance.

Ride out in a different sequence each time you restart the pattern, so your horse doesn't anticipate a routine. As a variation on the star pattern, where possible, turn off your trail partway back, and return to the barn on a different trail. Avoid routine; don't become predictable. Attempt to make every trail ride different so he doesn't anticipate what's going to happen next. Eventually, he should feel comfortable and safe enough with you that it doesn't matter.

This star pattern concept will be incorporated into all other techniques described in this chapter. It will also serve as a base line for your progress in solving this problem.

Won't Leave the Barn

What if you are saddled, ready to ride away from the barn, and you can't get your horse to leave? Rather than try to force him to leave the barn area, put him to work to make being right at the barn uncomfortable. Get him busy. Make as many transitions as possible: trot, canter, stops, backups, directional changes, circles, figure eights, go over obstacles, etc. Don't consider this punishment; just give him a productive job to do. Build his desire to stop and rest.

1/ If your horse prefers to be at the barn, ride him actively there, then head out on the star pattern again, letting him rest away from the barn.

Putting him to work means taking him to a higher activity level than an easy ride away from the barn would be. Stay positive; keep a smile on your face while doing something productive. Rather than punishing the horse because he wants to stay or go back to the barn, you are momentarily making the barn an uncomfortable place to be. You are giving him a choice, setting it up to make the right thing easy and the wrong thing difficult.

When you think he's ready for a rest, ride him just a little longer, then try again to ride him away from the barn. If he follows your direction, ride out just a short distance, stop, and let him rest. Let him be comfortable and relaxed; you might even step down and loosen your cinch.

Now ride him back to the barn and head out on another trail. If he resists leaving again, repeat putting him to work at the barn and resting away from the barn. Keep up this sequence until he starts to see the place he gets to rest is away from the barn, in the direction you want to go. He will also see he gets to return to the barn when you direct him there. Continue the star pattern and incrementally increase the distance out.

2/ If your horse rushed back, get him busy and active at the barn, then head out again.

151

Balks on the Trail

If your horse balks after you are out on the trail, put him to work at that spot just like you did back at the barn. When you are ready to give him a rest, ride him forward just beyond where he balked. Depending on your horse, either stop and rest or let him relax as you quietly walk forward. Then head back to the barn and work on active riding transition exercises there. When your horse is ready for a rest, head out again on the star pattern at a relaxed walk. Pretty soon your horse learns that wherever you ask him to go is always easier and more relaxing.

- -

The Dismount Option

Never encourage galloping or loping; it is always best to walk your horse back to the barn. Stay this side of trouble. **Be realistic about your own comfort level and ability to handle what's taking place.** If things really fall apart, you feel unsafe, and you have run out of alternatives, rather than risking an injury from a panicked horse, you may need to dismount. Only you can make this judgment decision about what is appropriate for you and your horse. However, should you choose to dismount, don't lead your horse back to the barn. Get him busy with proactive groundwork exercises. Your horse will not differentiate between you directing him from the ground or his back.

This may sound like you're giving in or letting your horse win. However, when people lose confidence horseback, usually something bad is going to happen and somebody is going to get hurt. Once you've relaxed and your confidence has recovered, mount up and start over—you will both be winners.

Disengage the Hindquarters and Bring Forequarters Toward Magnet

You've turned around, and you're riding back to the barn. You're walking on a loose rein, which is the best way to return home. When your horse's attention turns to the barn, he gets in a hurry, starts trotting, going faster than you want. You ask him to slow down, but he gets more excited, and now he really wants to go back to the barn.

Don't try to hold him back. The more you pull back equally with both reins, the more he lines up his skeleton and muscles, collects himself, and pretty quickly you are fighting with him.

He sees you as part of his problem rather than his solution. He needs to move his feet. They are hard to slow down at this moment, so direct them. Control what you can control, not what you cannot.

The moment he moves up into a trot, reach down one rein, bend his head and neck around, and ask him to disengage his hindquarters until he faces 180 degrees away from the barn. Maybe go 190 degrees and release his head, lean back slightly, bringing his frontquarters across. The magnet of the barn will make it easy for him to do a 170- to 180- degree turn on the haunches.

Immediately release the rein once he is pointed in the direction of the barn. This exercise is described in Chapter 2.

This is a modified one-rein stop. Rather than asking for a complete stop, keep your horse in continual motion. The stopping nature of disengaging the hindquarters and bringing his frontquarters on through will have slowed him down from a trot to a walk. Releasing the rein is your signal for him to walk. Each time your horse breaks into a trot, repeat the same procedure, bending the opposite side each time. Stay with this, smile, and remain relaxed and patient.

This can have a very calming, quieting effect on your horse. Rather than fighting your horse by holding him back, you are doing something productive that will help

1/ If your horse rushes back to the barn, make that difficult without holding him back. Here I am demonstrating slowing this filly down by disengaging the hindquarters until she is faced 180 degrees away from the barn.

2/ I release when she is pointed away from the barn. The magnet (the barn) will help bring her frontquarters across (pivot on hindquarters) facing the barn again. Then I'll ride forward on a loose rein.

in other areas. You are directing his feet, making the wrong thing difficult and the right thing easy, without being harsh or offensive.

Do as little with your legs and your reins as it takes to get the job done. You may have to do more, but always offer your horse a good deal first. Don't jerk his head or kick him in the belly. Let your horse's impulsion help you disengage his hindquarters, and let the barn draw his frontquarters to complete the turn. Using the magnet of the barn can be very productive in developing the feel, timing, and balance of bringing the frontquarters across.

Be aware of your horse's sensitivity level. If he's being sensitive to your direc-

153

tion, then offer him the same. If he's ignoring you, then you'll have to firm up to the point where you can redirect his attention. **This takes good judgment and experience.**

The only way to get experience is to live it, to ride your horse and create some wet saddle blankets from proactive, quality riding. When you are riding and working with your horse, take the opportunity to observe things you might not have before. Each time you ride your horse, you'll learn and understand more of what's taking place between the two of you.

Make Your Destination an Appealing Place

To reinforce that being out away from the barn is a good idea, instead of turning and riding straight back to the barn, stop and let your horse rest and relax. You could get down and eat a lunch or a snack. Loosen the cinch or maybe even take off the saddle. Let him graze or feed him a little grain you have brought along.

If you're riding during hot weather, plan to ride to a shady spot where you can give your horse a drink. Create comfort for your horse out on the trail as well as at the barn. Set things up so your idea of going on a trail ride becomes a more favorable idea to him. Most important is that your horse feels safe and comfortable with you wherever you direct him.

Partial Bend To Slow Feet

The partial bend is another form of using one rein to control your horse when he is rushing back toward the barn, or is chargey or jigging on the trail. Bend your horse's head and neck slightly (15-30 degrees) to one side. Limit the bend with the outside rein (opposite the bending side). To help keep your horse traveling straight, use your legs as a guide and keep your inside calf forward to prevent an inside turn. Adjust your leg position as needed to maintain the desired body alignment. This exercise is described in Chapter 2.

Do not use force or harshness. You're just aligning the horse and positioning his body. You don't have to use a lot of leg or rein pressure. Set him up and let him find

the release. Your objective is to slow his feet. When he drops down to a walk, immediately release rein and leg pressure. If he trots again, repeat bending him the opposite direction.

If your horse pushes his outside shoulder forward after you have bent his head to the inside, he is bracing through his hindquarters and loin area, because he wants to stay straight without bending. To line him back up on course, you may need to either bump him with your outside leg (your calf) or move your inside leg back to move his hindquarters over.

This control exercise works well because it is somewhat uncomfortable for the horse to continue rushing forward with his head and neck flexed. It is much more effective than pulling back with both reins equally, allowing your horse to push against the bit through his hindquarters. You'll find this exercise takes patience and may require some distance to get a change in your horse's feet. It is very effective with many applications. It also works well on a road or narrow trail where circling is difficult.

As you develop more responsiveness in your horse, it will take less to get him to slow his feet down. The key is the release. Once you release the rein, he gets a reward for slowing down. Alternate bending right and left to help build suppleness while you are solving the jigging-back-to-the-barn problem.

If he doesn't slow down to a walk when you bend him, you may need to complete a one-rein stop or use other means to get down to his feet. When you get back to the barn, head out again on the star pattern.

Serpentines and Figure Eights

This is another technique for a chargey horse heading back to the barn. Rather than try to contain his excess energy, direct it; put him to work, giving him a job to do. If the terrain where you are riding lends itself, experiment with riding your horse in serpentines and figure eights. Ride the serpentines and circles so they slowly spiral back to the barn. Be particular and ride your horse on a line as accurately as possible. Ride around trees, rocks, and other obstacles. You'll be solving this and other problems because your horse is get-

Never encourage galloping back to the barn. Walking on a loose rein is the best way to return home.

ting better at following your direction and leadership.

This is riding your horse proactively. Instead of reacting to your horse, you're directing him, giving him a job to do. I'm not suggesting working your horse to exhaustion, or using exhaustion as a tool to make the wrong thing difficult. Just put his energy to work and direct it.

Pretty soon your horse will welcome the idea of resting and relaxing. When he does, he gets to walk in a direct line back to the barn. When you get back to the barn, don't put him up yet, as that would be rewarding his barn-sour behavior. Unless he came home very quietly the last half of the ride, either head out again or actively ride him near the barn.

Turn Him Around and Head Out Again

Walking forward on a loose rein is the preferred way to return to the barn. However, if your horse gets chargey, another technique you can use is to turn him around, and head out away from the barn at a strong trot. When he settles down and travels on a loose rein, turn him around and head back to the barn. As long as he walks forward on a loose rein, let him travel comfortably back to the barn. If he

On the star pattern, heading back to the barn, two-tracking on a country road.

gets chargey again, then turn and ride away from the barn.

Obviously, the problem with this is you might end up farther and farther away from the barn. You have to make some judgments about whether this will work for you. You want your horse to realize every time he rushes, you turn him and go

If your horse wants to rush back to the barn, direct his extra energy. Give him a job to do by riding serpentines and figure eights, here using natural obstacles as markers.

away from the barn. As is true of all the suggestions discussed, if you work at this in a very patient manner without getting frustrated or angry, the horse will gain something. This exercise may not be appropriate for some horses or at some stages of training.

Get Ahead of Your Horse

This is another technique to experiment with when you head back to the barn. But this approach might not work with some horses. They will never settle down enough to come back to the walk before you return to the barn. As with the exercise just discussed, do this with a horse you have more control of, whose barn-sour problem is not severe, or who is nearly over the problem.

If you know your horse is going to break into a trot, ask him to trot before he does. Trot 10 or 15 strides and then ask him to walk 5 or 10 strides. Then go back up to a trot, then back down to a walk. If your horse can walk 10 or 15 strides toward the barn before he wants to trot, be ahead of him and ask him to trot before he volunteers. Then ask him to come back to

a walk. After five or ten strides, tip him up to a trot again—be proactive.

Being behind your horse's action—always reacting, disciplining, trying to correct and control him—can become very negative from the horse's point of view. If you stay mentally ahead of your horse, you get better at reading him, and he gets better at responding to your direction.

As with all these exercises, if you were unable to accomplish a relaxed walk back, ride at the barn for a while, working on productive exercises, or head out on the star pattern again.

Develop Straightness and a Faster Walk

Make positive and productive use of your horse's desire to head back to the barn. After you have progressed in solving this problem and can easily direct your horse, use the draw of the barn to help him develop straightness and a faster walk. When you ride him out and turn back toward the barn, notice how straight your horse travels when going somewhere he enjoys. Learn the feel of a faster walk when he is doing it on his own. Get in rhythm with his movement. When you get back to the barn, head out on another trail and start over. Your goal is to eventually have your horse willingly walk away from the barn as fast and as straight as he does coming back. When you have accomplished this you are well on your way to developing a willing partnership with your horse. Straightness and a fast walk are very desirable and you will use both in many other situations.

Gate-Sour

A variation of the barn-sour problem is a horse who is gate-sour. When you are riding in an arena, he may always be drawn toward the gate, because he knows it's where he came in and how he gets back to the barn.

If your horse ducks toward the gate and speeds up, then feels sluggish going away from the gate, here's a suggestion. Ride away from the gate, then loosen your reins with lots of slack. Allow him the choice to go back to the gate. When he gets there, don't let him stop and hang his head over the gate. Keeping the reins loose, start working your legs back and forth, bumping him with both calves, making it uncomfortable for him to stay at the gate. Keep him moving; don't let him ball up and stop. It might even be necessary for you to swat him a little with the tail of your mecate or your split reins. The instant he looks away and tries to move away from the gate, release your legs and pet him.

If things should fall apart, get him back under control by making a one-rein stop. If this exercise feels unsafe for you, then go back to more riding basics, or instead of a loose rein, work him in vigorous circles and figure eights at the gate.

When you release the pressure, predictably, he will turn back to the gate. Allow him to make that decision. Wait until he gets back to the gate so he will associate the discomfort with the gate. Then start bumping him again and release when he leaves the gate. You might have to repeat this several times. Most horses, after a while, will move away from the gate and stand. Let him stand and pet him; make it really comfortable there. Create a comfort zone for your horse with you in the middle. Wherever you direct your horse, you're taking his comfort zone with you.

You're allowing your horse the choice to make a mistake. When he makes the wrong choice—the gate—let it always be

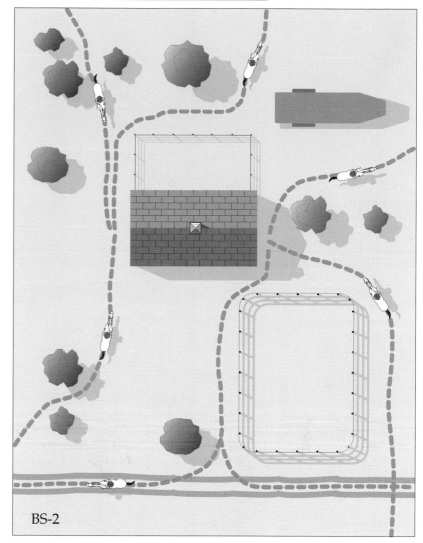

Star Pattern

more work for him than making the choice you want him to make—being away from the gate. Do this without making him feel he's being punished, threatened, or admonished. Allow your horse to work at these problems and sort these things out for himself—allow him to be a winner.

Get Him on Cattle

Putting the barn-sour horse on cattle will help to give him more meaning and a purpose to your riding—a real job. This makes riding more interesting, challenging, and rewarding. Horses seem to make a real positive transformation when they have the opportunity to work cattle. It's a natural for them. If your horse is not used to cattle, approach them so you don't overexpose him. Refer to the chapter on

Riding on cattle provides horse and rider more enjoyment, meaning, and purpose for leaving the barn.

Riding out in the open on cattle gives the horse a magnet to focus on, other than the barn.

spooking for an explanation of how I introduce green horses to cattle at my cow-working and working ranch clinics.

Tie Your Horse Up

When you ride back to the barn, instead of immediately turning your horse loose or putting him back in his stall or corral, tie him up, loosen his cinch, and let him stand there for a while. Let him learn that being back at the barn doesn't mean he's through for the day.

Leave him tied there for an hour or two. You might take his saddle off after a while. Later, come back with a bucket, offer a drink, and groom him. When you turn him loose, don't feed him until later. Break the pattern that every time he comes back

to the barn he gets fed, watered, and returned to his friends.

If he is sweaty, before you tie him up lead him around for a while to help cool him down. You could even lead him out to the trail, take a brush, and groom him there. I recommend you not walk off and leave a sweaty horse. It's important mentally as well as physically.

That's a good time to bond with him. Until he is cooled down, hang out with him and rub him. Everything you do needs to demonstrate positive leadership qualities.

Conclusion

This chapter has discussed several ideas to help with your barn-sour horse. If you find that one method makes more sense for you and your horse, start there. Then

158

Heading back to the barn on a loose rein, developing a faster walk. Riding alone with your horse can be an excellent way to develop a more willing partnership.

mix them up, rather than stick with any one particular approach. It will help keep you and your horse fresh. They all have more similarities than differences. Get creative, use as many approaches as possible, use your imagination and these principles to come up with your own.

Refer to the "as if" principle in the spooking chapter. The more confidence you have in yourself and your ability to ride your horse, the more confident and responsive he'll be. By contrast, the person who is short on confidence and is afraid probably will doubt his horse, making the barn even more attractive. If we think he's going to be bad or panic, then the horse interprets this as confirmation there is something he needs to be concerned about. It's a spiraling effect the rider creates.

Stay positive and optimistic; avoid anger. Create habits that are not aggressive or timid. Be a good leader—give direction and support. When humans get impatient, angry, or frustrated, it clouds their thinking. They lose their perspective and begin to blame the horse for the problem. Instead, take control of the situation and allow the horse to search for the answer. Reward the good, and discourage the not-so-good.

As you become more in tune with your horse, he becomes more hooked on you. This will solve many problems. Use these techniques, but even more important are the intangibles such as feel, timing, balance, and

Having ridden back to the barn, instead of immediately turning my filly loose, I have tied her up, loosened her cinch, and let her stand there for a while. If she were hot, I would cool her out first.

being aware of what your horse is thinking.

Helping your horse through your barn-sour problem can be a lot of fun if you can stay relaxed and positive. Observe your horse making progress. Observe his expression and feel him thinking and making decisions as you ride. Go with his flow and he'll go with your flow and you'll both be right on. You are developing a willing partnership.

6 SPOOKING

There are many things out there to spook a horse.

Horses Are Not Instinctively Brave Animals

SELF-PRESERVATION is very strong in horses. If it weren't, we might not have them here today to enjoy. Horses are prey animals who rely on flight as their principal means of defense. Anytime they perceive a threat, their natural instinct is to escape. Perception is reality for horses. They are very strong, athletic animals, and when motivated by fear, can cause great harm to themselves and their riders.

The same level of stimulus can cause varying degrees of fear and spooking in different horses. An extremely fearful horse will take off and run quite a distance, until satisfied everything's okay. Some horses will startle or jump a few steps, while others will react almost imperceptibly, not moving their feet from the track the rider is asking them to follow.

The horse does not purposely try to displease his rider by spooking. As did his ancestors in the wild, the horse has a keen awareness of his environment. If we want our horse to be brave, we have to be brave. For him to trust rather than fear his environment, he must gain confidence from the rider. The more confident the rider, the more confident the horse will be.

The goal of this chapter is to provide a developmental approach to help horse and rider reinforce trust in each other's ability to handle whatever comes along. The goal for the horse: to be aware of his environment, but checking in with his rider first anytime he is troubled. The goal for the rider: to be proactive, alert, and aware, directing his horse, helping him through his fear, communicating that spooking isn't necessary for survival.

The various exercises suggested are for confidence-building. They set up spooking situations to stretch your horse's comfort zone while you control the variables. There are also suggestions on how to handle real-

Spooking is a natural reaction to what the horse perceives as scary and threatening situations. Self-preservation is very strong in horses. When your horse spooks, go with his flow and pet him. If necessary use one rein to regain control. Then ride on as if nothing happened.

life circumstances as they come up. Before you begin, review the groundwork and riding information in Chapters 1 and 2. It also may be helpful to read the other chapters. As you proceed, develop your feel of the horse, looking to him to tell you how to adjust your approach.

Spiraling Effect

There can be a two-way spiraling effect with the spooking horse. Between horse and rider, spooking can become contagious. A rider often anticipates his horse will spook and rides nervously. The horse reads this and his anxiety level intensifies. Sure enough, the horse spooks at something. When the horse spooks, the rider spooks more, and the spiraling escalates.

Spooking may also come when the rider is daydreaming, coasting along, letting the horse go wherever the trail takes him. Pretty quick, something bothers the horse, and he checks in with his rider. If the rider is unaware or fails to support him, his horse will rely on his instincts. The horse spooks, unnerves the rider, starting the spiraling effect. In either of the above cases, the horse is reacting naturally to communicated fear.

If the rider remains relaxed and calm even when the horse spooks, they avoid the spiraling effect. As the horse perceives

This gelding is not too sure just yet about this newly constructed mailbox. Seek out opportunities to stretch your horse's comfort zone.

his human as his confident leader, spooking will begin to resolve itself.

When your horse spooks, balks, shies, or hesitates, don't kick him or punish him, as this will only deteriorate trust and confidence. Ride in balance, without pulling back or jerking on the reins when your horse spooks and jumps. Go with his flow a few strides and rub (pet) him. Then if more control is necessary, drift his hindquarters, riding on when he relaxes, or make a one-rein stop as described in Chapter 2.

Riding Proactively Reassures Your Horse

If the human is reacting to the horse instead of actively directing him, the horse may feel unsure about where he's being asked to go and about his rider's leadership abilities. When something comes along the horse may have otherwise not reacted to, he now spooks.

Instead of reacting to the horse, keep the horse responding to you. To help with your spooking problem, stay mentally ahead of your horse. You do not have to ride fast and hard; rather, stay active with transitions. Redirect your horse's attention by changing his focus, and he will have less inclination to spook. Head off a potential spook you may see ahead; be proactively redirecting your horse, rather than waiting and hoping you don't get a negative reaction. Riding proactively is fundamental to developing your horse's confidence.

An example: when stopped overlooking a steep bank drop-off, your horse may feel uneasy, ready to spook. Ask him to move before he does. This can be as simple as taking advantage of his heightened energy by doing something you

want to get better at anyway, such as moving the frontquarters across a half-turn (pivoting on the hindquarters), then riding off on a loose rein. You are making the situation productive, staying mentally ahead of your horse, and communicating that you will give him what he wants if he will wait for your direction.

Some horses are more thin-skinned and sensitive, more on the edge. They have very active minds. We need to be very proactive with these horses, exposing them to many things. Give them every chance to learn to respond to you in increasingly more stressful situations.

The "As If" Principle

Even if you are not confident, act and ride "as if" you are. Your horse won't know the difference. Soon you won't have to act, you will be. If all else fails, you can always rely on the one-rein stop to get your horse back under control.

An essential part of relaxing is for the rider to keep breathing. If the rider tenses up and stops breathing, the horse will tense up and become anxious. This tensing up can be conveyed to the horse through the rider's seat, legs, and too much rein pressure. Instead, ride forward relaxed, on a loose rein.

If any of these exercises are too big a stretch, practicing them while riding a more seasoned horse can help you later with your spooky horse. Even if this is not possible, you can tailor your approach to fit you and your horse.

Find Riding Obstacles

Initiating action helps develop confidence. Rider and horse stay mentally active. As you are working on overcoming spooking, challenge yourself and your horse to expand your comfort zones. Ride through and around obstacles—get creative and imaginative. Where possible (and permitted), get off the trail or take the more difficult route.

Your horse will become more sure of himself. When something comes along that might spook him, he's less apt to spook. Your horse's attention will start to

Ride on windy days. Ride by a haystack with a flapping tarp, acting as if it's not there.

focus more on you and his job. You will be thinking more about where to go next than about your horse spooking. This will put you in more control and your rides will be more interesting for you both. Your horse will develop the habit of being attentive, always waiting for your direction.

As the rider becomes more aware, he begins to sense when the horse starts to get troubled. The rider can then take proactive control, supporting the horse and heading off a potential spook before it occurs. When looking for interesting things to do, the rider is reinforcing the habit of actively directing, staying in the leadership role, keeping the horse aware and responding.

Avoid Sterile Environments

Within reason, don't worry about outside distractions. Use them for training, particularly at home in your familiar riding area. This will challenge your ability to keep your horse's attention despite disruptive noise or outside activity. When your horse gets distracted, redirect his focus back to you by giving him a job to do.

Riding on inclement weather days also helps build confidence. Riding during a blowing snowstorm can be interesting, challenging, and rewarding.

If his attention is off to the left, get him to look back to the right. Be consistent and disciplined within yourself. If you look where he's looking, it may validate his concerns. You are reacting to him instead of him responding to you. Instead, stay focused and redirect him.

1/ Work your horse off the fence. I am moving my slicker around above her. Note sluck in the halter rope in all these photos, as I am giving her a choice to stay.

2/ Next I rub the slicker all over her hip. She is taking a long hard look, but remaining calm.

3/ Get your horse used to all types of activity from all angles. This is also a good exercise for unstarted colts.

Ride on Windy and Bad Weather Days

Often we're inclined to avoid these days. Foul weather presents the rider with the opportunity to practice being focused and proactive. Windy days create even more distractions. If this is a concern, then get used to windy conditions closer to home. You could ride small circles, incrementally spiraling toward a flapping tarp over a haystack, or just ride on past acting "as if" it is not there. See diagram SP-1 and 2. Try to school yourself more than your horse. If you begin to worry, your horse will pick up on this, and transfer your concern into how he responds to you and the spooky object. Riding on windy and other inclement days will give you both many opportunities to develop confidence in each other.

Crossing a plastic tarp on the ground. This one is secured around poles so it cannot get bunched up or caught under a horse.

Set Up Situations— Add Stimulation

Challenge your horse around home where you control the variables before you head out on the trail and wait for a random

1/ *At a clinic, Kristi Plutt rides a young horse between a flag and the fence.*

2/ *Karen Steward rides her gelding past the flag. He is a little bothered so she is petting him. Note her slack reins.*

event to spook him. These exercises can also be accomplished on the ground before attempting them horseback.

Work your horse off the fence as described in Chapter 1. Sit on a high fence and get your horse to come to where you could mount. Rub a plastic bag, tarp, or slicker all over your horse so he learns to accept them. Don't overexpose him—approach in a manner fitting to your horse. Take it gradually until he can accept quite a bit of activity above, on either side, and against the saddle.

Next, ride past the slicker, tarp, or plastic bag you have left hanging on the fence, or secure a tarp on the ground to walk your horse across. If he spooks, shies, or hesitates, help your horse relax by staying calm, going with his movement, and rub-

Flagging colts at Winding River Ranch, Grand Lake, Colorado. They are learning to not be afraid of the flag, and to yield to pressure, just as they would in groundwork. This is equally good for the mare I'm riding, Abbey Lena, and gives her a job to do.

bing (petting) him, drifting his hindquarters or making a one-rein stop if necessary. You can do various riding exercises near the object, redirecting his attention from the spook. Soon you will be able to calmly ride by the object. He is learning it is okay to follow your direction instead of his flight instincts.

At my clinics I often use an exercise to help people practice supporting their horse in these scary situations. I ask them to ride on a loose rein through a narrow space between my horse and the fence while I hold a flag. Depending on the horse and rider involved, I'll either slowly shake the flag or just hold it quietly. This will spook some horses or make them hesitate to go forward. The rider is to keep looking straight ahead, rather than at his horse, me, or the flag. By picking out a distant object to ride straight toward, the rider will find that his horse is more likely to go forward. The rider's focus will give his horse direction and confidence.

When the horse and rider go between me and the fence, the horse may startle and/or rush forward. If the rider tenses up with his legs or grabs the reins, the horse might associate this with what spooked him. When we tense up we validate and encourage the horse's fear. The better response for the rider is to relax, go with the horse's flow, and pet him, while

When your horse spooks, go with the flow and pet him. If necessary use one rein to regain control. Then ride on like nothing happened.

leaving the reins alone. This supports the horse and avoids the spiraling effect. On the next trip around, the horse will exhibit more confidence. This may require persistence to overcome the human's instinctual urge to grab the reins. If relaxing and petting your horse does not settle him, then make a one-rein stop to regain control.

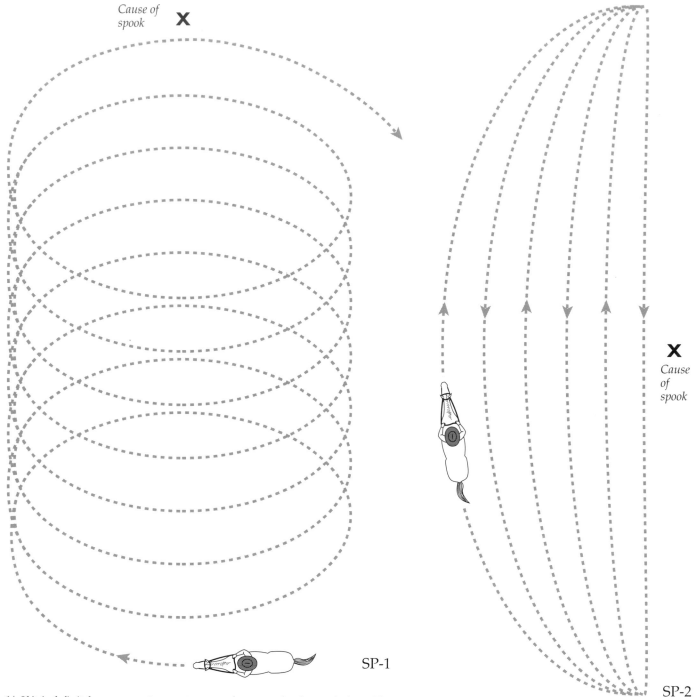

Cause of spook **X**

SP-1

X
Cause of spook

SP-2

1/ *If it is definitely necessary to accustom your horse to what he spooked at, ride away, then start spiraling circles toward the object. After you get as close as you need to, then ride off* **without** *asking him to put his nose on the object.*

2/ *This is the same concept as SP-1. Where the terrain dictates, this alternative may work easier.*

1/ *This old truck body created quite a spook for this gelding. As we ride on past, I am keeping him flexed toward the object.*

This is just an example of how to set up a stressful situation. Be creative, come up with your own. Anything out of the ordinary may be enough for a challenge. Try to not doubt your horse, so he will learn to not doubt you.

What To Do After Your Horse Spooks

There are several schools of thought on how to handle spooking. Many riders think when their horse spooks at something, they need to ride up and have their horse put his nose on the object to see it's nothing to be afraid of. I **don't** do this for several reasons.

Since the horse is a flight animal, his perception of danger tells him not to approach anything scary. Forcing him there goes against his nature. This might work in some cases, but may erode his overall confidence. Think of it from your own point of view. If you were afraid of something, you might not appreciate having it forced on you. If the human doesn't make an issue out of the spook, the horse will learn not to. A better solution is to just ride on. When your horse spooks, direct his increased energy into something useful and productive.

2/ *After several approaches and retreats as shown in diagrams SP-1 and 2, he is no longer bothered, and I ride on by **without** asking him to put his nose on it. It wouldn't even be necessary to ride by this close.*

If it is definitely necessary to get your horse accustomed to what he was spooking at, ride away, then start circling toward it. Make each approach a foot closer (see diagrams SP-1 and 2). It may take you many circles to work your way up to the

Horses see differently from humans. This diagram approximates their vision pattern.

Illustration courtesy of *Horse Industry Handbook* **published by American Youth Horse Council.**

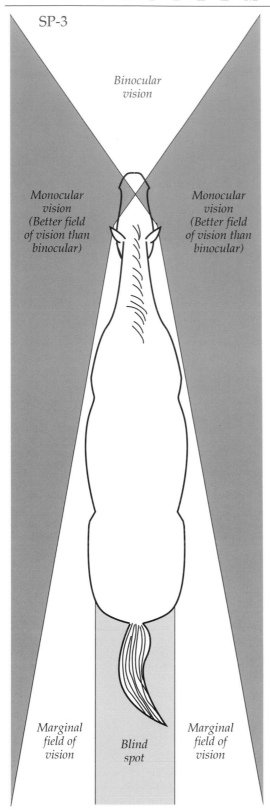

SP-3

Binocular vision

Monocular vision (Better field of vision than binocular)

Monocular vision (Better field of vision than binocular)

Marginal field of vision

Blind spot

Marginal field of vision

spook, but by the time you get there, your horse will have had so many approaches and retreats, he might no longer be bothered. Then just ride off **without** asking him to put his nose on the object.

Horses see and hear differently from humans (see diagram SP-3). When a horse's head is elevated, his vision is more effective at a long distance. When his head is lower, he sees better at a closer distance. This must be considered when we're trying to understand why a horse spooked.

Usually it is futile for us to try to second-guess what spooked the horse. It really doesn't matter anyway. We think he spooked at a specific object. However, maybe the horse spooked at something else, even farther away. If your horse spooked at a mailbox you've ridden past 50 times, it could be things looked different today. The time of day, cloud cover, sun reflection, etc., could all be factors in his perception compared with other days. Although we may know there is nothing to spook at, for the horse, perception is reality. Remember, he is naturally a vigilant prey animal whose decision not to spook could be deadly.

There are many things out there to spook a horse. So if you try to put his nose on everything, you might not have time for anything else. You could also build in more tendency to spook. Instead, keep looking ahead, continue to ride forward, and get your horse busy thinking about you and his job. It's much like when children get afraid. If you give them a big hug, get them busy with a game or a puzzle, they might forget to be afraid.

De-Spooking the Horse

It is not my goal to remove the horse's natural sensitivity and vigilance. I want my horses aware of their environment, rationally, not irrationally, so they help us both stay out of trouble. In helping people with spooking, my focus is on both rider and horse gaining mutual trust and respect, so that together they can confidently handle whatever comes along.

To accomplish this, I use an incremental approach-and-retreat strategy, rather than

Cattle help build a horse's confidence in his rider and environment. Starting a more fearful horse on the other side of the fence provides added security and might avoid a loss of confidence if the cattle turned back.

Photo by Kathleen Parrish

stimulus bombardment, which means flooding the horse with noisy and scary activity. I want to control the amount of stimulus presented based on the horse's reaction or response, giving him an opportunity to make choices and respond to the human, rather than become dull to stimulus bombardment. Flooding could also take something from the horse you want to leave alone. If these activities make the horse lose confidence, it might be hard to get it back. Don't ever betray the horse.

Horses naturally have tremendous faith in the human being. It is their natural instinct of self-preservation that the person needs to understand in order to gain their confidence.

If the horse understands that his rider is there to fill in for him and support him through to the other side of scary situations, he will gain confidence. Through a developmental approach, the horse can become more trusting in his rider instead of relying on his spooking instinct.

Get Your Horse on Cattle

Working your horse on cattle is an excellent opportunity to develop his confidence. Cattle work gives horses a real meaning and purpose to their training, enhancing horse and rider unity.

If your horse has not been exposed to cattle, start by riding with a friend whose horse is bold around cattle. Set up the situation so his horse moves the cattle. Once the cattle move, ride your horse alongside or just behind the companion horse. This will give your horse the idea he is affecting the cattle's movement.

At my cow working clinics, if a rider brings a horse who is afraid or leery of cattle, I set it up so there is a fence between this horse and the cattle. I have an experienced horse drive the cattle in a separate pen. This arranges things so the cattle stay across the fence and ahead of the inexperienced horse. This horse gains confidence

Ride out in a pasture when cattle are shaded up and lying down. Their movement as they get up and walk away will add to a horse's confidence.

After your horse has gained confidence, ride through the middle of a herd. This puts activity and movement on all sides, including his blind spot, at the same time.

having cattle move away from him as he trails them from his side of the fence. Pretty quick, he can move the cattle without support from the companion horse or the fence. I progressively build on this so eventually the horse can ride through the middle of a cattle herd.

Working with cattle will make a major change in your horse. As he gets more comfortable around cattle, ride out (with a companion horse) in a pasture when all the cattle are lying down or shaded up. Quietly ride through the herd and get all the cattle up. The cattle's motion and your horse knowing he has the power to move

172

Pulling a sled carrying a newborn calf to the barn with the mother cow following close behind. This is a great opportunity for a horse to have a real job while getting used to activity in his rear blind spot. Note: The rope is dallied, not tied to my saddle horn. If you don't have access to cattle, be creative and imaginative to come up with an alternative. **Photo by Steve Gulley**

them will help him overcome fear in other circumstances. Many horses develop a new, fresh attitude about their riding activities after working with cattle. They become bolder as they gain confidence in their rider and their environment.

As your horse gets used to working with cattle, and you find the opportunity, pull a calf sled during calving season. You may want to start with logging your horse first. Start by pulling the log or sled at an angle while backing your horse. Then pull forward off to the side and incrementally rotate the pull to behind the horse. Dally the rope to your horn so you can pop your dallies loose and even drop the rope if your horse gets troubled.

During calving season, if you pull a newborn calf to the barn in a sled, the mother cow will follow. Having developed your horse's ability to handle this activity in or near his blind spot will have a positive effect, transferring to other situations. You could also carry a calf with you in the saddle horseback. Experiment first with carrying your dog horseback. If you rope, drag calves to the branding fire

Author, Jeanne Orr, and Phil White holding dogs horseback. Every new experience will help your horse.

Photo by Carolyn Kupka

in the spring. Pasture-doctoring cattle alongside experienced horses also furthers your horse's education, giving him another real job.

If you do not have access to cattle, get creative—use your imagination to find alternatives. You may be surprised at what you can come up with.

173

1/ *Dragging a log horse back, commonly called "logging." Start by pulling at an angle while backing. Note: Initially I am holding the rope with just my hand. Therefore, if you don't have a horn, you can still do this.*

2/ *Now dallied (not tied hard and fast), I incrementally change the angle until I pull the log behind the horse. At any point I could pop my dallies and drop the rope to avoid a wreck.*

3/ Getting to work on several things at once. Her attention is distracted to another potential spook.

4/ After a moment of pause, she walks right on through the puddle, dragging the log behind.

1/ When encountering a vehicle approaching from behind, turn your horse and ride toward it rather than have it approach in his blind spot.

Sometimes facing up to scary objects is best, particularly something moving in your direction. Petting the horse gives security. Note my hand is still near the rein if more control is necessary.

Face Up to a Moving Scary Object

There is a time to turn and face up to what is spooking your horse. This applies mostly to moving objects. Facing a moving object is not the same as asking your horse to approach and put his nose on what spooks him. One example is a dog coming toward you. If you turn and ride away, it may encourage the dog to chase after your horse. You might turn him so the horse is facing the dog and stare it down. You have to read each situation, but often, turning and riding toward them will make dogs stop and turn away. Your horse would already be familiar with this if you've had him on cattle.

There are many times when an object, such as your neighbor's lawn mower, is moving in your direction. If you ride your horse away, it might spook him worse when the noise and movement approach his blind spot. It may be best to face up to the mower until it moves away again. If it is necessary to ride away from a moving object, ride away at an angle, such as the zigzag pattern, so your horse feels less pursued and the object stays out of his blind spot.

If the wind is blowing a plastic grocery bag your direction, circle around to the side while keeping your horse facing the object.

2/ As it passes, turn your horse like turning with a cow.

3/ Then follow the vehicle for a short distance or until it is gone.

When you get upwind, follow the bag as though you were driving a cow. This can be another proactive confidence-builder. These are a few situations where facing up to a scary object will help your horse put aside his fear and rely on his rider.

Turn With an Approaching Vehicle Like Turning With a Cow

When riding down country roads, vehicles like delivery trucks or even bicycles are often scary for horses. If a truck is approaching from behind, turn your horse and ride along the roadside or in the ditch, toward the oncoming vehicle. Keep your horse's nose slightly tipped toward the truck, two-tracking away if possible. As the truck passes, turn your horse just like turning with a cow, and follow until the truck is gone.

Avoid allowing the truck to approach in your horse's blind spot, scaring him more. Read each situation to determine what is the safest course of action. If your horse gets panicky, I recommend you stay mounted, but in some cases dismounting might be safer. However, if you don't have

When riding outside, have some means of control when dismounted. I ride with a traditional mecate rig, which includes a loop rein and lead. My rein is crossed over the horn so a horse is less apt to get a leg through it if he puts his head down.

good control on the halter rope from previous groundwork, you might be worse off. Your horse could pull away, run off, run through a fence, over you, or bolt into traffic. The better solution is to not put you and your horse in this predicament until you are sure you both can handle it.

When riding outside, have some means of control when you dismount. Mecate reins work really well for this. When you step down, cross the loop rein over the horn and use the mecate tail as your lead rope. If you ride with a halter under your bridle, you can leave the rein over his neck and control your horse with the halter rope. Prepare for contingencies before heading out on the trail, and use good judgment and safety.

Facing His Fears

Another exercise to help horses learn to overcome the spooking urge and face their fears makes use of a flag and plastic bag. The rider will need to have sufficient riding ability to control and direct his horse through this exercise. Reviewing the Groundwork and Riding Foundation chapters again may be helpful.

Starting about 20 feet away, ask a friend to walk a semicircle around your horse, quietly shaking the flag. Keep your horse on a slack rein, looking toward the flag as your friend walks back and forth. If your horse spooks, keep him facing the flag, with your hands wide apart on the reins. Allow him some drift and go with his flow. Reach down and pet your horse to give him a sense of security. Make a one-rein stop if needed. Allow him to relax before starting again. Continue the semicircle procedure, giving your horse a chance to become more accepting. As he does, your helper could walk closer to your horse, while continuing the semicircle. If he gets scared, have your helper reduce the pressure. Again, this requires feel, timing, and balance.

178

1/ This exercise will help your horse learn to face his fears. Using a flag, I am walking a semicircle around the front of Amy LeSatz's gelding. While keeping him facing the flag, Amy stays relaxed, supporting her horse with hands wide apart. Note her relaxed reins throughout all these photos.

2/ After first touching the flag to Amy's leg and then the horse's shoulder, I now rub the flag all over this gelding's body and legs.

3/ Moving the flag from left to right above their shoulders or hips can be very scary for horses because of the rear blind spot. See "changing eyes" section in Chapter 4. Accurately reading your horse's readiness for these exercises is essential to stay away from trouble.

4/ Adding a plastic shavings bag over the flag, I am now walking semicircles again.

5/ Amy rides circles both directions around me while I stand holding the bag. You can also do this with just the flag if your horse is more bothered, or start with this if it fits your horse better. Being able to initially move their feet rather than stand as in previous photo is better for some horses. Note this gelding's body expression—he was more troubled to the right than the left.

6/ Now I am approaching on the left with the bag touching Amy's leg. She keeps him looking my way.

7/ Approaching on the horse's right side. Amy stays relaxed while petting her horse. Note horse is more tense on right side.

8/ He is becoming more accepting, so we proceed. Amy and I are both holding the bag, moving it up and down.

9/ Amy turning loose of the bag, simulating what she would do if this gelding panicked later while she was carrying it around.

10/ Amy holds the bag again and is riding a slow circle while I still have my end. The gelding is accepting this, so I start to let go of my end.

11/ Amy is still riding the circle around me but now has the bag by herself.

12/ Still riding a circle, she has dropped the bag, and the gelding accepts this without getting more bothered. This really helped this gelding and Amy is now flagging other horses from him.

1/ *Preparing to drag the plastic shavings bag for the other horses to follow, I am checking out this gelding to make sure he can handle it first at a front angle before asking him to drag it in or near his blind spot, similar to the previous logging exercise.*

2/ *Notice Karen's and Amy's horses' expressions as they follow the bag. This is another confidence-builder.*

182

3/ Dragging a barrel; note the gray gelding's expression, showing more interest than fear.

Incrementally adjust the activity level of the flag. Eventually, the helper can shake the flag very actively, and your horse will stand. Although he may not be 100 percent relaxed, he will be more tolerant and accepting. As your horse shows signs of relaxing, or at least not elevating his fear, have your helper step back and/or ride away as a release, then start again. Continue this approach-and-retreat strategy.

Eventually, your friend can walk toward your horse at a 45-degree angle from the side, touching you on the leg and then your horse's shoulder with the flag. Do this several times on both sides. Then have him walk up to your horse shaking the flag. Next, have him quietly touch your horse all over his body with the flag.

When the flag is no longer troubling, hang a plastic wood shavings bag over the flag stick. Go back to the original distance, and start the procedure over again. Be careful to take enough time, because the bag can be scarier.

Don't overexpose your horse, as this can create more fear or a phobia. Allow your horse to accept it on his own terms, at a rate he can handle. If in doubt, have your helper ease off, and start again.

Next ride your horse in a circle around the person holding the bag. You could start with this tactic first if it fits your horse better. The other person stands in one spot and shakes the bag. Continue riding, making the circle smaller, until riding right by the shaking bag doesn't trouble your horse. If he starts to get scared, ease off by making the circle larger, then gradually smaller again.

When your horse is ready, reach out and hold on to the end of the bag. Slowly ride off with your friend walking alongside your horse. Move the bag down toward the ground, just as if it had been dropped, then move it back up. Do this on both sides. When this doesn't trouble the horse, the ground person can walk away with the flag while you are left holding the bag.

You could do the same thing by picking up the plastic bag from the fence, and rubbing it all over your horse and your saddle. If he wants to move off, go with him, directing and petting him. If things fall apart, drop the bag away from your horse (and the wind direction), ride away, and drift his hindquarters to a one-rein stop.

Anything you can help your horse learn to accept is valuable. Nosebags are a good way to feed grain and one more spooky thing horses learn to accept. Note: To prevent creating a pull-back problem, don't tie your horse up hard and fast while nosebagging him until you are very sure he can handle it.

If any of this is overexposing your horse, start from the ground and the fence, with your horse on the halter rope. This will be good slicker training too.

If you have a friend with a suitable horse, you could have him drag the shavings bag, a plastic tarp, barrel, or other object behind his horse (or from afoot). If he is horseback, he should dally the rope to his horn, not tie hard and fast. As he drags the object around, encourage your horse's curiosity to develop and follow the object from a comfortable distance. Don't let it come in behind him and don't step over the rope. Pretty soon, your horse will have his ears forward and want to follow the object like he is driving a cow. He will feel more in control, as if he is moving the scary object.

One day you may be able to drag a bag or barrel with your horse. However, increase the stimulus incrementally, as you can get yourself in a huge wreck in a hurry. When you start doing these things, you must be able to accurately read your horse's readiness.

Caution

These exercises are not mandatory to get your horse over spooking. They are just ideas for your consideration. If any of these suggestions seem too far beyond you or your horse's current ability, avoid them until you do more groundwork, riding foundation, and the other exercises first. Proceed very slowly; always err on the side of less stimulus, leaving room to build up to more. Once you've scared your horse more or created a phobia, it's harder to come back. Keep stretching you and your horse's comfort zones, but always stay within the parameters of common sense, safety, and good judgment. Certainly the horse who spooks, starts violently bucking, or runs off wildly is very dangerous. Perhaps solving this might require a knowledgeable, competent professional who can overcome the problem without force or fear.

Life Is Full of Surprises

Keep in mind that the solution to overcoming a spooking problem is dependent on the rider's ability to convey confidence, and not get afraid or angry. If the rider becomes unnerved or angry, it will elevate the horse's fear and validate his concerns. The more proactive and confident the rider, the more the horse will rely on him and the less likely he will be to spook.

However, there are no recipe, quick-fix cures for this or any other problem. Don't expect to solve spooking in one or even several sessions. Some horses will overcome this more quickly than others. Be realistic about solving spookiness. If you do all these exercises, don't be disappointed if the next time you ride out on the trail, your horse still spooks. However, recognize a change for the better. Your horse may still spook occasionally, but less frequently and less energetically. Over a period of time, you'll notice positive changes.

Be aware of the progress you are both making. Keep a positive, optimistic outlook. Be pleased rather than critical. See the glass of water as half-full, rather than half-empty. Pretty soon you'll realize your horse hasn't spooked in a long time.

Do not deny your horse his self-preservation; his nature is to spook. Give him reason to be confident in his rider and his world so he doesn't feel he needs to defend himself. Working on overcoming your spooking problem can create a stronger bond between you and your horse. The process can be interesting, challenging, and rewarding. Plan ahead and take each step slowly so you and your horse can enjoy and benefit from the experience. Your horse will learn to be as brave as you are. Good luck!

7 CROSSING WATER AND BRIDGES

MANY HORSE owners are denied trail riding enjoyment because of problems crossing water, bridges, or other obstacles. It would be a shame to miss a scenic trail ride with friends or an opportunity to help gather cattle because of a water crossing. This chapter will start with creek crossing and then discuss bridges and other obstacles. However, the principles, preparations, and strategies are similar. These ideas may also help prevent a future problem from developing.

If You Trail Ride, Crossing Water Is a Necessity

Trail crossings at creeks, bridges, and other obstacles do not have to spoil a good riding experience. With adequate preparation, you and your horse can obtain the skill and confidence to negotiate even the most challenging trail obstacles. This section will outline a developmental plan to help you resolve creek crossing problems,

Creeks, bridges, and other obstacles enhance a trail riding experience.

As your horse gains confidence, he will easily handle more challenging water crossings.

so they become fun, something you look forward to. The benefits will carry over into improved horsemanship.

The principles presented will apply equally well for a problem horse, a green horse, or a young horse who has never been asked to cross water. There are various approaches for reactions from several types of horses. If your horse is okay but you want to improve, getting him better now will help when you face a more challenging water crossing.

There are no recipes, magic techniques, or quick fixes for this or any other problem. **It is not the technique as much as the way in which you present it to your horse.** Give him a safe, positive reason to do what you want, reward him (release of pressure) when he tries, and your horse will think crossing water was his idea! It's all about allowing your horse to make choices. Encourage the choices you want and discourage the ones you don't. Be creative, use a combination of these techniques to come up with your own individual win-win solution.

A key to your success is being able to keep your horse's feet moving and directed. Develop your feel, timing, and balance, your ability to accurately read

The principles in this chapter apply equally to a problem horse or a colt never before asked to cross water.

Use obstacles back at your barn or in your pasture to learn to ride your horse straight. I am riding through a narrow opening between a large cottonwood and a steep irrigation ditch.

your horse, and adjust to fit him moment by moment. Keep a positive attitude and convey confidence throughout.

Why Should Your Horse Want To Cross Water?

It is important to understand why a horse might react as he does. Your horse doesn't purposely try to displease you or ruin your

trail riding enjoyment. Whether resisting from fear, lack of respect for his rider, or a combination of both, he is just doing what he thinks is right for his own self-preservation. The horse might not be accustomed to crossing water. Maybe there are no creeks where he's pastured or stabled, and he's never had a chance. However, there are situations where a horse would readily cross a creek where pastured, but wouldn't when asked by his rider.

The horse may balk because the water may pose, in his mind, a genuine threat to his survival. We might look at it and say, "You stupid horse, there's no way this can hurt you." But it doesn't matter what we think or what we know; it's the horse's perception that counts. The creek may only be a few inches deep, but to him it may look like a bottomless hole. If the rider gets frustrated or angry, trying to force him into compliance, the horse will feel threatened and become defensive. Now he associates water crossings with struggle and confrontation. This builds on itself, and he becomes sour on trying. If the rider is tentative or timid and doubts that the horse will cooperate, then the horse may live up to these expectations. Either situation elevates the horse's resistance, fear, and resentment level.

While working on this or any problem, the rider's attitude is felt by the horse. Don't let this become an ego battle, making it a contest or test of wills. The objective is to help the horse overcome his fear and resistance. To accomplish this, the rider gets the horse in a learning frame of mind so the horse feels secure following direction.

Be persistent while demonstrating confidence and patience. Let your horse work at it and don't be afraid to allow him to make mistakes—they are learning opportunities. Stay in a position of leadership, and you will see the project through to its successful completion.

Preliminary Work Back at the Barn: Ride Your Horse Straight

Rather than go on a trail ride and hope for the best, make a plan to devote ample

1/ Simulate a water crossing. I am riding this filly along the edge of a hose-created arena pond, allowing her to gain acceptance.

2/ Within a short time she is willing to walk all through the water without concern.

time back at the barn to strengthen foundation training for both you and your horse. This may seem time-consuming and a lot of work. However, taking the slower approach will give you a quicker, more permanent, positive result. It will speed success with less frustration and aggravation for both horse and rider.

Sufficient preparation is essential. Review the groundwork and riding information in Chapters 1 and 2. The other chapters also have ideas to assist you. Accomplishing these exercises will have a direct effect on your success when you get to a water crossings.

In solving this or any other problem, it is necessary to be able to ride your horse straight. This means your horse will go where you point him, with impulsion, proper body alignment, and go right or left when asked. Perhaps this is easy in a familiar area, but when you get to trail obstacles, your horse acts totally different. If so, incrementally work up to more challenging situations you set up at home, where you can control the variables while stretching both your comfort zones. Practice obtaining your horse's response and respect to go where you point him, regard-

1/ Kristi Plutt's mare is getting her first experience at a water crossing. She was quite troubled so I had Kristi ride back and forth parallel to the water.

2/ Once the mare made a change for the better, I ask Kristi to ride away, then take a fresh start. This takes pressure off the mare, rewarding her try.

less of obstacles, until this becomes consistent. Develop the habit of riding mentally ahead of your horse, proactively directing rather than reacting to him. Know how to reestablish control and how to redirect your horse when needed.

When riding trails and pastures, look for obstacles to negotiate. Avoid sauntering along, letting only the trail do the guiding. Be creative, get off the trail and find challenges—cross gullies, arroyos, ride around trees, rocks, and bushes, etc. Practice riding on an imaginary line, wherever you want your horse to go. You will both gain experience in more difficult situations as you cultivate your horse's interest, attention, and acceptance of following your guidance.

Simulate a Water Crossing at Home

One approach I sometimes use to help someone with this problem is to simulate a water crossing in an arena or pasture. Run water from a hose, making quite a pond—big enough so the horse can't jump over it. Keep the water running while working on this. If you feel pretty confident about yourself and your horse, you can skip this part, but you cannot hurt anything by spending this time at home first. However, read this section regardless, as this approach simulates the steps used at a real water crossing.

Ride your horse along the edge of the shallow pond. If he feels he's not going to be forced into something, he might build a little curiosity, and you might be able to

4/ *Although still showing slight hesitation, Kristi's mare is ready to give the water a try.*

3/ *Reapproaching the creek, the mare is willing to get a closer look. Her curiosity is starting to build and her fear to diminish.*

5/ *Kristi's patience, feel, timing, and balance have paid off. Her mare walks on across, showing confidence like a veteran.*

ride him right to it. He'll see it's really not a big threat, and you can ride him on across, or briefly in the water along the edge, and back out again.

If he feels insecure and can't cross your pond, don't force or fight him. Let him learn to relax and rest near the water. Keep him straight, facing the water. If he is nervous or fractious, to relieve his anxiety, ride him away and, if necessary, make a one-rein stop to reestablish control, rub (pet) him, then just start over again. Ride back to the water, but don't ask him to cross yet. If your horse will stop at or near the water, even for a few seconds, ride him away as a release. Your horse recognizes the reward when you **release pressure**. You're giving him what he wants, but you direct him. Your timing is very important here.

While you're trying to cross the water, keep looking forward by picking out an object on the other side to ride toward. Your focus gives your horse more direction from your body language.

Now ask your horse to approach your

191

1/ LuAnn Rigor's gelding is a high-energy horse with a history of water crossing problems. Here he was dancing and spinning around looking to escape.

2/ Rather than struggle with him at the creek, she is riding him away to put his energy to work trotting circles and figure eights.

3/ She has ridden him back to the creek to give him a rest, rubbing on him to make the creek a safe and comfortable place to be.

water pond again. If necessary, encourage forward movement with your legs, without doing too much or too little, but get a response. Excessive pounding or spurring can cause defensiveness, while not being firm enough or nagging may cause more resistance. Both develop a negative association, making it more difficult later.

If he's backing up or not going forward, encourage him with your legs. Bump him with your calf rather than your heels, to avoid tipping your upper body forward.

Use an out-inward motion rather than a front to back, to keep your legs under you for better balance. How much to encourage him forward with your legs is a matter of feel, timing, and balance. Some horses need only a little encouragement, others more. Be consistent in keeping your horse's feet moving and directed, while developing trust and confidence. The moment your horse moves toward the water, release your legs and let him walk forward on his own, rubbing him.

Pretty soon your horse will walk right across your water pond, or at least walk across the edge and out again. Don't make him stay in the water yet. When he does cross the water, ride him away from it, then stop, turn him around facing the water, rub his neck, and let him relax. Then ride across again. Soon, he'll be more comfortable crossing, then able to stand relaxed in the water. It won't be long before your horse gets more sure and is no longer concerned. With some horses this will come quickly, while others take longer. **Let your individual horse tell you what you need to do next.**

This simulated water crossing exercise provides horse and rider an opportunity to develop positive habits of respect, response, and release. This can serve as a preparation for a real creek crossing. You are elevating your horse's level of acceptance, recognizing when he is trying, and gaining his trust and respect.

4/ *After repeating the previous exercise a couple of times, he is now able to relax and direct his energy toward entering the creek.*

Heading Out for the Real Thing

When you are ready for the real thing, plan before you go. Scout ahead to find a shallow water crossing, 15 to 25 feet wide, flat entry and exit, with good solid footing. Avoid narrow creeks, as these often create additional problems when a horse leaps across. If you can find a wide, flat, shallow place, it really makes things easier to start.

When you head out, go with the intent of working only on the creek crossing. Make this a separate project. Spend your whole day, if necessary. Start early and stay late; pack a lunch. With this time frame in mind, you'll probably finish early. For safety reasons, it's best to take someone with you. They can also provide moral support.

If your friend is mounted on a dependable horse, you can always let his horse cross the water first, and have your horse follow right behind. Or the companion horse can draw your horse from the other side. There's certainly nothing wrong with this. However, my recommendation is to begin the project with your friend as an observer, not a helper. If you depend on another horse and rider to get you across, your horse is missing what you want him to learn. Your real goal is for your horse to confidently take direction from you, to go anywhere you ask him to go, regardless of obstacles or terrain.

5/ *LuAnn's patience, feel, timing, and balance have paid off. Her gelding has a new perspective on water crossing.*

Note: If after a while you and your horse are not making progress, it may be appropriate to use the companion horse's help. If you follow his horse across or cross with them already on the other side, do so just once. Then start again, working on your own, without the companion horse's help. In this way you become less dependent on a coaching horse. Your horse will develop more acceptance following your direction.

1/ Howard Reinstein's 2-year old-colt is having his first trail ride and water crossing experience. Howard helps him stay relaxed as the colt picks up his right front, ready to walk forward.

2/ He is petting his colt to give reassurance.

3/ This colt is now comfortable enough to lower his head and drink.

4/ After drinking, he started pawing and Howard asks him to move forward to prevent him from lying down in the water.

1/ *Once your horse crosses without hesitation or fear, ride him up and down the creek.*

When you initially ride up to the creek, there may be a point at which your horse balks or stops, refusing to go forward. Avoid hitting him at that moment with your legs, spurs, or crop, as this could validate the horse's fear and resistance. If he does balk, just relax, wait a couple seconds, then ask him to move his feet forward, even if not toward the water. Better yet, be proactive, use your feel and timing to figure out where he might hesitate. Stop him just before he gets there, rub (pet) him, then ride a short distance away. Let him relax a moment, then ride back toward the creek again, and stop.

Then encourage your horse to take one step forward. You're not asking him to enter the creek, but move one step. **If you keep your goal to one more step forward rather than all the way into the creek, you will get across sooner.** However, at the same time expect your horse to keep trying and don't settle for less. This is kind of a gray area, but this is why horses are so much fun to work with. You have to learn to accurately read them and make good decisions on how to proceed. If you stand there and let your horse check out the situation, he might willingly walk into the water on his own. I've had horses do this many times and it's kind of amazing.

If he resists going forward, then you need to decide what procedure best fits you and your horse. If he's panicky, you may want to back him up a step or two, or even ride him away from the creek a few feet and circle back to the same spot and let him relax, then start again. The next time you approach the creek, he may get a little closer. Your goal is to get one step closer to the water. You might even find your horse will just walk right up to the creek. When he gets there, don't overencourage him to go forward. Let him stand there, relax, and explore the situation. Allow him to put his nose down and check out the creek. Continue with this approach-and-retreat strategy, attempting to ride your horse away from the water before he tries to leave.

If he's not panicky, encourage him forward a little with your seat and legs, but not to the point of forcing him. With your hands wide apart on the reins, keep him straight, facing the water where you want to cross. Pretty soon he'll relax, and may start to get curious; he is trying. Let him stand there relaxed or ride him away, then start again. When you consistently get your horse's response and you can direct and support his movement, successfully crossing the water is very close.

A mistake riders often make is continuing or increasing pressure, rather than releasing pressure when the horse tries. The horse then sees the creek as an undesirable place. Instead, make the horse feel as safe and comfortable crossing creeks as any place else you ask him to go. This approach is similar to trailer loading. You are creating a situation where your horse perceives no pressure at or near the creek. Therefore, he is much more inclined to consider crossing.

While you are working at this, visit with your friend. This will help you stay relaxed, positive, and breathing normally. Stay concentrated on what you are asking your horse to do, keeping your demeanor businesslike and matter-of-fact. Your horse will sense this and the water crossing will be no big deal. Because you are relaxed, your horse will be more relaxed.

Soon your horse will learn that going forward, where you direct him—in this case toward the creek—is always the path of least resistance. Pretty soon, with only slight encouragement, your horse will walk right into the creek.

The High-Energy, Won't-Stand-Still Horse

Some horses have difficulty standing still; they have a lot of energy. If they feel insecure or too confined when you encourage them to cross the creek, they might rear, buck, or attempt to run off. This type horse requires more work back at the barn to get this energy directed and under control. On the plus side, these horses can be easier because they have lots of impulsion—it takes very little to get them to move their feet.

If you get resistance at the creek with a high-energy horse and he is dancing all around, ride him far enough away to have room to start trotting or loping. Put him to work with productive exercises, vigorously riding circles or figure eights. Direct the horse's energy in a positive way, but don't try to exhaust him.

After a few minutes your horse will build up a desire to rest. To let him rest, return to the creek where you started. Let him catch his breath and relax while you rub him. Let him stand there until his pulse and respiration come back to normal. This makes being near the creek a safe, comfortable place. Then ask him to take one step forward. If he won't go forward or he starts dancing around again, ride away and work at trotting or loping circles and figure eights again. Do whatever exercises you feel safe with, but keep him busy and working. This is not for

2/ Riding up a creek with the added challenge of steep canyon walls.

punishment; rather you are directing his life and energy in a positive way.

When your horse again has a desire to rest, ride back to the water as before. Keep the horse facing the creek crossing and pet him. Now ask him to take another step forward. If he does, don't ask for another. Just stop, relax, and pet him. It is very important you read your own individual horse and be willing to adjust to what is best to do next.

If he's ready, ride your horse right on into the creek. However, a lot of times you might think because you got one step forward, he'll walk in, but instead he'll resist,

Kristi offering her mare lots of opportunities to be in the water.

Continue presenting more challenging water crossings to your horse.

dance around, or escape and run off. If this happens, just get control and start over. There will continue to be times when your horse will hesitate, but keep his feet active and directed. With this type horse, it probably won't be a problem.

If your horse resists by backing up, don't pull back on your reins. Instead, keep him straight, with your hands wide apart, facing toward the water, and bump him lightly with your legs as described before, but be careful. If you get tense and pull back abruptly on the reins, he could rear or flip over. Just make backing up a little uncomfortable for him, but not unbearable. Keep him from getting panicky or feeling overconfined. When he quits backing, release and start again.

Make this process gradual, where you're not trying to do it all at once. However, there is a real feel, timing, and balance factor here. Although you should be methodical, don't draw things out so your horse loses interest or learns more resistance. Keep him active, busy working at it and in a learning frame of mind. Notice if your horse make changes for the better and reward him.

Pretty soon you'll find your horse will just walk right into the creek, because you have built a positive habit of response with respect. Your horse has learned the path of least resistance is in the direction you point him.

The Sluggish Horse

If your horse is the opposite of the high-energy type, you will have to liven him up and get him responsive to go forward when you ask. However, the creek is not the place to work on this. Instead, get him

As you progress, look for more challenges, such as crossings with a steeper entry.

responsive back at the barn or another familiar area. You may need to really bump him with your legs (calves) and/or the tail of your mecate, halter rope, or a crop. When he consistently moves out energetically with you lightly asking, then go to the creek crossing.

If he reverts back to sluggish when you start at the creek, ride him a short distance away as with the high-energy horse description. However, instead of trotting or loping circles and figure eights, you will work on him moving out with energy and life from a halt to walk to trot and/or lope, as you did back at the barn. At times you may have to work at making the wrong thing (not moving out when asked) difficult, actively encouraging him to keep busy working at it. The goal is for your horse to move his feet when you ask and then use this impulsion to direct him.

As soon as you have your sluggish horse consistently responding to your direction to move out, ride him back to the creek, taking his increased energy with you. If he is not fearful or panicky, carry his impulsion on forward and he may just walk right into the water.

LuAnn is reinforcing her gelding's willingness to take on more difficult crossings. Note Sheri Gulley's horse's expression; one ear is attentive to her and the other forward.

Once You Are in the Water

Once you get the horse willingly going into the creek, don't ask him to stay in the water just yet. Ride him across to the other

This filly is taking a drink before entering the creek from a steep bank. This would not be a good place to start solving a water crossing problem.

Amy LeSatz riding well balanced out a steep creek bank.

side, turn him back facing the water, stop, and let him relax. Be careful he doesn't race or charge across. After a short rest, ride him back across.

After he has crossed several times, ride him out into the water, asking him to stand and relax. He may even want to take a drink. A word of warning: If your horse starts pawing, he may attempt to lie down, especially if he is hot and his back itches. If he paws or you feel his feet gather under him, quickly get him moving forward.

How many crossings to make depends on the horse. For some, three or four times will be enough. Don't drill it into him. Leave him alone; let it be enough for now. Do something else for a while, then come back. You could cross some horses numerous times. Learn to read the individual horse and know when to quit.

Once you've got your horse really good, where he doesn't hesitate, ride him up and down the creek. Give him a lot of opportunity to be in the water, as long as he remains comfortable and relaxed. Make it fun. If at any point he gets scared, quietly ride him out and start over. However, since you have not forced your horse to get in the water and you have kept him quiet and relaxed, he'll probably stay in a good, learning frame of mind.

As your horse gets better at this creek crossing, you'll want to start finding other

1/ Narrow ditches and creeks can be very difficult because of the horse's natural tendency to jump. Avoid these until you have greater control of your horse's feet. If you feel your horse prepare to lunge forward, back him up and take a fresh start. Where possible, approach at an angle close to parallel, until your horse learns to relax and will walk across. Then incrementally work up to crossing perpendicularly.

2/ Never doubt your horse. The young Thoroughbred gelding I'm riding was very unsure about walking into this narrow creek, but thirsty enough to get down on his knees. At least he didn't lunge across.

Photo by Carolyn Kupka

3/ *After your horse starts walking across narrow creeks, seek them out to expose him to many situations.*

Photo by Carolyn Kupka

Riding under a bridge through the creek is another challenge for horse and rider.

Photo by Ty Wyant

1/ This bridge is challenging for horses because of the high side walls and the echoing noise the concrete walkway makes.

2/ At least you won't get your feet wet if you start by leading your horse across, as Sheri Gulley is demonstrating.

3/ Don't allow your horse to rush across.

4/ Narrow bridges without side rails can be more challenging for some horses and riders. Use the same principles for bridges as with water crossings, adjusting to fit each individual horse.

1/ These tunnels under the highway connect two riding areas. Tunnels are another fun and interesting challenge.

2/ Note bird exiting as I enter the tunnel. Just another day at the office for my mare, Dee Lena.

locations. Since you have been working at a slow, quiet creek, gradually work up to more challenging ones that are rushing, noisy, and deeper. Eventually you'll want to be able to ride your horse into a crossing with a steeper, sloped entry.

Make sure your horse never gets chargey. Sometimes at steeper spots, they'll rush and charge into the water and up the other side. Slow the horse down before you enter the water. If he's not scared, you might even discourage this by stopping your horse in the water parallel to the flow. Then when he is waiting for your direction, turn him and ride him slowly out.

Regressions are common and just an expected part of the training cycle. Anytime things fall apart, go back to an easier

3/ Lots of opportunities: tunnels, creeks, and steep banks.

4/ Like gates and other crossings, use common trail courtesy. As Steve LeSatz is demonstrating, riders should wait until everyone is through the obstacle before riding off.

creek crossing for a refresher. Continue to achieve step-by-step progress and your water crossing problems will quickly become history.

Narrow Creeks and Ditches

Narrow creeks and ditches seem to be one of the biggest aggravations for people. Horses tend to want to jump them rather than step across. Discouraging this jumping can sometimes be difficult. Therefore, avoid these narrow creeks and ditches until you have established a great deal of control of your horse's feet and have mastered wider creek crossings. This is another one of those situations where I make use of the partial bend to slow the feet described in Chapter 2. Also, your ability to ask your horse for one step at a time becomes very important in this situation.

To get started, select a flat, safe location. Approach these narrow crossings as close to parallel as possible, making them appear wider to the horse. If at any time you feel your horse gather up, preparing to jump, back him up or ride away, then return and start over. If your horse leaps over the narrow creek or ditch, turn him

5/ This tunnel is too low to stay mounted, so we are leading our horses through.

At a trail ride clinic, I am demonstrating how to avoid getting your knees bumped going through a gate. If the horse gets too close to one side, use your leg (left in this example) to move him over. You can also use your hand to assist your leg by pushing against the post.

There are many obstacles along the trail such as this manmade concrete dike. Developing a strong riding foundation will carry over to all situations.

Snowdrifts are another trail obstacle you and your horse can learn to readily negotiate.

it wet and handy to cross through each day you ride. Also, take advantage of riding after a heavy rain when the ground is wet and muddy. Using the approach-and-retreat exercises already described, your horse can learn to gain trust and confidence crossing boggy areas, just as he has with other trail obstacles.

If you can avoid a bog on a trail ride, it may be your best option, as they can be more dangerous than they appear. Having worked through simulated bog exercises, at least you will be able to negotiate one if no other option is available.

Bridges and Other Trail Obstacles

Successfully crossing bridges is much like crossing water. Use all the same principles and similar techniques. Horses resist bridges for much the same reasons as water. They are noisy, look strange, and the footing seems insecure.

You can start by having your horse follow a dependable horse across the bridge. However, for the same reasons as mentioned earlier, I prefer to accomplish this first with my horse taking direction from me, not another horse. Take the time to become proficient at the preliminary groundwork and riding foundations before arriving at the bridge, and your success will be more quickly achieved.

You can start by leading your horse across the bridge. At least you won't get your feet wet. Just be careful he doesn't get scared, rush, and pull away from you, or worse yet, jump on top of you. If this might be the case, do more preliminary groundwork. If you lead him across, next time drive him across by walking alongside him, directing with the tail of your mecate or halter rope. Once you have accomplished this, mount up and ride across.

If you start with riding rather than leading, use the same approach as with the water crossing. There is no right or wrong in your selection of how to get started. What's important is to start with what is appropriate for you and your horse's ability and experience. Generally speaking, bridges are easier than creek crossings.

If your horse is afraid of crossing bridges, pick a wide, safe one that makes a

around and start over. Try to prevent this jumping across. However, he may have to do this several times until he can step across. As your horse accepts stepping across parallel, gradually change the angle of approach each time you cross, until you have crossed perpendicular. Stay consistent and patient. Don't give up and don't doubt your horse; it will all work out.

Bogs

Bogs come in many varieties and locations. Bogs are much more difficult to work through in the backcountry with a troubled horse than are creeks and bridges. They can also be more hazardous, causing pulled ligaments and tendons, etc.

If bogs are a problem for you and your horse, I recommend setting up simulated bogs at home to master before going out on the trail or pasture for the real thing. Setting this up may require some earth moving with a shovel or tractor. Make the bog large, but not deep, and wide enough that your horse cannot jump across, with ample working room nearby. Build your simulated bog where you can easily keep

minimum of noise. It's best if the planks are close together so he can't see the water or arroyo below.

Eventually work up to increasingly difficult situations. Avoid unsafe bridges. As you become more proficient, spend several sessions trailering your horse out to various locations where there are creeks and bridges to cross. For now, make your trail ride objectives center on bridges and creeks rather than covering distance and miles.

Where I live there are tunnels, under highways, we ride our horses through. These are a lot of fun. Use the same approach to get your horse through a tunnel.

As you get better at these things, you will find you don't need to take as long with your training sessions—success will come quickly. Continue incrementally stretching out your comfort zones while keeping things safe and positive. Work up to where you and your horse have mastered every safe bridge and creek accessible in your area.

Utilize the approach-and-retreat concepts I've discussed through all these problems. Use your imagination, be creative and come up with your own combination of these techniques that work best for your horse. Soon you will be riding the trails, and there just won't be anything out there your horse is not willing to cross, whether it's stepping over a log, crossing a creek, bridge, tunnel, a winter snowdrift, or any obstacle, man-made or natural.

Your individual success will depend not on a specific technique, but on how you present it to your horse. It will depend on your feel, timing, and balance—your ability to accurately read your horse and to adjust as he makes changes. Keep a positive, optimistic outlook. Soon, you and your horse will be enjoying the trails, able to go anywhere you choose, looking forward to obstacles with enthusiasm. Good luck!

With preparation and practice, creeks and other trail obstacles will become something you and your horse look forward to, especially on a warm, high country day.

Photo by Carolyn Kupka

8 HERD-BOUND

The Horse's Perception

INSTINCTIVELY, the horse knows the safest place to be is with the herd. Wild horses survive by living in a strong social hierarchy with safety in numbers. When the herd moves off, all the horses move together. Although our horses are domesticated, their self-preservation and social instincts remain. This becomes a problem when the horse's intent, which is to be with the other horses, differs from the rider's. If the other horses you are riding with trot or lope off and you ask your horse to walk, he has to choose between his natural instincts and your guidance.

The concepts and techniques in Chapters 1, 2, and 5 will be helpful when you start working on your herd-bound problem. Herd-bound behavior is very similar to barn-sour; however, due to horses' natural instincts, the herd-bound problem can be more ingrained. The chapters mentioned include suggestions for a chargey horse or

Riding with a group in the open country can bring out herd-bound behaviors. These riders are all traveling about the same pace, which helps horses stay calm and relaxed in a herd.

one who jigs on the trail. Also review in Chapter 4 the exercises on getting your horse mentally hooked on you in the round corral. All these problems can be rewarding and enjoyable to overcome.

Typical Symptoms

When you are riding with others, herd-bound behavior means the horse's attention is directed more to the other horses than to the rider. It is difficult to maintain control when other horses travel faster, slower, or in a different direction. If the rider wants to leave the group, the horse gets upset from separation anxiety. Even when the group stays together, some horses just won't settle down, constantly jigging or wanting to go to the front of the herd. In these cases, the horse is relying on his instincts, rather than accepting guidance from his rider. Keep in mind that herd-bound behavior is really a symptom, although we refer to it as a problem.

It is easy for riders to inadvertently encourage herd-bound behavior. Riding in a group can bring out the worst if a solid foundation does not exist between horse and human. If the rider allows the trail and other horses to determine direction, then attempts to redirect the horse, the horse will probably resist, perceiving the rider as a problem. If the rider repeatedly gives up and lets the horse go with the other horses, this rewards herd-bound behavior. The horse builds on this, knowing if he resists long enough, he will be allowed to rejoin the herd. These and other human actions can cause or perpetuate the problem.

Riding With Awareness

To help a herd-bound horse, being a proactive rider demonstrates effective leadership and develops mutual trust, confidence, and respect. For example, when you're riding at a walk in a group, be aware of the others. If the other horses start trotting and you get caught unaware, particularly if you are riding near the back of the group, your horse is probably going to trot.

These riders are well spread out yet staying together enough to minimize herd-bound behavior. They are riding proactively, keeping their horses directed and attentive.

Horses are naturally herd animals with a strong sense of self-preservation.

Before heading out on the trail to work on a herd-bound problem, first review the foundation exercises in Chapter 1 and Chapter 2, including being able to ride through all your horse's gaits on a loose rein.

Your horse is now taking direction from the other horses. If you allow this, you have reinforced the herd behavior. Stay more aware; trot your horse first. If the group doesn't trot, slow him back down. This could provide many opportunities for walk-to-trot-to-walk transitions. At least you're riding proactively, ahead of the action. However, be subtle and try not to create problems for other horses riding with you. **Always use common courtesy when riding with others.**

When the group stops to open and close a gate, as each rider goes through, he should stop and turn his horse facing the person closing the gate, and wait. This allows the last rider to close the gate without having a troubled horse.

Whenever the group is leaving to head out on the trail, there is often a waiting or lag time until it is your turn to move out. Often, horses get anxious and fidgety when they see the other horses leave ahead of them. Instead of sitting inactively waiting your turn, get your horse's feet moving around the immediate area. Watch, and when it's your turn, have him ready to immediately head out. Being proactive will help your horse stay calm and attentive instead of nervous and irritated.

While riding, if your horse's mind begins to drift, do something to get him busy and attentive to you. Until you

Use common trail courtesy. This group has stopped and turned their horses facing the dismounted rider, who has tightened her cinch. They are waiting until she is mounted and ready to ride off. This safety courtesy minimizes herd-bound behaviors.

resolve this problem, ride with greater awareness than normal. It's the little things that make the difference.

Set Up Situations

When you are out riding and your horse starts acting herd-bound is not the best time to begin problem-solving. Plan ahead and set up these situations. Safely expose your horse to the circumstances that could bring out this behavior, and allow him to learn he does not need to feel insecure. This is working developmentally, rather than reactively. Your horse needs to be in a good learning frame of mind and attentive to you before you start the exercises to follow.

Know how to make a one-rein stop, in case your horse gets fractious. However, stopping can escalate your horse into panic if the other riders keep moving, creating more distance between you and the herd. Unless the other riders stop or ride back to you, asking your horse to stop could possibly make the situation worse. **For good trail riding safety, when someone is in trouble with his horse, the closest rider should ride back to him and**

Riders stopped, facing gate, waiting for the other riders.

211

This type gate is not safe to open and close without dismounting. Lloyd Britton with his molly mule Lucille, who might leave him or be difficult to mount if the other horses rode off, works to get the gate closed. The other riders' courtesy of waiting helps minimize herd-bound behavior.

take responsibility to tell the others to hold up. This may help the troubled horse settle down, and it makes positive use of herd instincts.

When you head out on the trail to begin working with this problem, you will need cooperative friends to help you. Control as many variables as possible, mainly the actions of the other horses and selecting your riding partners wisely. As with all techniques, the suggestions in this chapter are only as effective as the manner in which the human presents them to the horse. Keep a positive, optimistic outlook, and it will all work out.

Walk-Trot-Walk

This is an excellent approach-and-retreat exercise to get started on solving herd-bound problems. Select open, relatively flat riding terrain. A long jeep or irrigation road or wide trail is ideal. Begin riding at a walk with two other riders. While the other horses continue walking, start by trotting 100-150 feet (or other appropriate distance) down the trail, then slow to a walk. Immediately, one of the other riders should start trotting and ride past you another 100-150 feet, then slow to a walk. Both your horse and the other rider's horse should be walking on a loose rein at this moment.

After the second rider passes you, if your horse decides he needs to trot to catch up with the horse ahead, ask him to come back to a walk (using any of the appropriate examples in Chapter 2 such as partial bend to slow the feet). Don't hold your horse back from trotting; ask for a walk, release when he does, then ride on a loose rein. Allow him to make a mistake. Each time he breaks into a trot, bring him back to a walk and release. If you can't maintain a walk on a loose rein, the distance between you and the rider ahead may be too great at this time. If your horse can't handle this distance, you can cut it down next time.

When the second rider has passed you at a trot and at the prescribed distance and

The trail leads out to the left. Rather than sitting watching the other horses leave, the riders on the right are proactive, keeping their horses busy while waiting their turn to ride out after stopping at a gate.

begins walking, the third rider, still behind you, will trot his horse past you and the front rider, go on a specified distance, then slow his horse to a walk and proceed on a loose rein. When the third rider comes to a walk, if your horse is walking forward on a loose rein, ask him to trot and pass the two horses ahead of you, go a specified distance, and again slow down to a walk, then ride on a loose rein.

Continue this walk-trot-walk leapfrogging exercise, adjusting the distances to fit the comfort levels of the horses involved. Your horses have a chance to be together, then apart, then together. Try to minimize taking the problem horse out of sight of the other horses at this time. Keep adjusting distances, and make sure you're able to walk your horse on a loose rein, without holding him back. You can do this exercise for miles, and it's amazing the positive effect it has on horses. See diagram HB-1.

Be aware of your body rhythm, because it needs to stay in a walk when you want your horse to walk. If he moves up to the trot when you don't want him to, your body rhythm shouldn't follow his trot.

It is best to slow up a herd-bound horse when headed downhill. The riders in front are helping by not getting too far ahead.

Walk-Trot-Walk Exercise.

A/ Start out by riding together, single file, with the least confident horse in front. B/ When all three horses are walking quietly, the first horse should trot ahead 100-150 feet, then begin walking on a loose rein. C/ When No. 1 is walking quietly, No. 2 should move out at a trot, passing No. 1 and slowing to a walk, 100-150 feet in front. D/ Then No. 3 begins trotting, passing both No. 1 and No. 2 and easing to a walk after traveling 100-150 feet ahead. Then start the sequence all over again.

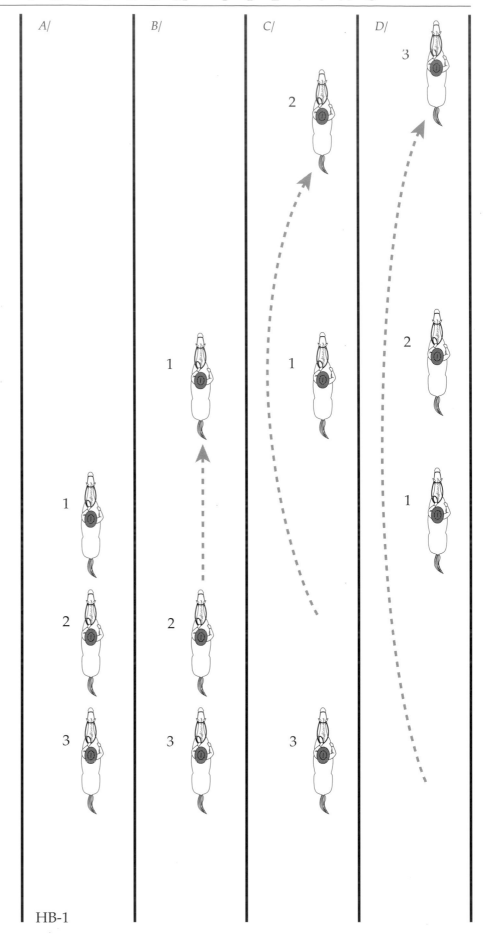

HB-1

Walk-Trot-Walk. The rider in the middle is trotting past the first and second riders. The riders in front and back are offering their horses a choice to stay at a walk.

Note the slack reins on the lead horse walking as Lloyd's mule, Lucille, trots by to take the lead, practicing the walk-trot-walk exercise. Steve Patterson's Paint Horse is having trouble staying at a walk, so Steve is slowing him up. Then he will release his rein, allowing him to again walk forward on a loose rein. If his horse continues to have trouble, we may have to shorten the distance between horses for a while.

Stay in a walking rhythm with your body, and bring him back down to a walk, with as little rein as needed, then release. If your horse can't tolerate this exercise, practice more basic ones in Chapter 2 to help you both get more in tune with each other.

Riding in Tandem

When two riders are out riding side by side down a road or trail, it is easy to get involved in conversation and forget about the horses. To avoid establishing or per-petuating herd-bound behavior, occasionally practice riding separately for short periods. Get off the trail (where permitted) and give your horse a job to do by riding around a bush or tree while the other rider stays on the trail. Then come back, and after riding in tandem for a few strides, the second rider could get off the trail, then come back. Continue alternating intermittently as you ride down the trail. Pretty soon, both riders can leave, going

1/ *Riding in tandem, then splitting apart for a short distance. These two geldings are herdmates, and the one I am riding for the owner is the most troubled by separation from the herd.*

2/ *After being apart for just a short distance, I have ridden this gelding back to his herdmate for a while before splitting apart again.*

opposite directions for a short distance. Don't create separation anxiety by traveling too far at first.

If this increases the anxiety level in your horse, ride back to the other horse, but immediately leave, circle back, and repeat. When you feel your horse relax, ride alongside the other horse again for a while, then start the procedure over again.

Herd-Bound to a Buddy

Sometimes a horse will be herd-bound to a specific horse. This next exercise will help get his attention on you instead of just his herdmate. If you are riding the herd-bound horse, have a friend ride the buddy horse. In a large arena with good footing, have your friend sit on his horse at one end about 150 feet away, leaving plenty of room around them and the fence. On the other end, facing the buddy horse, drop your reins on your horse's neck, but don't ask him to move. Give him a choice whether to stay there or let his herd instincts pull him toward his buddy. See Diagram HB-2.

Your horse will probably start moving toward the other horse. Allow him to go toward the magnet, his herd buddy. This is much like the gate exercise in the Barn-Sour chapter. Once he gets to the other horse, get him busy. Actively trot or lope some circles around his buddy. Keep doing this until your horse decides he'd like to rest, or he's thinking he might want to move away, because his idea is turning into a lot of work.

Once you feel him wanting to rest or move away, then ride him back to the other end of the arena. Turn him around toward his buddy, stop and drop the reins on his neck again, but don't ask him to move. Allow him to rest and pet him.

He may immediately want to go back to his herdmate. Let him go and then start trotting or loping circles around his buddy again. Change the direction of your circles. Incorporate figure eights or any other transitional type of maneuver. The purpose is to make the wrong thing difficult, not to punish or fatigue the horse. You won't let him stand and rest next to his buddy. He gets to rest at the other end of the arena with you.

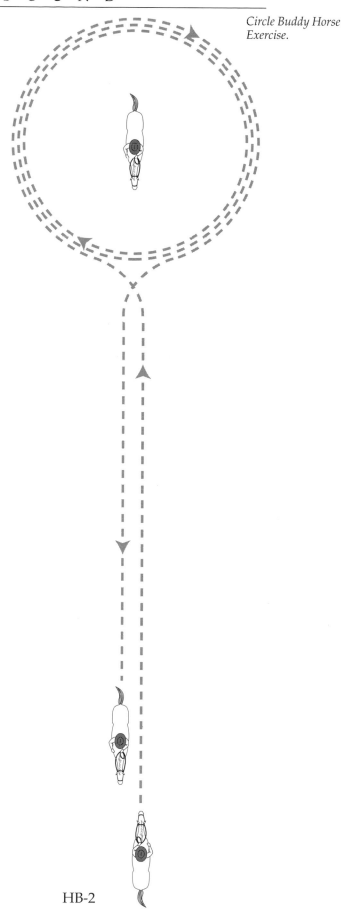

Circle Buddy Horse Exercise.

HB-2

217

1/ *I am riding this roan mare for a clinic participant who was having difficulty getting her to go the direction she wanted because the mare was herd-bound. This sequence shows a variation on the exercise diagrammed in HB-2.*

2/ *After spacing the other riders out, I am getting this mare real busy when she wants to hang out with the other horses.*

Exercise good judgment. Stay positive and keep him working when he wants to go back to his buddy. After several trips, depending on how strong the attraction, most horses will choose to stand at the other end of the arena and rest. After he has rested and is still content to stand there, walk him toward the buddy horse. Ride him around the other horse at a quiet walk. You can even let him stand next to the buddy horse for a few seconds, then ride him back to the other end of the arena.

In helping your horse learn to be comfortable away from his herdmates, you're not trying to make him stay away from them all the time. The objective is to be able to come and go as you please. A good time to ride him back to his buddies is when he is content being away. Don't wait too long; he may get anxious. Timing is important.

3/ *I won't make her stay away, but I will show her that being with the other horses will turn into a lot of work.*

4/ *She is starting to get the idea, so I will ease off when she willingly moves away from the other horses. I will then allow her to stop and rest on a loose rein, away from the other horses.*

Then ride away again, setting up another opportunity to come and go, incrementally staying away longer as your horse can accept this. This is an example of the approach-and-retreat concept.

There are many variations of these exercises, adjusted to fit the terrain, the horses, and the people involved. You could have someone stand holding the buddy horse, tie him at one end inside or outside of the arena, or turn him loose in an adjoining corral. You could very easily do the same exercise outside in a pasture. However, the arena may offer a certain amount of security for horse and rider. Use your own creativity and come up with your own variations.

Get your horse magnetized to something other than just other horses, such as cattle.

The goal is getting the horse to accept guidance from you, rather than following his herd instinct. You expand your horse's comfort zone and take it with you wherever you go. Your horse learns to depend on you for his safety and comfort, rather than the barn or other horses.

The Up-Front Horse

Horses who must be in the lead, another form of herd-bound, will benefit from this next exercise. The goal is for your horse to be content, following your leadership, to travel in the front, middle, or back of the group. This exercise works best with a larger group of four or more riders. Be sure you ride with friends who are cooperative. Also allow ample time and distance for your horse to make a positive change. He will need to separate and compare the difference between what he wants to do and what you ask him to do. He will need to learn that his choice

causes him considerably more work compared to your direction, which brings him more rest and relaxation. Then his choice will be to follow your direction.

As you are riding up the trail with other horses, if your horse rushes forward to be in the lead, rather than holding him back, let him go to the front. Keep a safe speed and gait. When he gets there, ride him forward past the front horse, maybe 30-40 yards. Then turn around and trot all the way to the back of the group. Just as you get to the last horse, turn your horse around and ride along relaxed on a loose rein. If he feels like he has to go to the front again, let him go. Once he gets there, ride him on past as before, turn him around and trot to the back once more. See diagram HB-3.

Continue this exercise until your horse decides his idea is more work than yours. He gets a chance to be everywhere among this group of horses, but the back is the only place he gets to travel at a walk. Containing a horse who wants to go forward will often add fuel to the fire, making things worse. Throughout this exercise, you're being

220

proactive, directing rather than holding him back or containing him. This exercise will have a good effect on your horse, with a more lasting, positive outcome.

Serpentines and Zigzags

Riding your horse in serpentine and zigzag (snake trail) patterns also works well to direct the excess energy and activity level that herd behavior brings out. Let him cover more ground without putting more distance between your horse and the horses in front of you. Use trees, rocks, bushes, and other natural obstacles as your markers. Keep your serpentines and zigzags moving forward instead of backward. Everyone in your riding group can do this at the same time, depending on terrain. Just keep trail courtesy in mind.

Don't Ride Nose to Tail

When riding on a narrow, single-file trail, a horse will often crowd up on the horse in front of him. This is neither safe nor good trail etiquette. Maintain a mini-mum one or two horse lengths between riders. If a horse crowds up on another horse and the rider starts pulling back on the reins trying to hold or force him to stay back, the horse could become troubled, more herd-bound, and start jigging. There are more productive ways to solve this.

This exercise will require a cooperative rider in front of you. The front rider will use the tail of his mecate, halter rope, or anything similar. He will reach back and flip the tail of his rope so your horse runs into it when he crowds. You won't hold your horse back. Just keep his nose straight, so he runs into his own pressure. This isn't punishing your horse; you're just letting him learn that when he crowds, he runs into something that bumps him on the nose. Aim for the nose, avoiding the horse's eyes and ears.

This procedure imitates herd behavior. When one horse crowds another, the front horse often will kick back. When the rider in front swings his mecate back and

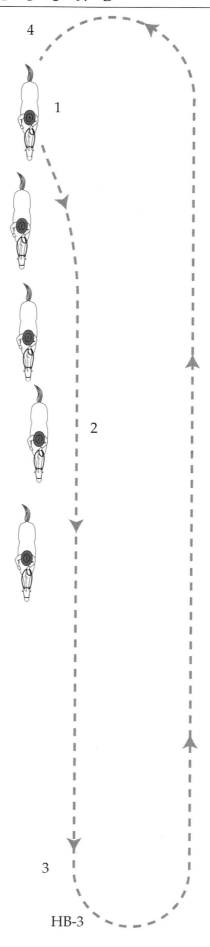

The Up-Front Horse Exercise. Due to space limitations, this diagram depicts horses riding too close together. For safety and courtesy try to maintain a minimum of one horse length behind horse in front of you.

Start this exercise by riding your horse at or near the rear of the group. 1/ If he starts to trot, slow him back to a walk, then release the reins. If he won't walk on a loose rein, let him move past the other riders. 2/ Keep him moving until he's 25 to 30 yards in front. 3/ Then, without slowing, turn and ride to the rear of the group. 4/ Ask him to walk on a loose rein. If he wants to go to the front again, repeat the exercise.

HB-3

1/ *Tracy Speich's mare (on the right) wants to charge ahead, so instead of forcing her to stay back, she is actively riding her forward, then on past the lead for a short distance.*

2/ *Now Tracy is riding back to the rear. She will turn around when she reaches the last rider, then give her mare a choice to walk calmly forward on a loose rein.*

222

These riders are evenly spaced, traveling forward without crowding up on another horse, showing good trail courtesy.

bumps your horse on the nose, it simulates the real situation of a lead horse kicking a crowding horse.

This may seem like an unpleasant thing to do to your horse. However, it's much less traumatic than constantly overconfining by pulling back or jerking on the reins. This should not be harsh or abusive, just effective. Timing is important. Experiencing this a couple of times can have a positive effect on horses. Your horse may form a whole different idea about crowding another horse from behind. After he has run into his own pressure (the rope) a few times, often just hand movement from the rider in front will be enough.

Riders whose horses have a tendency to kick often tie a ribbon in the tail when on a trail ride. It's a warning not to ride up behind them. However, I recommend we all take the responsibility to not allow our horses to crowd. If the horse in front kicks us, it's not his fault. It's just like a vehicle accident on the road. Whenever a driver rear-ends another vehicle, it's always the rear driver's fault; he gets the ticket. The same is true of riding on the trails.

Get Him To Wait for Your Direction

With a calmer, patient horse and rider there is a similar technique to try. When your horse crowds up and puts his nose

When riding up a slope or steep hill it is sometimes good to have the horse and rider in front not get too far ahead and wait for the horse bringing up the rear. Sam and Nick Gulley demonstrate here as I approach on my mare, Dee Lena.

on the front horse's butt, slow him to a stop, with a soft feel. This may be a good time to use the partial-bend-to-slow-the-feet exercise. Release the reins and ask him to stand there on a loose rein until the horse in front moves off a few steps. Then while he is standing on a loose rein, ask your horse to walk forward.

Initially, you'll have to let the distance between horses be somewhat short,

Gathering cattle out in the open with other horses is an excellent opportunity to develop a horse's confidence in his rider.

Sorting out pairs on my filly Brownie while the other horses and riders hold the herd in a rodear.

Moving a large herd will help encourage a herd-bound horse to think about the job at hand rather than where the other horses are.

Cattle work has a positive effect on horse and rider working as a team. If you don't have access to cattle, get creative and use your imagination to come up with an alternative.

When herd-bound problems decrease, riding with other horses in open country can be a pleasure rather than a hassle.

because your horse can't stand there very long without moving on his own. The objective is to ask him to move forward while he's standing still on a loose rein. All you want is for your horse to stand still for only a second at first, waiting for your signal to go forward.

Build on the distance and time. After doing this a number of times, when he's stopped standing with a loose rein, you'll begin to feel his body language asking to move, but still awaiting your signal. Immediately ask him to move out. When he is really tuning in to you like this, you are making progress that will carry over into other areas. Horses will really learn to wait for you if you are consistent and respectful with them.

Similarly, if your horse starts to trot, whether with a group or alone, and you didn't ask him to, stop or walk him. When he'll stand or walk on a loose rein for a second, move him off at a trot. This may not sound like it has much value, or it might sound like you're giving in to your horse. However, it is on your timetable, and he has to wait for your communication. Your horse will learn that he gets what he wants by waiting for you. Giving your horse what he wants in this way builds trust and respect. This will have a very positive effect on your horse over a period of time, along with all the other good habits you are developing. Be creative, finding various riding situations to experiment with this and other exercises without overexposing your horse.

Make Lots of Transitions

When riding with a group, making lots of transitions keeps your horse attentive and focused on you rather than his herd-mates. A transition is any change of direction, speed, or gait. Try trotting your horse 10 strides, then bring him back to a walk for 5 strides, then ask him to trot again, and repeat. Work on two-tracking while riding down the trail or a road. Look for obstacles to ride around. Then see how straight you can ride your horse by picking out an object to ride toward. Use any of the riding exercises in Chapter 2 to help you become more focused and proactive. Do these exercises without stressing the other horses, bringing out their herd-bound behavior. Use good trail riding courtesy.

Often when you're working with a herd-bound horse, he'll whinny back at his buddies. Instead of punishing him, refocus his attention by giving him a job to do. The ideal is to catch him just before he whinnies and distract him. Avoid overexposing your horse by taking him too far from the herd. Refer to the barn-sour star pattern suggestions.

Much of problem-solving is in redirecting the horse's focus. When the horse is not tuned in to you, his attention will be on something else, which often gets you into trouble.

Get Your Horse on Cattle

As you and your horse advance, look for more opportunities. Like trail riding, moving cattle offers a chance to ride out in the open with other horses, providing more positive experiences in varying situations and circumstances. Getting your horse on cattle can build up his confidence and get him more focused on you and whatever job you give him. Cattle work always seems to have a positive effect on horse and rider working together as a team.

Develop Straightness and a Faster Walk

Make positive use of your horse's desire to be with the herd. After you have advanced through solving this problem and can easily direct and support your horse, you can now use this "problem" to benefit you and your horse. This is a more advanced level technique. Let the draw of another horse ahead of you help him develop straightness and a faster walk. However, he should still wait for you to direct speed and gait. Learn the feel of a faster walk and observe how straight your horse is when drawn by another horse. Get in rhythm with his movement. If things fall apart, go back to the earlier exercises before trying this again. Your

goal is to eventually have your horse willingly walk away from the herd as fast and as straight as he walks in their direction.

Conclusion

These approach-and-retreat exercise suggestions will help broaden your and your horse's comfort zones. If you can expand near, but not reaching, his limit, then ease off, letting him relax, he'll develop more trust and confidence in you.

There will be times when you'll step too far out of his comfort zone and get a negative reaction. Just work through it, regain control, smile, and start over. If you're with a group, have a prearranged agreement that when one rider is in trouble, the nearest rider will ride back to the troubled horse. You can use the herd behavior to get out of trouble. Don't overexpose your horse by putting him in a situation that he perceives as sink-or-swim.

Solving all the riding problems we encounter has a common thread. Set up the situation so your horse makes the right choice by taking the path of least resistance. The goal is to develop your horse's trust, confidence, and respect in his leader. When the horse perceives that being with his rider and following his direction gives him equal or greater safety and comfort than the herd, the horse and rider develop a willing partnership, and problems resolve themselves.

Be creative and imaginative to come up with ways to fit your particular situation, your horse, the terrain, and people you ride with. Make this interesting and rewarding for your horse, and you'll both enjoy solving your herd-bound problem.

9 PULLS BACK WHEN TIED

HORSES WITHOUT a pull-back problem know how to move their feet when tied, accepting restriction and confinement. The opposite are horses who pull back. They are like a time bomb and are potentially dangerous to themselves and their humans. This is possibly the most difficult of all horse problems, and it's not easy to fix.

To get the problem manageable may require a great amount of feel, timing, balance, and experience from the human. This chapter is designed for **prevention** as much as for suggesting solutions.

Your horse does not pull back intentionally to displease or cause you aggravation. The horse's self-preservation instincts cause him to fear restraint, because it takes away his only defense—flight. In his mind, being tied up creates a high level of vulnerability, and he just doesn't know what else to do to protect himself. Despite this, if given a chance to learn to accept restriction, horses can learn very early to become dependable while tied up, even for long periods.

Most pull-back problems are caused by improper early training or lack of good

If given a chance to learn to accept restriction and confinement, horses can become dependable, even when tied for long periods.

judgment by humans. Putting the horse in a sink-or-swim situation he cannot handle might cause him to pull back. For example: tying a horse solid before he has had an opportunity to learn to yield to pressure while confined; tying to unstable posts or tie rails; or tying in areas where the horse can get overexposed to something unfamiliar or scary. If he breaks loose, his pulling back has been rewarded. If he doesn't break loose, he may severely injure himself.

The best solution is preventing the problem. Awareness of the steps you can take to help your horse learn to tie well is preventive medicine. Give him the opportunity to learn to accept restriction and confinement while yielding to pressure.

The pull-back solution lies in the preparation steps before you tie your horse again. This approach also applies to the never-tied young green horse. The pull-back horse may take more time at various steps, however. Do not tie your horse up with multiple halters and ropes to a tree so he cannot break loose. Although this may solve the problem for a few, it may injure more horses than it helps. **Avoid tying your horse up until you have made considerable progress in the preparation steps.**

The objective of this chapter is to help your horse learn an alternative to pulling back, which is moving his feet within a confined area while he relaxes and overcomes his fear of restraint. He needs to learn that his answer is moving his feet right, left, forward, or a combination of all three while yielding to pressure, instead of pulling backward. After discussing how to prepare your horse to accept being tied, I will suggest some guidelines to help you avoid a future pull-back problem.

Getting Started

Start with the groundwork in Chapter 1. Getting your horse good on the halter rope is very crucial and cannot be overlooked; it is a very important step. When you bend your horse one direction and he moves his hindquarters in the opposite direction, you are preparing your horse to lead and be tied. At virtually every phase of groundwork, your horse is learning to yield to and from pressure. This is what being tied is all about.

The rope-over-the-hocks exercise is excellent for teaching your horse to give to

229

Practicing the semicircle exercise. I hold the halter rope as though this filly is tied. She is moving her feet in a semicircle in response to my shaking the flag in my right hand.

Rather than pull back, your horse should immediately lead up if you quickly speed up, even if it surprises him.

1/ To help your horse accept more restriction and confinement, begin leading by using the halter rope on a foot. I am rubbing it up and down this filly's front leg in a light seesaw motion to accustom her to the feel of the rope.

2/ With constant pressure on the halter rope around her pastern, I asked her to step forward. I am now starting to release. At first, you release when any foot moves, not just the one with the rope. Note slack in the halter rope back to her head.

1/ I use an extra soft (3xxx) nylon lariat with a Brannaman metal honda for leading by a rope around the foot.

2/ Stay in a small working area such as a round corral for this exercise. With the loop around this filly's pastern, I have asked her to step forward and am already releasing, putting slack in the rope. Note I am off at an angle instead of directly in front of her.

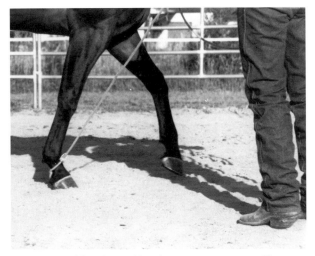

3/ This metal honda quickly releases pressure around her pastern when I release.

4/ She readily accepts leading in response to light pressure. Note I have the halter rope and lariat coils in my right hand, and am leading her with my left hand. I switch to the opposite hand when working on her left side.

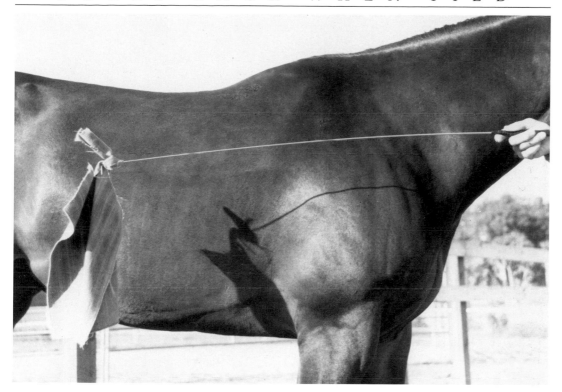

The flag I use for these exercises is a stainless steel antenna rod with canvas tied to the end.

pressure and think his way out of confinement. In the semicircle exercise, in effect you are the tie post, and you are teaching your horse what to do and where to go with his feet when tied.

While practicing the leading exercises in Chapter 1, quickly move off from a walk to a trot. Your horse should immediately lead up right behind you. Even if it surprises him when slack comes out of the halter rope and pulls against him, his feet should come forward immediately without pulling back. This is one good test to determine if your horse will stand tied safely.

While backing your horse with your hand on the halter as in Chapter 1, ask him to immediately walk forward from the back-up. If your horse braces before coming forward, this will carry through to pulling back. Work through this until your horse quickly moves forward without hesitation.

Do the round corral exercises in Chapter 4 even if your horse is easy to catch. Pay particular attention to the changing-eyes section; it will help him be more comfortable with movements while tied.

Lead by a Rope on a Foot

Much of problem-solving is about freeing up the horse's feet, which is really freeing up his mind so he doesn't feel he has to use flight for self-preservation. This starts with the groundwork and carries throughout. Yielding to pressure while accepting a degree of restriction and confinement will further your horse's development. Teach him to accept and then lead by a rope on his foot. Before starting this, be sure you and your horse are solid with all the groundwork in Chapter 1.

Starting with a front foot, run the tail of your halter rope around your horse's pastern. Rub him up and down lightly in a seesaw motion, then hold with a constant forward pressure at a 30- to 45-degree angle off his shoulder. Keep slack in the rope between your hand and his head. Don't try to pull his foot out from under him. Let him think his way through this and learn to come off his own pressure.

*1/ Dally to a tie post. This shows how **not** to dally the rope around the tie post. The rope going back to the halter is in my left hand. If she pulled back, it could potentially bind up against the rope in my right hand, making it difficult or impossible to slowly slip the dally. This could create too much of a sink-or-swim situation. The correct dally would have the rope in my right hand go over the top of the rope going back to the horse (in my left hand).*

When he leans your direction or moves a foot (any foot at first), release, pet him, and start again. If he gets bothered, hang on without pulling; just go with him when he moves. However, if things really fall apart, you could drop the tail of the halter rope, and start over again. With the right approach, he will soon lead by a front foot, without pressure against the rope. Alternate to both front feet.

While doing these exercises, stand off to the side of your horse's front shoulder.

Don't get directly in front of him; you might inadvertently drive him backwards, making his pulling back worse.

This next exercise is not to be taken lightly as there is a degree of risk involved. If not presented correctly, it could easily result in injury to you and/or your horse, potentially making your horse more fearful.

After your horse fully accepts leading by the halter rope on his front feet, place a lariat loop around his pastern. Stay in a small working area with your horse haltered. Using an extra-soft nylon lariat with

2/ *This shows how the nylon halter rope (25 to 30 feet long) should be dallied around the post. Standing on this filly's left side (out of photo) I am using my flag, asking her to step her hindquarters over to her right, in a semicircle. Note gate hinge bolt on post to keep rope from slipping down.*

3/ *If she were to pull back, I would let the halter rope slowly slip through my left hand, making pulling back difficult, but not sink-or-swim. The flag is in my right hand.*

4/ *I have switched sides and am flagging her over to her left.*

metal honda, such as a Brannaman honda, which works best for a horse rope. When you release the pressure on the rope, the metal honda opens quicker and easier than a tied honda. Don't use a flat nylon line, as it is more apt to burn your horse.

Holding on to the tail of your halter rope, let your horse circle around you in the corral, initially just wearing the rope on his foot. First accompany the horse, then ask him to accompany you, then you accompany each other. Allowing him to wear the

PB-1

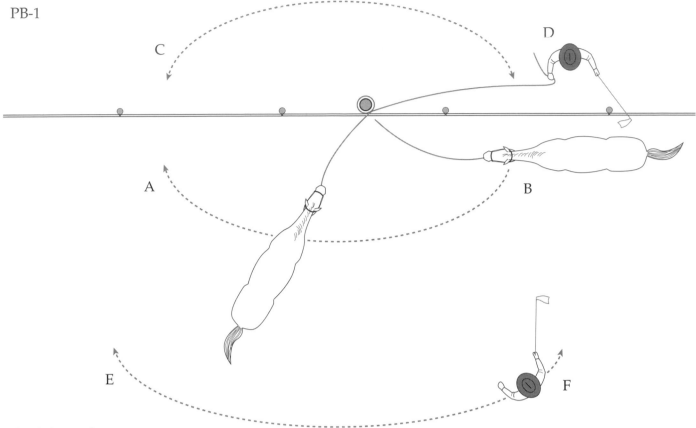

Flag the horse so he always has a place to go, moving from A to B to A, stepping over side to side, moving his hindquarters as in disengaging. Let him stand and relax a few moments after he moves over before starting again. If one person is working the horse, move from C to D to C while flagging the horse from A to B to A. Continually reposition yourself to avoid flagging directly in front of the horse. If two people are available, the second person flags the horse while moving from E to F to E, while the other person holds the halter rope, moving from C to D to C. Only one person flags at a time; both avoid standing directly in front of the horse.

rope and get used to it before you ask anything of him is accompanying him first.

When he stops, pet him and let him relax. Then ask him to lead up with slight rope pressure on his foot. Leave slack in your halter rope unless you need to regain control. After he will freely lead up, stand off to the side and put a slight backward pressure on the rope to encourage him to slow down and stop. Then release and pet him.

Get this good with all four feet, one at a time, starting with the front feet. Be cautious—the hind feet may be more trouble for your horse. Go slowly and get your horse to operate from a feel, not pressure. If you are not comfortable with this, proceed extra carefully or seek a competent professional.

The purpose is to free up your horse's feet, so don't force him. Give him time to think. This exercise also helps you develop feel, timing, balance, position, and release.

Dally to a Tie Post

This exercise makes use of a large-diameter (12-inch) round tie post buried 4 feet,

and about 8 feet tall above ground, a 25- to 30-foot, 5/8-inch nylon halter rope, and a flag. Dally your rope one turn around the post as high as possible, leaving from 4 to 6 feet of slack between your horse and the post. Your dally must come from bottom to top to prevent binding up as shown in photo. Keep your rope from slipping down the post as you work with your horse by installing a gate hinge bolt (or similar device) behind the post near the top. Take your dally above this bolt. Be careful to not get your hands hung up in the rope. Have a sharp pocketknife handy at all times in case of emergency. Use caution when you set this up to prevent causing a pull-back before you even get started.

Having the rope dallied as high as possible lessens the chance of injury or breaking loose. **When tied high, the horse's leverage to pull back is also reduced.**

If your horse pulls back, slowly slipping the dally around the large-diameter post will create enough friction to make pulling back difficult and a great deal of work. This avoids putting your horse in a sink-or-swim situation, while he learns to yield to pressure.

2/ Although she is not completely comfortable with the heightened stimulus, she is stepping over to her right in a semicircle rather than pulling back. In these later stages of training, it is important to stretch a horse's comfort zone by incrementally creating more stressful conditions.

3/ I have switched sides, still on the outside of the fence. She is moving to her left away from the flag. Note the dally is still from bottom to top with the rope over the top going back to my right hand.

Before you start with your horse, experiment by having a friend hold the rope while you pull back. You'll quickly see how much work it is when your friend allows the rope to slowly slide through his hand as he holds back against your pull.

This exercise works best with two people, but can be accomplished alone. I prefer a post set next to a fence, but a free-standing post will work. See Diagram PB-1. Standing off to either side, use your flag to direct your horse in a semicircle. Go easy at first, don't try to scare him. Your objective is to have him move his feet away from pressure. As an alternative to pulling back, his option is to move around side to side,

1/ *Before tying to an inner tube, I have run the longer halter rope through the tube, flopping it around to get her familiar with it. Also, I move the horse side to side in a semicircle before tying her to the tube.*

2/ *Now she is tied to the tube with her regular halter rope. I am using my flag to ask her to step over to her left. Note how the inner tube is tied around post with a small doubled nylon rope above the hinge bolt.*

stepping his hindquarters over. If you have a friend helping, one of you can hold the tail of the halter rope while the other uses the flag. Only one person at a time should flag the horse.

Caution: Once the horse starts to move over to the side, release the flag pressure and step away to prevent driving him back, thus encouraging a pull-back.

If he pulls back instead of stepping over, allow him to work at it by letting the rope slide very slowly through your hand. When he comes forward off the pressure, approach him from the side, reassure him by rubbing him and letting him relax. Readjust the rope, then start again.

As your horse gets fluid and free with moving his feet, not pulling on the rope, get more vigorous with the flag. Don't try to make him pull back, just help him to learn to think under incrementally more stressful conditions, while keeping him in a learning frame of mind.

Do this exercise with your horse moving side to side many times and for several sessions. Review the groundwork with your horse preceding each session. Be very thorough, spending lots of time reviewing each step before moving on. He may not pull back for several sessions, but then experience a regression. Be patient and don't take anything for granted. You are asking your horse to stretch far out of his comfort zone. Help him by staying calm and relaxed. He will progressively get better.

Tie to an Inner Tube

When your horse has made consider-able progress, you can test tying hard and fast. This is approaching a sink-or-swim situation, so accurately reading your horse's readiness is imperative. **Don't be in a hurry and wish you had done more preparation after it's too late.**

Tying to an inner tube is an intermediate step. However, you may need to tie this way for a long time before tying hard and fast.

Tie a deflated truck inner tube to your tie post as shown in the photo. Use a new tube, without tears or rot. Run your halter rope through the center, hold on to the tail and flop it around to get your horse accustomed to the tube moving. Before tying, move him side to side again as already described. If he pulls back, keep the angle between horse and halter rope narrow, so

3/ *She has stepped over to her left. This shows the halter rope tied to the tube with a quick-release bowline knot. She has enough length to not feel overconfined. Note my flag in the lower right-hand corner of the photo.*

4/ *It may be necessary to use this tying method for a long time before it is safe to tie hard and fast.*

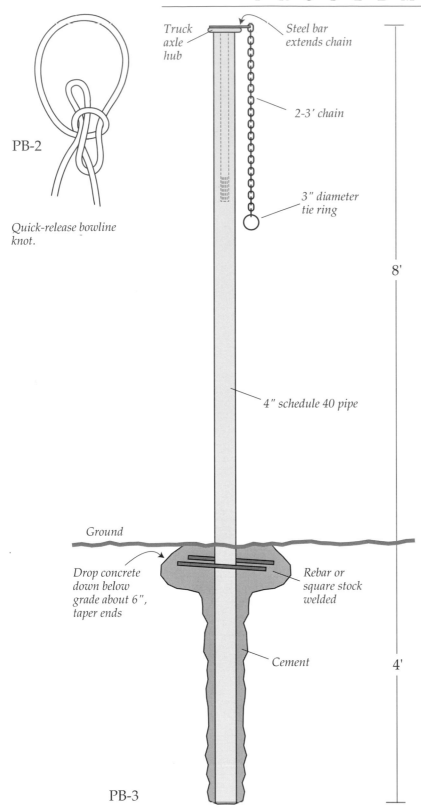

PB-2

Quick-release bowline knot.

Truck axle hub

Steel bar extends chain

2-3' chain

3" diameter tie ring

8'

4" schedule 40 pipe

Ground

Drop concrete down below grade about 6", taper ends

Rebar or square stock welded

Cement

4'

PB-3

Permanent tie post—horse can move 360 degrees while tied.

This tie post stands 8 feet tall and has a 1,000-pound-capacity caster welded at the top, providing 360-degree rotation. This caster system is the easiest to rig up.

he pulls against the tube. If he does pull, go back to the dally post procedure again.

When you are satisfied he is not likely to pull back, tie him to the tube with a quick-release bowline knot. See Diagram PB-2. Tie long enough to not overconfine him, and short enough to not allow him to step over the rope if he puts his head down.

When he is tied, if he does pull back, the stretching of the tube will be similar to you slipping the rope over the dally post. Remember to tie the tube as high as possible. Also, do not use a snap on your halter rope—it breaks too easily, or could flop around, hitting him on the jaw, perhaps making him pull back. Tie your halter rope to your halter with a half-hitch or a bowline knot.

You can leave your horse tied longer each session. If you leave the immediate area while he's tied, keep him within your view.

Permanent Tie Post

This is the best and safest idea I have seen for tying horses. In an open, flat area, bury a 12-foot length of 4-inch, Schedule 40 pipe about 4 feet deep. (This pipe is available at pipe supply stores.) At the top of the pipe, rig a swivel that can move freely 360 degrees. Connect a stout chain to the swivel and let it hang down the pole to a height of 5 to 6 feet. Connect a metal ring to the chain end as your halter rope tie point. See Diagram PB-3 for specifications.

When your tied horse walks around the pole, the swivel rotates, preventing the halter rope from wrapping around and binding up. If your horse pulls back, he pulls against the top of the pole, at 8 feet, and his pull lifts his front end. This minimizes his leverage, reducing the chance of injury or breaking loose.

Caution: Use a strong, well-made halter and halter rope without a snap. Tie long enough so your horse can lower his head and relax, but not so long he could get a foot over the halter rope. Maintain level ground around the pole.

Build your tie post in an open area where your horse cannot hit or get hung up on anything as he moves around or if he pulls back. Locate the post where you can most easily view your horse while you are doing other things around your property. If you build more than one of these tie posts, allow enough space between so horses cannot get close to each other.

Never Take Tying for Granted

Once you are this far along, your horse is beginning to learn how to handle being tied. Don't doubt your horse, but **don't take him for granted either.** Don't be disappointed; you may never solve this 100

This tie post, also 8 feet tall, has a truck axle hub inserted at the top to provide 360-degree rotation. Note quick-release bowline knot.

241

1/ Some tips and guide-lines. Don't tie colts for the first several saddlings. To maintain control, I have the halter rope draped over my left arm. Note how I hold the saddle while placing the blanket. This filly has enough ground manners to stand quietly while I work around her.

2/ With the halter rope still draped over my left arm, note my position as I buckle the back cinch. I use the same position for the front cinch.

percent. Things may work out fine while he is tied to your tie post at home. However, being tied at a strange place, tied to your trailer away from home, etc., may bring out a regression. Continue to use good judgment on **how** and **where** you tie your horse.

Some Tips and Guidelines

• Your approach is more important than any technique. It's not what you do (the technique), but how you go about doing it (your approach, understanding of, and presentation to your horse).

• When leading, don't pull straight forward if he pulls against you. Get off to the side and bend him and have his hindquarters step over. Stay out of the front triangle when he pulls against you. See Diagram GW-12. Poor ground handling habits by humans can create or perpetuate a pull-back problem.

• Don't tie a colt for the first several saddlings. The added confinement the saddle and cinch represent may cause him to pull back. After he wears the saddle as comfortably as he wears his mane and tail, it will probably be okay to tie him while saddling. Immediately after saddling, untie and lead him past you both directions to untrack and free up his feet, relaxing him mentally.

• Older pull-back horses may exhibit a similar problem when being saddled. It may be best to not tie them hard and fast while saddling. Instead, dally-tie or drape the halter rope over your arm.

• Don't tie to anything that can break, pull loose, or move: cross rails, weak posts, flimsy trailer ties, the mirrors on your truck, trailers not hooked up, etc.

• Don't initially teach your horse to tie using your trailer. Start with the dally post. Later accustom him to being tied to your trailer with a similar procedure.

• Avoid snaps on your halter rope; they seem to always break, and are often the weak link. Instead tie directly to your halter with a half-hitch or bowline knot. See Diagram PB-2.

• Avoid halters with buckles and metal

1/ *With this filly dally-tied to the trailer, I walk behind her to switch sides instead of ducking under her neck, which could cause a pull-back.*

2/ *After snugging up the cinches, I untie her and untrack her feet by leading her past me to my left. This frees up the feet and the mind, making her feel less confined and less apt to pull back than if she were to first move her feet while still tied. The added restriction of the cinch can cause a pull-back.*

When tying out on the trail, this is my preferred method. Having thrown the halter rope over a stout horizontal green tree limb, I have tied off with a quick-release bowline knot. My mare can now relax in the shade with her head down and a leg cocked while I have lunch. Be sure to check local regulations before tying on public lands.

244

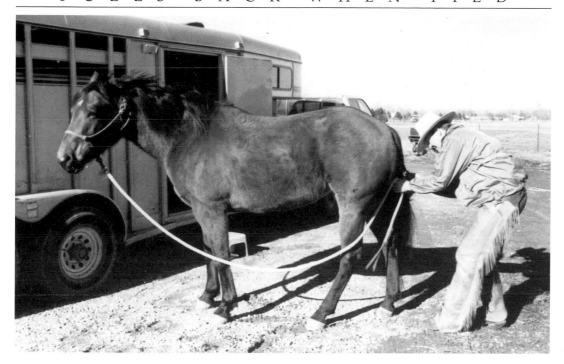

Part of being a halter-broke horse is not only being well-trained to tie but also to stand patiently without being tied while we work around him. Also, to avoid a potential pull-back, never tie a horse for nonroutine activities such as clipping, deworming, vaccinating, etc.

rings, which are another weak link.

• Tie high. Your tie point is best when it is higher than your horse's poll (about 6 feet on most horses). This minimizes his leverage if he does pull back. Avoid tying low.

• Tie long—long enough so your horse can relax while standing with his head down. If tied too short, he cannot relax and feels overconfined. As a rule of thumb, the longest you would ever tie him would allow him to just barely put his nose on the ground to eat or drink, with all the slack out of the halter rope. This minimizes the chance of him getting a foot over the rope.

• Don't tie where the ground slopes away, or on uneven ground with rocks, holes, etc.

• Avoid using cross-ties. From the horse's point of view, they are overly restricting and confining, making it difficult for him to step his hindquarters over to relieve his restraint anxiety. Instead, tie with just one line.

• When tying out on the trail, tie to a stout, horizontal tree limb above his head (and above your saddle horn), not to the trunk. Too often the tie rope will slip down the trunk. Loop your halter rope over the limb and tie off with a quick-release bowline knot. Do not tie to dead trees or limbs.

Note: Before tying your horse anywhere on public lands, check local regulations for tying stock. In most backcountry areas, regulations prohibit tying to trees, and

This panel would not be strong enough to tie to. I am demonstrating how to dally-tie instead of tying hard and fast. Test this by pulling on the halter rope between the panel and the horse's halter. The rope should be snug, but slip very slowly with a firm pull. If it doesn't, adjust with one less dally or wrap, or one more. If a horse pulls back, the objective is for the rope to slowly slip enough to give the horse time to yield before pulling the entire rope free, similar to the dally-tie post exercise. This method is for tying for short periods, while the handler remains in the immediate area.

require tying to picket lines.

• Don't bridle or unbridle your horse when he is tied. Don't tie hard and fast with the bridle reins.

• Never mount a horse while he is tied.

• Don't tie a horse while clipping, deworming, vaccinating, or for other nonroutine activities. If your horse will not stand patiently with your halter rope over

These two horses both have pull-back problems, but they have learned to stand quietly, here while dally-tied to the trailer. **Never take tying for granted,** *as you may never solve this problem absolutely 100 percent. The pull-back problem is potentially a major risk for injury to both horse and human, as well as a real inconvenience. Taking the necessary steps to* **prevent** *this problem from ever beginning or reoccurring is well worth the time and effort.*

your arm, work through more Chapter 1 groundwork exercises first.

• Don't tie hard and fast to a metal fence panel, even if it is connected solidly to a post. Instead tie to the post. If there is no post, dally-tie to the rail.

• Learn to dally-tie: Instead of tying hard and fast to a panel or other point, take one to several turns or dallies around the top rail. Test it to make sure, if your horse does pull back, the dallies will slip slightly, creating enough friction to give him time to think and step forward.

• **Be thoughtful and careful how you walk up to your horse to untie him.** Approach a pull-back horse so that you do not drive him back or encourage him to pull back. Generally, instead of walking straight at the horse's forehead, I approach from the side or the hip and make sure he is aware of my intentions. I sometimes ask him to shift his hindquarters to the side, then reach up and untie his halter rope.

• While a horse is tied, don't walk under his neck to change sides. Instead, walk around behind or untie him before changing sides.

• These suggestions are not an exhaustive list. Rather than get locked into do's and don'ts, **use common sense and good judgment!** Always adjust to fit your horse and the situation.

Conclusion

Provide your horse an opportunity to think, learn, and make choices. Give him time to learn that being tied is safe and comfortable, and does not threaten his self-preservation. Don't put him in a sink-or-swim situation until you are sure he will be okay. Just remember, this problem may never be totally and completely solved, so use good judgment and common sense whenever you tie your horse.

A horse's pull-back problem is a human-caused problem. You may not have been the cause of your horse's problem; maybe he had it before you owned him. However, from now on, do your best to make being tied acceptable to him and keep him away from situations that could make the problem reoccur. Help him to gain trust, confidence, and respect in his human and the situation.

The ideas and suggestions outlined in this chapter are not a recipe or mechanical process. Stay flexible, adapting your approach to fit your individual horse moment by moment as you go along. All the preparation you do to free up his mind and feet **before** you tie him will determine how he handles it **when** you tie him. Your horse will have a new perspective on being tied when he learns that **if** he can move his feet in a thoughtful way, he will be okay, and **when** he moves his feet, he will be okay.

246